Healing Tomorrow's Mothers

Healing Tomorrow's Mothers

A True Account of how an
Extraordinary Group Home Strove
to Bring Hope and Healing to At
Risk Teens

Mary Kay Lutzow & Danel Burchby

Kyla Brown

SSB

CONTENTS

CONTENTS

Paperback Edition
ISBN: 979-8-9888543-6-4

Editor, Kyla Brown

Photo credits: Mary Kay Lutzow

SSB, First printing 2024

Disclaimer

The book is written through the eyes of the narrators, and small details of fact may be incorrect or conflated. This is a true story of our lived experience relevant to operating a non-profit entity serving adolescent girls. Some names and details have been changed to protect privacy and conversations may have been edited for brevity. All efforts have been executed to present accurate, reliable, complete information. This book was written by memory, and ours are imperfect. We've done our best to be faithful to our experiences, and when possible, have consulted others who were also present during that time. We also relied on letters, logs, and conversations we've had with many people who appear in these pages. Recollections and stories in this book are subject to the fallible memories of the writers. Neither author is engaged in rendering professional advice to the individual reader. The ideas and interventions contained in this book are not intended as a substitute for consulting with a professional treatment provider. Neither author is liable for any damages caused by using the ideas or suggestions in this book.

1

Founding Mothers

God, grant me the serenity to accept the things I cannot change,
the courage to change the things I can,
and the wisdom to know the difference

Mary Kay

Over the course of my 10-year career with Candlelight Vision Corp (CVC) I've had so much to be proud of. From such seemingly small accomplishments as seeing a terrified young girl accept a hug, to creating an agency offering multi-levels of care for vulnerable adolescents. None of these accomplishments would have been possible without the dedication and commitment of a key group of people I consider to be the *"Founding Mothers."*

My final career path in life as a certified Drug and Alcohol Counselor began in 1987; I had been a Certified K-8 elementary school teacher in a previous lifetime teaching second grade. As Tom, my husband, and I embarked into the parenting arena, we were starry eyed idealists committed to not putting our children into childcare. Thus, we worked opposite shifts to each other from the time Nora, our oldest, was two.

The seeds of the vision for residential care were born out of common experiences shared by like-minded women. Working at a co-ed residential program known as Freedom House, I fell in love with the residential treatment model. The possibilities and opportunities to really effect transformational change were abundantly clear. It was at Freedom House where I came to know Michele Hutchinson and Marn Gibson.

I was familiar with Michele before she applied for her position there, and recommended her to the hiring committee of Freedom House. She was a friend through church, a fellow mom who had been up to her ears in child-rearing at the same time I was, and we spent some of our hours home with the children together. I knew that the hiring committee would not regret their decision to hire her. Michele brought insight and common sense to the team. She was always looking for what was driving the kids' behaviors and yet had no problem establishing clear and definitive boundaries by communicating what was or was not acceptable. The kids were generally respectful to her as Michele had a way of laying the rubber on the road without threatening their autonomy. Throughout our time together she proved herself to be a reliable team member, consistent with professionals. community, and clients.

After working at Freedom House with Michele, I was later blessed with the opportunity to work with her again at the girls' group home on the reservations of the Oneida Tribe of Indians. This time the tables had turned and, since she now managed that facility, she was the one advocating for me in the hiring process for a drug and alcohol counselor position at the girl's adolescent group home in Oneida. Michele had established herself as a valuable and respected team member with the tribal administration. She was instrumental in my being hired and welcomed into the AODA team at Oneida. Our philosophies of grace and accountability once again benefited the children we worked with.

Years later when Tom and I were considering purchasing what would eventually be A Better Choice Group Home, I would turn to her for wisdom and expertise. Michele was a wizard when it came to state regulations and knowing how to write and implement policy and procedure. We spent endless hours developing schedules, program structure, and numerous programs that would contribute to the goal of mending broken children. This concept began to appear like a viable and feasible adventure, not to mention terrifying and exciting.

During our time together at Freedom House, there was another strong professional that had joined the team. Her name was Marn Gibson. Marn was compassionate, empathetic, and a stickler for details. She had the uncanny ability of sensing when boundaries were crossed and when to draw the red line, standing firm in her expectations of those around her. Marn had been an invaluable member of the Freedom House team. I was the family therapist, and she was the case manager working directly with the clients. We had worked closely together regarding family issues and how they reflected in the child's treatment and progress.

Michele and I turned to Marn and pitched the philosophy and intent of what at this time was still a concept and unfulfilled dream. Marn was as cautiously optimistic as Michele and I were. The three of us were like-minded in more ways than one. Not only did we share ideals in our approach to adolescent development and recovery, but we also shared a common faith and belief system that was crucial to our work. While Candlelight Vision Corp., the eventual non-profit entity, was not a faith-based program, every phase of development was covered in prayer and, I believe, in God's direction. The belief was led by a God through whom all things were possible and whom loved unconditionally and whom we were tasked to emulate.

Throughout this process I would argue with God. That He really needed to find someone else who was smarter and more well equipped than I to complete this project for Him. It was at these times He would remind me of the scripture that states "He will use the least among us..." Well, Lord, no argument there. I was left with the only other choice: to listen and obey. He ended up providing me with three honorary sisters who, in his graciousness, were certainly capable and competent, Marn, Michele and soon after, Danel Burchby.

Marn, with her keen eye for detail, was tasked with writing the business plan that we would take to the bank seeking funds for this mission.

Marn dutifully poured herself into the business plan. She researched, verified, and polished the dream into a professional masterpiece that wowed the bank and its decision makers. We heard from the president of the bank that indeed the business plan was one of the most well written and professional documents that he had seen in his tenure at the bank. It was a proud moment when they funded not only the mortgage, but program costs, startup costs, and remodeling costs. Finally, our dream was becoming a reality.

The fourth compadre on the administration team joined us a few months later. She was solidly embedded in the social work scene but was home with a new baby when this idea came to fruition. Danel was everything and more than we could have hoped for. A state licensed social worker, she immediately understood and identified with our vision. Danel brought a valuable depth to our programming that expanded the vision and program for A Better Choice Group Home, the very first of our programs, and later all of the programs that would make up Candlelight Vision Corp. She brought her ideas and programming elements that only solidified our reputation as an agency that would meet the needs of many families and children.

Danel and I developed a presentation on our philosophy and program. The administrative team decided together that we did not want to limit ourselves to a single county for placement of children. We would seek placement contracts throughout the state. That decision was central to protecting program autonomy as well as preventing interference with our program philosophy. It would also keep us out of individual county political frays that are a natural part of bureaucracy.

After some long work days, even longer work evenings, and plenty of coffee and whiteout, Danel and I took to the road with our agency presentation highlighting what we were offering and why we believed it would be effective. And most importantly, we believed for our referral sources, how it would save dollars in the long run to invest in treating troubled adolescents before they, and later their children too, became entrenched in the system. Introducing ourselves and our program to numerous counties and referral sources across the state became an essential part of our job description, as we were continually seeking to spread the word to any and all placement agencies throughout Wisconsin. After those initial trips and presentations, we continued our travel adventures, going to prescreen potential clients that were referred to us for years to come.

I will forever be grateful to the founding mothers. The time, dedication, and loyalty of these three women who poured themselves into developing an extraordinary program that planted seeds and made lifelong impacts on so many people.

2

Making Dreams a Reality: Mary Kay and Tom's story

~ The ABC House

Mary Kay

On June 9, 2008, Candlelight Vision Corp. (CVC) was 10 years old. As we reminisced about the events of the last decade of our life, Tom and I mused, *'If we knew then what we know today would we still have bought that first house?'* Neither one of us ever answered that question, but if pushed to answer I believe the answer would have been yes. We were blessed with a naiveté that protected us from becoming lost in logistics, statutes and self-doubt that could have prevented so many miracles. As with anything, it's what you don't know that gets in the way.

And there was plenty that we were blissfully unaware of. But graciously those things did not reveal themselves all at once. Only in part, one crisis at a time, did we have to tackle each hardship that came our way. Each battle was vindicated by the privilege of watching children and families find purpose and meaning in their pain. There were many losses and defeats along the way, for staff, families, and those angry, wounded teens who couldn't or wouldn't surrender to life on life's terms. I guess in retrospect Garth Brooks answers the question of if we had known in his song *The Dance* where he wisely sings, "I COULD HAVE MISSED THE PAIN, BUT I'D HAVE HAD TO MISS THE DANCE." We had to dance; we knew no other way.

In 1997 Tom and I came to realize that we had unwittingly become part of the sandwich generation. While we were raising kids and being loving, doting grandparents to two very active grandsons, my mother developed breast cancer and, shortly after that, Alzheimer's. Tom was well established in his role of Domestic Engineer, as he was the full time stay-at-home parent to four feisty adolescent ladies placed in our treatment foster home. We were also launching our youngest daughter from the nest to her freshman year at university. I was working some fairly normal but intense hours. Watching my mother, a very bright, intelligent Registered Nurse slip slowly but most certainly from reality into a dark and encompassing abyss was one of the most painful experiences I had encountered. It was surpassed only by the despair of my father as her lack of reality became his daily trial.

One of the hobbies that Tom and I shared in those days was to explore "couldjas" on Sunday afternoons. We would scan the Open Houses in the newspaper, go exploring real-estate nightmares, and then spend the rest of the afternoon discussing "couldja do this and couldja do that" to create a silk purse out of a sow's ear. Inevitably we were planning apartments for the kids we had in care, or an Independent Living House for kids who were aging out of care with no place to go. Although Tom was the most practical of our team, we always shared a heart for kids that were hurting. Helping children that were in distress and pain, often showing it through antisocial behaviors, was a passion that we and our children share. Our two adult daughters joined me working at the group home as Case Managers at different times throughout the years.

One Sunday a dear friend of ours, Anne Van Roy, who also happened to be a realtor, told us of this "diamond in the rough home" in a nearby town. So, with our usual curiosity, we decided we would go look. That's all we ever did was look - when there was time. Well, we went to look at an old homestead house in a pretty run-down area on the main drag of this small town. Neither one of us were prepared for what happened next. We fell in love with the potential of a very old, very needy, property. It had a front and back staircase and this amazing round wall. The "couldja" process was soon in full swing. One of the deciding factors was that I could leave my job and be more autonomous (ha!) thus having more time to assist and support my father in caring for my mother. That Sunday was the day that our hobby of looking at houses became our obsession. Renovating this property to house wounded children became our mission. We closed on the house in November and began renovating from top to bottom, inside to outside in February of 1998. It truly was a family affair, every waking moment for every able-bodied family member and friend was engulfed by creating an environment that would prove to be a safe place for children to feel and heal.

Renovating an entire house at once turned out to be quite the undertaking. It also proved to be good practice for what was to come with the children in the sense that contractors often behave much like adolescents. The plasterer whined that the electrician was putting too many holes in the ceiling. Everything was a crisis. They made promises that they had no intention of keeping. Molehills became mountains and mountains became molehills and nothing, absolutely nothing, happened on time. I found myself longing for some feisty foster child to be in my face changing my name. At least I knew how to deal with that!

So many wonderful people came to assist and donated their time in making this house a home: staff to be, parents of foster children we had in our home, our dear friends. Our daughters Nora and Leah painted their hearts out. Of course, Nora reminded us with each brush stroke that she "hated the color pink" and Leah hovered over me reminding me frequently that women of my age "had bad hips so should be careful on that ladder." Tom and our son Brian hung perilously from the scaffolding at the top of the house removing asphalt siding. All the while my son in-law played tag with my seven- and eight-year-old grandsons up the front staircase and down the back. With a June first deadline, we were working 12-to-14-hour days. There was no time for Calgon moments. Tom limped down the steps every night, only to crawl out of bed the next morning, have 3 naproxen 2 cups of coffee and head for the house to start another 14-hour day. The Lutzows were on a mission, and towards the end it was best accomplished if we stayed on different floors from each other, or at least in different rooms.

Tom was an absolute saint, and his humor and patience got us through many stressful moments. I overheard him telling a contractor one day "Let's just cut to the chase on this. I always get the last word and here it is...ask Mary Kay." They both laughed heartily and I snuck back upstairs giggling at how handily he had passed the buck, hopeful that he was outgrowing his "if you can't see it from the highway, don't worry about it" motto.

In the meantime, there were state licensing standards to meet and hoops to jump through. A neighborhood meeting where we needed to notify and meet with the neighbors was required as this was to be a house in which at risk teenagers would live. Not everyone's favorite neighbors. We researched and got names of every person living in the area; we created a mailing list and sent out invitations to a dinner meeting. I was familiar with how ugly these meetings could be, and my anxiety was through the roof. I cooked a dinner of beef bourguignon with desserts and coffee for the meeting. On the evening of the meeting, there was a huge snowstorm and the only people there were soon-to-be staff. We did eat well, however. There were no phone calls, no boisterous neighbors, and lots of leftovers. I figured we had crossed that hurdle rather handily; wouldn't you think the fact that no one came or called meant no one was objecting?

No such luck. We later found out that the Chief of Police was objecting to the development of the program. He felt the city was going to be overburdened by calls about delinquent teenagers. The message was he may need more police officers to respond to our facility. After hiring an attorney and borrowing a rolling measuring device from a friend, we walked off the distance (in a major sleet storm mind you) between our facility and another CBRF (Community Based Residential Facility) in the area, ensuring we met the standards for distance outlined in a request from local authorities. Two meetings later the City Council granted our exception. The Chief of Police kissed me on the cheek, said congratulations, and promised to support us any way he could.

I am very proud of how CVC's relationship with the police department developed; Each staff person that was hired learned that we do not call the police unless there are no other options. One of the greatest compliments we have ever received was when one of the officers responding to an incident at the house told staff, "We know that when you guys call you need someone to respond." A deal was struck, and it was a win-win situation. I got a kiss from the Chief, and we wouldn't call his officers because some darling child called us a rude name or refused to go to bed.

We were unable to open June 1st because the siding wasn't done, but by June 9th the beds were made, and the program was in place. The siding got done, we passed State inspection, and our first clients were placed. The learning curve had begun. One week later I placed my mother in an Alzheimer's specific group home and she, just like our clients at the group home, begged, threatened, cajoled, manipulated, guilt tripped, wept, and hoped beyond hope to go home. While my father, my brothers and I wept and second guessed and reassured each other that this was what was necessary to keep mom safe, empathy was with every breath I took as I personally and professionally experienced the circle of life with its series of peaks and valleys, joys and heartbreaks. It's a great life if you don't weaken, and for the next ten years there would be no time to weaken.

A Better Choice Group Home, quickly known as ABC, was located on the main thoroughfare of a small town right at the end of an aging residential district and very near the beginning of the downtown area. The city was pleased that an aging eyesore had received a face lift, and quite frankly improved the aesthetics on that corner immensely. Unfortunately, ABC became a rose between two thorns, with two landlords on either side of us who shared the same mentality as the noted slumlord Leona Helmsley. It was often challenging to say the least.

We had some entrepreneurial young men next door on the one side that we strongly suspected were growing and dealing marijuana out of the basement. Occasionally as the mood struck them, they would moon our girls, and I'm not talking the harvest moon. Don't get me wrong, our girls were rarely offended, and would sometimes reciprocate. However, the last straw occurred when an officer came to visit one day with a piece of paper containing the picture and statistics on the new downstairs tenant next door - a registered sex offender!

That pretty much sealed the deal; we could not run a credible program and protect the already vulnerable young ladies in our charge with these obstacles looming in our path. Already, the first place the police checked for runaways was in the basement next door. Every truant child in the School District was in and out of that house all day long scoring on the crop growing in the basement. The very connections we were trying to break were cutting through our backyard on a consistent basis. It was clear the financial investment we had in this property, not to mention our commitment and obligation to provide a healthy environment, was threatened by the existence of these neighbors.

What to do? The fact of the matter was I knew exactly what we had to do. We had to buy that house. In my mind it was that simple. Unfortunately, the bank required two signatures on the mortgage papers, and that guy that slept next to me at night didn't always identify "simple" under the same terms as I did. I was right, Tom was, shall we say, less than enthusiastic. He reminded me of the time required to renovate A Better Choice, and the physical and emotional toll on the family. He reminded me of the condition of the neighboring property and what it would take to bring that property up to code and licensing standards. One by one, each of the concerns he had presented turned out to have a feasible and reasonable solution.

Over the next couple of years in operation, we noticed a pattern in the County's willingness to place girls out of their home. County Social Service Departments were the only referral source for the teens placed with us and they were waiting longer and longer to place teens with us. On one hand it is understandable, and totally defensible from a treatment approach. On the other hand, the unintended consequence was that the girls we were getting were much like the resistant strains of bacteria cropping up in the scientific world. Because they had first been put through a myriad of other treatment interventions, both inpatient and outpatient, they were much more treatment savvy. They were continuously apprising us of our limitations and their rights. It would generally take at least 30 days, some massive power plays, and numerous calls to social workers and family members to finally settle in. And that was usually after a minimum two-week honeymoon while they cased the joint, assessing just where everyone's Achilles heel was, and when and how the best time to draw back the arrow was. Therefore, that often-discussed brown stuff would usually hit the fan at approximately six to eight weeks into the program. Weathering that storm was imperative to find the windows of opportunity to connect and make change for these young women.

As county money got scarcer and budgets got tighter, another pattern we noticed was treatment monies for older 16 year olds and 17 year olds were becoming tighter by the day. They were soon to be of the age where they would be funded by another department's budget. If the system could just hold out long enough for them to violate a law, that would put them on a corrections budget or in the case of mental illness, the young adult budget. There were only so many juvenile dollars to go around and they had to be spent as judiciously as possible. Now, I'm not usually known to be a woman of few words, but this whole cycle to me can be summed up by an old commercial selling tires for your car, YOU CAN PAY ME NOW... OR YOU CAN PAY ME LATER! The obvious inference of course is that you're going to pay one way or the other. In these cases, we are either going to pay somehow for these children now or we will continue to pay for them as a society long into their adult years, and, in the case of the population we serve, those damages would rock the cradles of generations to come.

In assessing this pattern of placing cycles it became apparent to us that there were many, many young ladies aging out of care, or not being offered services due to their age. These girls were unprepared to function in the real world. They would quickly burn out the Social Service and Human Service system and often ended up in dependent abusive relationships, or in corrections. Different budgets yes but the same boat nonetheless - OUR TAX DOLLARS. Thus, the development of our next program, Tender Loving Care Transitional Living Center (TLC^2).

In the year 2000, two years after we opened ABC, we opened Tender Loving Care Transitional Living Center (TLC^2), both incorporated now under the new name Candlelight Vision Corp (CVC). The name and the purpose, "people perish for lack of vision" was created by Michelle, one of the Founding Mothers of Candlelight Vision Corp.

This was yet another one of those times that God had kept us blissfully in the dark. Had we known what the future held, we would not have made the move to purchase the second house. That probably would have been better for us as individuals, but not the children CVC was committed to serving. There are numerous young ladies that come to mind whose own children would be living totally dismal lives if it were not for the transitional skills, healing, and self-confidence their now grown mothers gained from the time they spent at TLC^2.

This transitional home was to embody many of the same philosophies A Better Choice Group Home encompassed: accountability, honesty, respect for self and others, and safety. But it would differ in the goal. While clients at ABC were far and wide going to be returning to their family of origin, the clients of TLC^2 were aging out of the system and likely going to be on their own once discharged. Given this difference, TLC^2 was heavily focused on independent living skills, both practical and concrete, i.e. budgeting, bus routes, and GED tests, as well as the softer skills of socially acceptable language, assertive communication, and hygiene expectations at a job.

After being glaringly confronted with the issue of older teens aging out of care and ending up on a different county department's caseload, we bought the second property in the spring of 1999 and immediately began renovating. In answer to Tom's question, "just who do you suppose is going to do the work on that place?" We hired a very capable and reasonably priced "Jack of all trades." We knew that we had already burnt out our friends and family so "Jack" became a crucial part of realizing our vision. Plans were made, priorities established, paint and equipment purchased. We were on a roll. Both Tom and I were very impressed with the abilities of this "jack." After a short time, however, a pattern developed of no "jack" on Mondays, then there was no "jack" on Fridays. To say the least, I was an unhappy camper. Although very capable, "jack" was not very dependable. We finally got the downstairs completed behind schedule due to "jack's" ever lengthening weekends but completed, nonetheless. At this point we parted ways.

Now that which we had feared the most had come upon us. The entire upstairs which, if you remember, was occupied by the entrepreneurial young men who operated their business out of the basement was to be offices and group rooms and had yet to begin being renovated. I was working an average of 10 to 12 hours per day, and Tom still had four feisty, creative adolescent girls to care for at home. Once again, we were forced to call on all the people that still loved us and vigorously supported the call of Candlelight's vision. The first order of business was to eliminate the danger that anyone spending too much time upstairs or breathed too deeply would test positive for cannabis. It appeared the young gentleman either had to do a lot of product testing or they believed so deeply in the organic plants they raised and sold that they consumed as much as they sold. Suffice it to say that if there was a drug dog on the city police force, they could have made the hit from the other side of the street. Eventually heads cleared, the vision formed, and by the grace of God and our faithful friends and family TLC^2 was ready to open.

Exhausted and once again vowing NEVER AGAIN would we do such an undertaking, Tom and I went "Up North" as they call it in the Midwest, to escape and re-energize. Such trips where it was just the two of us were rare indeed as the piece of property we had in the woods, housed, fed and slept up to twenty or more people on any given weekend. But this time it was going to be just ours; little did we know the dark journey that would begin that weekend.

It was the end of summer in 2000; we had been so occupied with the renovation and licensing of TLC^2 that we had not been "north" all summer. It had been rainy most of the preceding month. What we had longed for the most was to sit quietly in front of the campfire watching the flames flicker and enjoy the smell of outdoors and burning wood that seemed to wipe your mind clear and allow you to just be in the moment, to connect again with a sense of nature an earthy basic spiritual well-being.

None of that was going to happen with a wet fire pit and wet wood. That night, the process of emptying the pit and getting a fire started became one of the most frightening experiences of a lifetime. There was a sudden blowback from the pit that set Tom on fire. The entire front of my husband was flaming as he ran away from the fire pit, stripping his cotton T-shirt up and over his face to escape the flames. He threw the shirt and slapped out the flames on the front of his jeans with his hands, while I powerlessly screamed for help in an empty forest.

Following the ambulance to the nearest hospital 20 minutes away took what seemed like a lifetime, and yet a blur that still seems surreal. Like watching a movie frozen in time all I could do was continue to repeat over and over the same prayer, "Dear God, let him be okay."

At the rural hospital the doctors examined him, cleaned away as much of the debris and scorched skin as they were capable of, and sent us to our family hospital an hour away. They stated, as we were to hear numerous times in the future, two things had made the difference between being transported by me in our vehicle rather than needing a helicopter. One, that he was not wearing a nylon or rayon shirt or pants, and two, that he had the presence of mind to respond as he did, removing the shirt, despite the resulting burns to his face and hands. Had there been any more debris or insult to the burned area he would have been on the helicopter instead. Good thing I couldn't reach him prior to how he responded. I would have had him "stop, drop and roll," which would have left his burned area caked with dirt, sand, and pine needles.

Tom was admitted overnight at the local hospital in order to further treat and clean his burns that were about his face and neck, and to be observed for symptoms of shock. He was released the next day with lots of instructions and an appointment with a specialist.

Although it was very painful, Tom was faithful to the routine established by the doctor. Within a month or so, his face was almost entirely healed with little to no scarring. There remained only one trouble spot on the right side of his neck. The specialist shared that it was a traumatized lymph node that was just going to take time to heal. As time went on, that "traumatized" lymph node continued to get larger and larger. It was obvious that Tom was concerned, although he made no mention of it, relying heavily on the "traumatized lymph node" diagnosis. I tried not to hound him, or overreact, as this usually triggered his resistance, and getting medical treatment took even longer.

Since he already was seeing the Burn Specialist every other week, I decided to wait for that appointment to say something. As it turns out, I didn't have to draw the doctor's attention to anything; he immediately made arrangements for Tom to see an Eye, Ear and Throat surgeon. We would later learn that he also specialized in Oncology. That appointment took a week. By the time Tom went to see Dr. Shaw, the lump on his neck had grown from the size of a walnut to the size of a golf ball. Our oldest daughter had already been on the internet and arranged for a Navigator from the American Cancer Society. I, on the other hand, was allowing my denial to protect me from my fears. Two of our children were unavailable and we decided not to tell them anything until we had solid information to give them. This resulted in Nora, our oldest, being the only one of our children aware that this journey had begun and the only one holding things together. She was a rock and a fountain of knowledge thanks to her contact with the Navigator. Our youngest daughter was out of the country, and we hadn't even told her about Tom being burned, let alone the growing lump on her father's neck.

Dr. Shaw immediately arranged for a biopsy that confirmed everyone's worst fear. Tom was diagnosed with 4th stage head and neck cancer.

Life as we knew it stopped. Looking back over those months I'm reminded of the Footprints poem, I can assure you that the footprints in the sand did not belong to me. Memories of those days remain clouded. I do remember attending a cancer support group, where I received literature on death and grieving.

Approximately three years prior to that, my health insurance company decided that they were no longer going to cover the prescribing doctor that had managed my maintenance medication for over a decade. Our current internist decided, in all his wisdom, that my medication regime was outdated and there were many newer medications on the market that would certainly work more effectively. Thus began the demise of my functional effectiveness. Despite numerous return visits and complaints regarding my continued compromised function he refused to return me to my previous medication regime.

It was a very gradual decline. Probably the people around me noticed that deterioration far before I was able to acknowledge it. Although I was having concerns about my ability to recall things, and there were some episodes of what I referred to as brief check-outs (later I would learn that these were microsleeps), the day that I could no longer deny that something serious was happening was the day I was zooming along the highway. I was watching a car on the on-ramp to gauge my speed to allow him access. The next recollection I had was being halfway across the bridge, which was a fair distance from where I had begun to observe it. Wow, that was scary! I immediately called my internist and asked for a referral. After I explained what had happened, I was referred to a Neurologist. It took some time to be able to see her, but she ran some tests, an MRI, and CAT scan

The good doctor diagnosed me with sleep apnea and reported that my lapse of awareness was indeed an episode of "microsleep" a phenomenon that occurs when a sleep deprived brain grabs an opportunity of non-stimulated quiet time to catch up on zzzz's. This explained earlier episodes that had been occurring with an alarming frequency. Episodes where I would be in staffing and zone out, coming back into an awareness of my absence and try to reorient myself to the discussion at hand.

With a new treatment regime for my apnea and despite our admonitions to "NEVER AGAIN" take on a large undertaking, Candlelight grew to include our third program, PRN (Providing Respite Needs), a freestanding prefabricated home on the "campus" (two parcels of land) later in its years that offered respite to clients who were in danger of being placed out of the home as a intervention to attempt to support families to be able to parent effectively by offering respite from the child regularly. Though the stories ahead of you focus heavily on the group home ABC, you will find a recollection or story or two from both TLC[2] and PRN within these pages.

I wish I could tell you there was a storybook ending to this chapter of our lives of rainbows and warm cuddly goodbyes, but unfortunately that was not the case. For eleven years Candlelight Vision Corp, the staff, the clients and their families, counties, social workers, finances, and the demands of business occupied my waking and most of my sleeping moments. People would say things like "I don't know how you do it." Often staff would be telling me to "go home," and even on occasions clients would tell me I should leave - although often their motives were questionable. I am certainly not telling you this was a one (wo)man show. Quite the contrary, there was a core of dedicated loyal team members that poured their hearts and souls into those programs. The longevity of our Admin Team (the A-Team we called ourselves) was admirable. There were many trials and tribulations, not the least of which were the financial impacts of census, insurance, hiring and training. It was Gary, our gifted accountant, who immediately identified some financial issues and set them straight. All in all, there was always an answer, it may not always have been the answer we were looking for, but God was faithful to provide the answers we needed.

While this narrative is a recount of many people's experiences in relation to the treatment and healing process of adolescents, it encompasses our own healing processes as well. We stayed for the dance despite the pain. Garth Brooks would have been proud.

3

Building Our Reputation

Danel

Getting settled in as a new program and agency in the community was not without its pitfalls and frustrations. As an unknown entity and one not affiliated with a larger agency like Lutheran Social Services or Family Services, it was a major undertaking to begin to build a reputation of integrity and quality within the community and the networks of other agencies that work with the same population we were serving. There can be suspicions and cynicism, and sometimes just plain fear of the unknown. Unfortunately, sometimes that fear and suspicion came from other agencies that could have been collaborating with us.

As a group home licensed by the State, CVC was subject to certain regulations and governed by a licensing agent, including standards for staff education and training, maintaining the physical property, programming for the clients, confidentiality, and of course, safety of all involved. Group homes come up for re-licensing every two years, at which time the licensing agent would make a check of all required material as well as the physical property to ensure everything was up to par. We were assigned Linda Robinson.

Early on, we received referrals from the immediately surrounding counties. To start, we made contacts with the counties we were most familiar with and could build upon our personal reputations with those contacts to build trust and a partnership to serve these young women that most counties were shipping off to far away residential care or group homes, weakening ties to their own families and making it difficult to complete family counseling. Winnebago was one such county. Mary Kay had been a solid provider of treatment foster care services dating back many years and was showing success with the toughest placements, including sexually abused and delinquent female adolescents. I worked for County Human Services as a social worker, liaising with the out of home placements throughout the state and had contacts within the county and a reputation as a hard worker with an eye on what's best for the client.

The front-line social workers that carried the caseloads appeared excited there was to be a new option for placement for adolescent girls in their community. Our home county was our biggest referral source by far. We had a supervising county worker designated to receive requests from the front-line workers for group home placement and then, in turn, refer them to group homes she thought they would be appropriate for.

Since CVC did not specialize, unlike those providing only Alcohol and Drug services or only accepting placement of sexually abused kids, most adolescents that were deemed appropriate for group home level care we could work with. We worked hard at developing a reputation with referral sources. We believed there was good in every child and there was hope for better choices and healthier relationships. Additionally, we did not give up easily. We would put up with runaways and not let the client sabotage her placement just to get away from the structure and rules. This seemed to have the effect of better behavior and not as much energy put into trying to get "kicked out" as they realized it was easier to work their treatment program and be allowed to go home. County workers liked this too as we did not often ask them to scramble to find a new placement for a client we did not want any more. Every feasible intervention was used before we would ask the county to find another placement for a child that was disruptive and only then if it was determined that the adolescent was a danger to herself, others, or the therapeutic milieu of the home. Two clients exemplify this principle we held as we attempted to outstay their patterns and walk with them through thick and thin.

~ a core board member of Candlelight
Vision Corp.

—Anniemae—

Mary Kay

Behavior disruptions and misbehaviors by our residents were often by design, a way they had learned to push others away so as not to have to make an attachment, or as a power play to get what they wanted. One such case was Anniemae. Anniemae was a child of the system, growing up for the past twelve years in numerous different foster homes when her parents were unable to or chose not to care for her. Throughout this time, Anniemae had woven a fantasy life for herself, one in which she had many expensive possessions waiting for her, many friends, and more riches to come. The truth was much harsher. She had only recently found out who her father was and he was currently serving a twenty year prison sentence for sexually abusing his step-son. Her mother had left her with a friend at age three and never returned for her. Thirteen foster homes dotted Anniemae's background. She had disrupted each foster home after a certain amount of time by accusing the foster home of mistreatment, by running away, or by behaving so badly that she would be removed. She simply seemed incapable of forming a healthy attachment and when it appeared she was getting close to another person, feelings of fear and inadequacy kicked in and fueled behaviors so insufferable and instilled such fear in her caretakers that they felt they had no choice but to have her removed. In this way, Anniemae moved between homes, maintaining her dream that someday someone (other than her present caretaker) would rescue her and she would live happily ever after.

Anniemae repeated this pattern at the group home. A beautiful girl, with dark brown hair and eyes and a slim build, Anniemae could pull at your heartstrings with just a look. Her pleasant manners made you want to help her and make things better for her. Dressing more maturely than most girls her age, she looked at times like the quintessential college freshman. Anniemae, though, was easily frustrated by limits and expectations, pulling away quickly, cursing and seething when told "no." She earned numerous consequences with her behaviors and quick cruelty to others. Another group home may have been happy to ask for her removal after the first few instances, given there was no family to work with and provide incentive. CVC stuck it out and Anniemae remained with us until she was eighteen.

—Erin—

Other times behaviors were simply a social skills issue, where residents had not learned to cope with not getting what they wanted in an age-appropriate way. A good example of this is Erin. Erin was a slight young lady with blonde hair she kept up in a ponytail. She had two involved parents that hated each other, but were very invested in Erin. Unfortunately, Erin had been shown some particularly intolerable behaviors, which she learned were effective in pushing people away, as well as bullying people into getting what she wanted. Erin had simply been taught to tantrum, and tantrum she did.

We often saw a screaming Erin kicking her feet on the floor and furniture, pounding her fists, and even holding her breath. Erin was fourteen at the time, had been expelled from school, and was now on her way to being asked to stop attending the alternative school she was at.

"Fuck you! Fuck you! Fuck you! Fuck you....you're such a fat bitch who never should have been born. I hate this fucking place. AAAAAAaaaaaaaaaaaaaaagggghhhhhhhhhhhhhh," emanated from the living room during one such tantrum when she was not allowed to smoke a cigarette.

Erin was disruptive on a regular basis, but never as much as when she was with her parents or had just seen them. Her parents, especially her mother, showed literally some of the same behaviors. Social skills were in short supply in that household. As easy as it would have been to ask for Erin's removal in order to quiet down the house, it would have left Erin free to repeat her pattern at another placement and have the satisfaction that if she did not like the rules, a few strategically placed screams could get her somewhere else. It would also have precluded her from learning any new skills to help her cope with the anxiety of not being in control. We stuck it out with Erin as her tantrums slowly declined.

~ Five ABC residents playing at the local park

4

Defining Success

Danel

Success can be as simple as a shift in attitude, a glimpse of a client looking outside herself, or a moment of maturity and insight. We hope and pray these moments turn into a lifetime of new patterns, but we are content to be grateful for the moment and know it may soon pass to be replaced by old, easier ways of thinking.

Savannah gave us an example of how fleeting these moments can be, yet also an example of a true change beginning to take seed in a young mind. The following are both messages written by Savannah to Mary Kay, the Treatment Director who worked very closely with the girls. Mary Kay gave her heart and soul to her work with each individual adolescent, knowing that in each one, though hurting in some way, is the potential for a strong young woman who could make a difference. She knew encouraging this potential required a delicate balance of accountability, unconditional regard, and generous doses of nurturing.

A handwritten letter was left on the kitchen table one day after the girls had left for school. Savannah's large, roundish handwriting was apparent on the envelope. It was addressed to Mary Kay. Savannah was on Phase C, over halfway through with her program at ABC. Though prone to stubbornness and poor attitude at times, Savannah had made true progress in changing her ways of thinking and working through her placing issues and underlying family problems. She was usually dressed in semi-Goth clothes and retained her pitch-black hair. Her makeup though, had taken on a more understated look of late and her pretty blue eyes were more apparent as she wore her hair away from her face.

With some anticipation, Mary Kay opened the envelope. As she read the words, she sat down at the table and tears began to come:

"Dear Mrs. Lutzow,

I would like to show you my appreciation for the hard work and the time you spend on the many girls in the house. Many girls need you for support and guidance. You help us make better choices in our lives. By providing us with new and healthy programs, we will become people that are more responsible. The way you handle everything just comes out so right, that sometimes I wonder if you really are an angel. You make it easier for me to relate things in my life to you because you are honest and open about yourself. This helps me get many things off my chest and out in the open so I do not feel so stressed.

The tender loving care that you provided helped me more to become a better person, and someone I can now trust and love. You are my inspiration, because of all of your hard work. If I had to handle so many things, it would leave me discombobulated. I now believe that there are people like you in this world that I will come to meet in my life, and I will not be alone in my years to come. You were also there to guide me through my spiritual awakenings, and everything that had to do with my family. All I know is that you replaced the care and love that was missing in my life when I was a child.

I especially appreciate all of the tools and techniques you have provided me with to take on this long trip called life. My thought process has improved a great deal, and I can handle situations in a completely different matter. My tools will help a long time in life with school, family, work and other relationships in my life. I am so grateful for all of the things you have offered. You have also taught me to love myself and to praise myself, this will help me to get through life a lot easier. Thank you.

Sincerely,

Savannah

One of the things that made this letter so amazing was that only a few weeks earlier, Savannah was going through a rough patch. Old behaviors were emerging that we hadn't seen since her placement. She earned consequences and did not seem to care one way or the other about her future. In one of her more disruptive moments, she was sent to the Learning Center by Mary Kay to have some time to think without distraction.

The Learning Center was simply a desk placed in a quiet corner that staff could easily check on but gave privacy of thought and removed an audience from a tantruming child. Girls could either be sent to the Learning Center by a staff member, usually with an assignment, or could choose to go there on her own in order to self-intervene in negative behaviors or regulate their emotions. A staff member had taken to placing inspirational quotes on the wall by the Learning Center the week Savannah had been sent there. As protocol dictated, she was continually checked on and when calm, she was allowed to return to the general milieu of the group.

Soon after, a sharp-sighted staff noted the quote had been torn down and was lying tucked into a corner by the desk's left front leg. As she picked it up she noticed, in large roundish handwriting, obviously Savannah's, the following scribbled in angry strokes:

"I'm gunna kill Mary Kay à Cunt, SlimFast Bitch, Fat Ass"

Mary Kay was soon in possession of the now defaced inspirational quotation. She quietly tucked it away in her desk. She now has both of Savannah's notes and keeps them stored next to each other to remind her not to get too full of herself and of course of the power love and nurturing to command permanent change.

5

Pre-Screening Clients

Danel and Mary Kay

One of the most enjoyable parts of the job was pre-screening potential clients. County Health and Human Service agencies referred girls for placement after they had been through the court system and deemed appropriate for out-of-home placement, specifically to a group home. At this point, the case worker would decide which group home he or she wished to place their client and send out referral information, most often consisting of the most recent court report, delinquency history - which is equivalent to an adult's "rap sheet," social history, and any other pertinent information such as school or counseling reports, past placement history, medical history, etc. Most case workers would also make a phone call to CVC to inquire about open beds and the appropriateness of their referral while informally answering any questions we had such as special education needs, past abuse history, social skills, independent living skills needs, and alcohol and drug use history.

When CVC had an open bed at any one of the group homes, as part of the clinical leadership team, we would interview potential clients to see how we felt they might fit into the group home as well as what benefit they might receive from the treatment we offered. Most often we could determine by the paperwork and the case worker's phone call if we would be likely to accept a child or not, but the pre-screening interview process was helpful to be able to connect with the client, reduce her anxiety, and really get a feel for someone despite what they "looked like on paper." The significance of the interview came from knowing that case workers could and often did "spin" a girl's paper to look one way or the other in hopes of matching more easily to a placement. Being stung a few times by inaccurate information, we were vigilant about seeing the girls in person or at the very least interviewing them by phone to get a personal feel for their mindset.

Now of course we were aware that the girls, most likely, did not wanted to be placed. These were not voluntary clients. In fact, some were extremely set against being placed. We learned to look past the verbal abuse and other strategies we saw over and over again for trying not to get accepted and look at whether we could work with the behaviors they presented, whether we could meet their needs, whether the girls were in touch with their feelings or had any insight into their behaviors, whether they would respond to groups, and whether they were safe for the milieu in the group home that we already had. Sometimes a girl would be appropriate for the group home, but not with the mix of clients that were already placed there.

An example is a girl who might have a history of running away and being gone for long periods of time. Normally, this is an appropriate placement as we work with the county and the family to put a safety plan in place. However, when we have three or four other girls who we believe are on the cusp of running, a new placement coming in could urge or convince the other clients or provide the means to run, putting them in danger. A girl might offer to hide another girl, show her how to stay on the run longer, or introduce her to friends and acquaintances that will help her go "underground." This may happen for several reasons. One, a girl might not want to run alone. Two, a girl might like to have that kind of power over another. Or three, the girl might need or want something from another girl such as money, a diversion for the staff, or a scapegoat if they get caught. Another example of appropriate issues but inappropriate timing is if a girl has a certain gang involvement and we believed that would constitute a danger to the other girls or has the potential for physical conflict in the house. We would decline such a placement.

Other reasons girls were not accepted were if we believed we could not meet their needs. For example, if a girl had a recent history of a suicide attempt, the pre-screening process helps us determine where her suicidal ideation is at that time. A group home is not equipped to handle actively suicidal clients. If a girl has such extreme mental health needs, needs for physical restraint due to aggressive behaviors, or other issues that may jeopardize the client or the rest of the clients, we ethically need to ask the county to seek other placement, sometimes at a higher level of care.

The pre-screening process is helpful on so many levels, not the least of which is reducing some of the client's anxieties about being shipped off to an unknown place. Oftentimes their minds fill in the gaps of what might take place at a group home or at times, they may have gotten information about the group home from a client who left on unhappy terms who might angrily lash out about staff, the rules, or the program. During the pre-screening interview, the client is allowed to ask questions and interview us as well, thereby getting answers from the source. At times, the pre-screening interviews are as funny as they are helpful and provide a welcome comic relief of sorts.

6

Pre-Screening Interviews: The good, the bad, and the funny

Danel

Because we were responsible for the therapeutic milieu and process, Mary Kay, the Director, and I, as the Lead Social Worker were the ones most often conducting the pre-screening interviews. Though we preferred for the girls to come to the group home for the interview, arranging transportation and their legal status often interfered and we would end up traveling to their current placement. I remember a time when a client was doing her best to not get accepted. This young lady was placed at shelter care, a "holding tank" of sorts for adolescents. Boys and girls, sometimes as young as 11, who were in between or awaiting placement in foster homes, group homes, or child care institutions temporarily lived here. Others may be placed there for several days after a family fight or runaway in order for things to cool down at home. Built as a big ranch style house, our county's shelter care was somewhat homier than other counties. Our neighboring county's shelter care facilities were locked and more institutionalized.

The girl we were interviewing this day was pretty invested in having us turn her down for placement. Thirteen years old with goth black dyed hair and several piercings outside of her ears, this girl was angry at the world and not afraid to show it. Every other word out of her mouth was a cuss word. She rose off the couch and began pacing the room as we moved from asking her if we could answer any questions for her to beginning our standard questions about her, her family, and her situation that brought her to this point. Her voice rose to a shout from the first question about the spelling of her last name. A bigger girl, she moved with confidence and anger, throwing cushions off the couch, and stomping her feet. We, nevertheless, persevered, as we could sense it was an act meant to scare us off. Moving on despite not getting many answers, I asked an easy question on a scale of least to worst anxiety producing.

"What's your mom's name?"

A string of epithets followed before the question even completely left my mouth.

"GoddamnmotherfuckeralwaysinmybusinessshitIcan'tbelievethis-goddamnshit-FUCK!"

When she came up for air, I quickly saw my last chance at engaging this girl. Poising my pencil above my questionnaire and putting on a face like it was critical this be recorded, I asked with a straight face,

"Wow! That's a pretty long name! Does she go by anything shorter?"

Silence. Her eyes cut up to me and I saw a quick smirk. The ice was broken. We didn't acknowledge her prior behavior, just simply moved on from where we left off. She didn't answer every question or sit perfectly still but we managed to get what we needed and hopefully left her feeling a whole lot more comfortable than when she began the interview.

Another favorite pre-screening story of mine is a young lady Mary Kay and I went to an interview. She was placed in an alternative school in a neighboring town and the teacher agreed to let us come and see her there. Hanna was referred by a county known for only placing extremely difficult adolescents who had exhausted every other form of intervention. We had, in the past, really struggled with their placements, feeding our skepticism going in.

Hanna was a 17-year-old, who appeared unusually naive and imma-ture for a group home placement. A solidly built girl who hunched her shoulders when she walked, but kept her head up trying to look tough. Short blonde hair was cropped to her head, looking slightly unkempt. Hanna had good eye contact and portrayed a very important, tough, and unruffled demeanor. Eager to interview, Hanna plopped down on the chair and let us know she was ready to answer any questions we had. She breezed through the interview and seemed to be very open. We then began asking her about her past and current drug and alcohol use. Hanna apparently saw this as a prime time to inflate herself and her "coolness." We immediately recognized some of her answers as ex-aggerated. This is not uncommon. Though some, maybe most, clients will minimize their drug and alcohol use because they think it will play out better for them if adults do not believe they have a problem. Para-doxically, some kids maximize their use and try to impress people with their tales of excessive drug use to scare people away. Typically, we ask a client what drugs they have tried, how often they use it, and how much they use at a time. Hanna's answers were suspect.

"What other drugs have you used?"

"Acid"

"How much do you use at a time?"

"Two or three pills. I don't know. My friend gave them to me"

Hmmmmm...this didn't sound right....

"Pills, really? Are you sure they were acid? Maybe she gave you some other kind of pill?"

Hanna narrowed her eyes at us now, thinking she may have been insulted. "Yes, of course, I'm sure. I saw the box."

Okay, this made less sense the deeper we got into the conversation. One last try: "I'm not sure acid comes in a box...what did it say?"

Hanna huffed now, sure we were either disrespecting her or totally clueless, and said in a raised voice, "It said RIGHT ON THE BOX 'Ant – ACID.'"

I caught myself, saying nothing and certainly not looking at Mary Kay or betraying a smile, as I realized Hanna had most certainly eaten a couple of harmless Tums tablets that she believed were hard core drugs. We went on, suppressing grins and simply moved to the next question, allowing Hanna to save face.

Sometimes pre-screening interviews took on a life of their own not only from the clients but from the circumstances and surroundings.

We arrived at the prison in the early afternoon after a two and half-hour drive stretched too close to four hours because Mary Kay and I had gotten lost – *again*! Keep in mind this trip pre-dated GPS. Never mind that we had made this trip dozens of times, we had somehow managed to get on a road neither one of us recognized and made several more wrong turns trying to correct our mistake, becoming hopelessly turned around. We pulled over at an intersection next to a tavern and in sight of a county highway sign. Frustrated, we called Southern Oaks Girls School, our destination, to explain our tardiness and ask for directions.

"We are across from Happy's Bar on County Highway N," I explained to the control officer.

"No, you can't be," he shot back.

"What??" I thought. *"Didn't he hear me?"*

"I am," I cleverly replied. "I can see it from here."

After several rounds of this same refrain, he put on another officer who managed to figure out we had crossed the county line and were on a *different* County N than the first officer assumed. Forty minutes later and a grand total of an hour and a half late, we pulled into the parking lot at Southern Oaks.

Southern Oaks Girls' School (SOGS), now defunct, was built in October of 1994 as the secure juvenile correctional facility for adjudicated female youth. It housed adolescent females who had been adjudicated (convicted) of offenses ranging from theft to operating a motor vehicle without the owner's consent to drug and alcohol related offenses to homicide. Any female under 18 in the state that was sentenced to corrections as a juvenile ended up at Southern Oaks Girls' School. Its two buildings, Main and Annex, were located on 2.8 acres of land just south of Milwaukee. Southern Oaks was built after overcrowding at Lincoln Hills School due to the increase in female adolescent offenders and the inherent problems with a co-ed population that made a separate facility necessary.

In 2011, Southern Oaks Girls' School was closed after maintaining only 20%-30% capacity. This was due to a decrease in serious crime by youth as well as counties using alternatives to corrections placements. At the time, though, Southern Oaks was in full use. Technically a secure correctional facility, it was, for all intents and purposes, a prison with barbed wire atop high fences, uniforms, and locked cells. In other ways Southern Oaks made efforts at recognizing its population by providing cheerily painted day rooms, colorful posters inviting residents to join Girl Scouts (meetings held inside the fence, of course), and an activity schedule featuring arts and crafts, mentors, and cooking. As you entered the lobby, you waited to be buzzed in the doors by central control. Passing through one set of doors, you are trapped in a four by eight foot space as the second set of doors is programmed to stay closed until the first set is locked again.

In the lobby, visitors then walk through a metal detector and pass their picture ID through a drawer to be examined by the officers behind the mirrored glass of the central control office. After signing in, we are buzzed into the unit where an escort will take us to pre-screen our potential client. Usually, we are allowed to interview a client in the visitor area, but since our interviewee, Shanda, had been placed in Touchstone, the equivalent of "the hole" or solitary confinement, she no longer had the privilege of meeting us in that luxurious of a space. Our escort, a largish woman whose keys jangled against her leg as she walked, led us to the unit Shanda was being held on. She explained Shanda was close to her release but may have jeopardized this due to her recent behaviors, which apparently include flashing some construction workers who were completing a project on the facility grounds.

When a resident of SOGS violated a rule, they were written up, or for more serious offenses given a hearing and a consequence if found guilty of that offense. All offenses from violence to passing notes and sharing clothes affect the resident's permanent records and may affect her release. Unlike adult offenders who are given specific sentences or at least a range of time, juvenile offenders are placed on one year supervision terms, which can be extended at a court hearing upon the recommendation of the county case worker. Therefore, a juvenile's sentence is, in fact, indeterminate, and her release date is based upon behaviors while in the institution. Every few months, the resident faces OJOR (Office of Juvenile Offender Review), a one-woman committee, to review her progress, or lack thereof. The county case worker, parents, and in-house social worker, as well as the resident are invited to the OJOR. Typical recommendations are: review again in 60, 90 or 120 days, or recommend for release. Shanda was getting close to being recommended for release as her county case worker had asked us to interview her for post-corrections placement upon her release. However, her recent antics may have put this on hold.

We reached the unit and were led into a small room with three chairs and a table pushed to the side. There were no windows. Mary Kay and I selected our chairs and were told Shanda would be brought in shortly. After a few minutes the jingle of keys alerted us that Shanda was on her way. 16-year-old Shanda came through the doors with a small smile on her face. Her long, shaggy dark hair spilled into her eyes and her large frame was draped in the SOGS uniform of navy-blue pants and an ill-fitting white button-down shirt. What caught both of our eyes though, was that Shanda was completely shackled. Both hands and feet were manacled so she was unable to push her hair out of her eyes, or tuck her shirt in. Her escort sat her down in the free chair, let us know how to reach her when we were done, and made a move to leave. Mary Kay asked quickly if the handcuffs could be removed during the interview.

"No, sorry. Policy," the escort stated. "They need to stay on."

Stunned, we conducted our first interview of a tethered client. Unfortunately, some of the difficult questions we asked elicited tears from Shanda and, unable to wipe her eyes or nose, she sniffed through parts of the interview, not complaining. Shanda was obviously rough around the edges and lacked social skills and impulse control. Severely sexually abused, she was also dealing with a younger brother dying of leukemia. We accepted her and she soon earned her release from SOGS to come to CVC.

Though Shanda was successfully released from SOGS to CVC, others have been able to successfully sabotage their releases.

Mary Kay and I interviewed a 14-year-old young lady at an urban high school at midday, as her social worker could not get time away to transport her to the group home for an interview. Somehow we managed to find our way to the school without getting lost, and pulled into the parking lot of a massive institutional brick structure, proudly claiming the name of one of this city's toughest schools. With a high dropout rate and violent incidents increasing, this school had its hands full. Several police cars were pulled up to the yellow curb in front of the circle drive. We found a parking space and weaved our way through a crowd of teens just released for the lunch hour. Several minutes later, we had found the office and were explaining our presence to an overwhelmed looking secretary who flipped through pages of a calendar while claiming she would "figure out where we were supposed to be." Finally, she located the right page and informed us we were to be in a different office down the hall for the *alternative students* – read: behavioral problems.

More weaving through the crowds of high school kids, most taller than us, and we nudged open the doorway to find a clot of people blocking the office from the inside. We recognized police uniforms and connected them to the cars outside. Stepping back, we paused and decided to approach the door after a few more minutes. Voices emanated from the office.

"WHAT??? I dint DO IT!!"

"The Hell you ARE takin' my shit!"

"WhatEVER."

When the voices died down a bit, we successfully navigated our way into the Alternative Office, which now had a line of surly looking teenagers sitting on a bench with a police officer at each end holding down the fort. Now about thirty minutes late for our appointment, we gingerly approached the secretary after she appeared to be done communicating with the officer and re-explained our presence.

"Bria? Bria *who*??" demanded the secretary.

Mary Kay repeated her name as well as the social worker's name who had set up the visit, only to be answered by one of the kids doing bench time.

"She's absent today – skipped out."

Our hopes were dashed--traveling two hours and navigating our way through the chaos at the school, only to be told Bria decided not to show up to school today. As we were digesting this news, the secretary fired back at the student,

"Don't be shooting off your mouth."

Turning to Mary Kay she read off her attendance sheet, "Bria is showing up for her fourth hour, but not for the first three. I'll call her counselor to get you a room, Honey, while she's still here."

Whew! Progress. We did meet with Bria that day, got her story, and accepted her into CVC. Bria was in foster care at that time and had only been attending the school for about three months, interrupted by runaways and truancy.

This was just a glimpse of Bria and many other kids' daily lives, attending school and trying to learn with innumerable distractions, including the police, or sometimes not even attending, either out of boredom, being overwhelmed, or being too distracted by their own life issues to think about dealing with interacting with 2,500 other teenagers on a daily basis.

Bria often skipped school to spend time with her boyfriend. As she put it, he gave her relief. A safe place. A place where she wasn't reminded that she was failing four subjects and had difficulty keeping up with the reading assignments. A place where she wasn't in danger of being pulled into a verbal or physical fight between other students, who both tried to intimidate her and gain her alliance. She had quickly learned she was one of thousands, and the truancy officer never managed to make it to her home. She was a hash mark on an attendance page, and it was much easier to quietly fail her classes than to plot her course through high school alone.

Another pre-screening adventure took place, again at Southern Oaks Girls' School. A new county had called CVC to inquire about placement. As a non-profit whose existence depended on providing exceptional service to girls, we were always excited about hearing from new counties. New referrals meant our reputation was spreading and hopefully it was becoming known that we were making a difference in the lives of young people and their families. The new case worker completed the referral process and faxed over the paperwork we had asked for. We noticed immediately that the paperwork consisted of several times the amount of information we usually received...this was red flag number one. Sifting through the mounds of reports, includ- ing numerous reports from SOGS disciplinary committee, a pattern emerged...self-harm, threats to others, hallucinations.

Though Abby had not had an incident of violence or extreme self- harm in over six months, the accounts were harrowing. She had used her bra to try to suffocate herself while simultaneously trying to drown her- self in the toilet while serving her time in Touchstone solitary confine- ment. What really caught our eye was the fact that the county SWAT team had been called in numerous times to deescalate a situation she had created, or to subdue her enough to transport her to a Mental Health Institute, where she had been a patient over five times while a resident at SOGS. This was all highly unusual. SOGS has their own security force that carries handcuffs and pepper spray; it was extraordinary that they would call, much less *repeatedly* call, a county law enforcement agency to deal with an out-of-control teen. SOGS also has their own mental health unit including physicians and psychiatric nurses. It was unheard of, at least to us, that they would utilize a Mental Health Hospital that was over two hours away.

Despite our misgivings, this was a new county and we wanted to put forth the effort to please them by at least going to see Abby. We had already decided she was not appropriate for group home placement by reading her reports. Mary Kay and I read from the voluminous file during the two-hour drive, sometimes laughing in shock or literally dropping our jaws at the extent of her antics. She had been tased numerous times and been placed in Touchstone over a dozen times for lengthy periods during her one-year stay at Southern Oaks. However, we did notice that her behaviors had calmed during the last six months she was there, and we pored over the psychiatrist's report to see if medication management had been responsible for this change. It turned out that both medication and therapy had been initiated, which had seemed to give Abby some relief from her mental health symptoms and enable her to control some of the more dangerous and unacceptable behaviors. She was quite a bright girl, we realized, looking over her school averages, though she had not attended public school for the past three years.

"Hmmmm...interesting case," we thought as we drew up to the doors and prepared to meet Abby. A brief wait in the visitor room passed while we read the signs that indicated no soda was allowed for residents and everyone was expected to use the bathroom one at a time. Abby appeared at the doorway with her escort. She had a shiny, round face with large brown eyes and stringy brown hair. Her institution clothes fit snugly. She looked up at us shyly at first, but then exuded confidence as she shook our hands and began to talk. Her story flowed out of her without shame. Raised by grandparents after her mother took off. No father. She described fights with her sisters until her grandparents couldn't handle her anymore. Stolen cars. Verbal and auditory hallucinations started four years ago – usually telling her to hurt herself or others. Self-harm by cutting, choking, rubbing skin off her arms, and banging her head. Dialectical Behavior Therapy appeared to have helped quite a bit. If she came to us, she would need a new DBT therapist for sure.

DBT is a type of therapy that has grown in popularity as a way to treat adults and older adolescents that exhibit symptoms of Borderline Personality Disorder, a collection of behaviors such as self-destructiveness, extreme difficulty managing anxiety, difficulty with relationships, impulsive behaviors, and distorted perceptions of the world. Studies show it manifests itself primarily in emotionally vulnerable individuals who grow up in an "invalidating environment," often having a history of abandonment.

DBT offers skills to cope more effectively, emphasizing self-acceptance. It teaches specific behavioral techniques that can help a person both accept that change is needed, and implement that change in a non-shaming way. Borderline Personality Disorder (BPD) is notoriously difficult to treat, and requires a strong commitment to treatment from both the therapist and the patient. Therapists often shy away from patients presenting a BPD diagnosis, as they can be difficult to work with, make accusations, and have notoriously poor insight. They are known for their "I love you, I hate you" way of relating to people, which can drive even the most patient and understanding provider to limit the number of patients with that diagnosis they take on. DBT has offered some promising results with this population.

Mouths agape, we listened. And listened. And listened. Finally, Abby was spent. She looked up at us expectantly, proud of her efforts and wishing to be accepted. Despite the group home being a court-ordered placement, we do run into clients who truly wish to be placed with us. In Abby's case, she simply had nowhere else to go after corrections, and she wanted to be wanted by someone. We asked her our questions, and probed deeper into her past behaviors, making it clear what would be acceptable and not acceptable at the group home. At some points we pushed her a bit to see how she would react, reciting some rules she might not like, and asking her what would happen if she wasn't accepted. Abby showed remarkable frustration tolerance to our questions and answered them maturely and confidently. She had obviously prepared for this interview. This was apparent when we were about to leave and she pulled out a list of questions written neatly on a piece of torn loose-leaf paper (spiral notebooks were contraband at SOGS, as the metal spiral could be used as a weapon).

Despite having been there almost two hours, we sat back down and patiently answered each question:

"Will I have a roommate?"

"Yes, everyone has a roommate, there are no single rooms."

"Can I bring my journal?"

"Yes, you can have a journal, but staff may read it if there are concerns."

"Is music allowed?"

"Yes, certain music is allowed, after you are off orientation."

This announcement met with her immediate displeasure, and she began negotiating. It was obvious Abby was used to trying to negotiate rules, and she was going to struggle with having the same expectations as everyone else. We continued calmly, over her protests.

"You may listen to certain approved radio stations. No burned CDs, mp3 players or ipods are allowed, as staff can't be aware of what you are listening to. Only music that meets the criteria of responsibility is allowed."

This required a bit more explaining. At the group home we had a continuum of behaviors featured prominently on a large poster in the living room, detailing behaviors that fell into categories of responsible, irresponsible, arrestable, and extreme criminal. This is part of the Truthought ™ curriculum we used at CVC. . Behaviors such as "balances hard work, fulfillment of obligations, and recreation," and "makes choices for the good of self and others" fall into the responsible category.

Other behaviors such as "unreliable, inconsiderate, and careless," and "routinely lies to get by" fell into the irresponsible category. "Feels successful because offenses have gone undetected," and "deceptive and secretive, thinks of self as better than others" were under arrestable, and behaviors such as "commits crimes and used drugs and alcohol to feel superior" were listed under extreme criminal. Referenced quite a bit at the group home, and used for self-reflection, the continuum of behavior gave staff a concrete tool for measuring the appropriateness of music, a staple in a teenager's life. If staff was unfamiliar with a song, the girl was required to submit the lyrics and determine whether that song encouraged behaviors that fell into the responsible column of the continuum. If so, it was deemed okay to listen to.

Without verbal communication Mary Kay and I met eyes, and we instantly knew we wanted to give this girl a chance despite what she "looked like on paper." We had connected and we felt she deserved a chance. Besides, if she didn't come to us, who would take her? She was lucky just to get an interview from us. And that only happened because she came from a new county. We didn't reveal these thoughts to Abby, telling her only we would take it back to the team to discuss and be in contact with her county case worker; our usual spiel at the end of an interview. She politely thanked us and waited compliantly for her escort.

"Well, what do you think?" I asked unwilling to be the first to verbally commit to wanting to accept her.

"She sure was different than I thought," Mary Kay replied.

"Yeah," I said. We drove in silence for a while.

"We could try and find a DBT therapist for her," Mary Kay suggested.

"She did present herself very well and has been pretty stable for the past six months," I came back with. "I can't believe we are thinking about taking her."

"I know. This could be bad," Mary Kay acknowledged.

Thus went our conversation all the way back, including a stop for lunch. By the end of our drive, we were committed to at least trying to put together a plan with the county, CVC and outside providers that would ensure we gave Abby the best chance of success at the group home. We still had to sell the idea to the team, as they had input whether this placement was good for the group home and for Abby.

Several weeks later we had contacted and struck a deal with a DBT therapist to treat Abby at our group room rather than his office, and to reduce his fees to an amount the county was willing to pay, as her state health insurance assigned to children in care did not cover his fees. The county was on board as well with a safety plan of having Abby immediately removed to a mental health facility if she became unmanageable. SOGS pitched in by agreeing to release her on a two-week trial visit. In other words, Abby would remain a Southern Oaks resident, under state custody, for her first two weeks at CVC; able to be returned to incarceration if her behaviors did not fall under "group home" level of care. CVC staff had some buy-in, though several were reluctant to try making this work for a child who didn't have much hope left.

We brought in a trainer to counsel staff on how to handle and react to any hallucinations Abby might have: to validate *her*, not her hallucinations, while "grounding her" with reality-provoking statements such as, "You are here at the group home," "You are safe," and "You are with me in the living room right before supper time." The goal was to curtail the visions or voices without provoking anxiety in Abby, thereby possibly heading off her self-destructive behaviors.

7

Abby: the rest of the story

Danel

Abby, as with all the girls coming out of Southern Oaks, began her stay at CVC very unspectacularly. Because SOGS primarily used behavior modification techniques with rewards and consequences, the residents who left there usually continued to behave well, hoping to gain privileges quickly, and avoid punishments. Abby called us "ma'am" and asked before she did anything. We followed her safety plan to the letter and had a few opportunities to use our newly learned grounding techniques when she began talking to herself during groups and staring off into space, claiming the doll in the corner was telling her to move and controlled her arms. We felt quite proud of ourselves when she recovered from these episodes and appeared grateful for our support.

For a girl with some social anxiety, it was perhaps not the best timing for our first annual CVC *Beauty Brigade Live* Fashion Show to occur just one week after Abby arrived at CVC. The girls were not required to walk the runway, only to help with the show in some way. Though Abby declined to model, eager to make friends, she pitched in with serving food to the guests. Halfway through the show, I saw Abby bolt from the room as I sat with my friends, a guest for the night. I quietly excused myself and took off after her, worried she was thinking of running away. I found her quickly in the corner of an adjacent room, breathing heavily. She explained to me she wasn't able to "do it."

"What do you mean," I asked. "No one is expecting you to *do* anything."

"You know, *be there*."

"Well, you can hang out by me if you want,"

"No!" she exclaimed.

She then bolted towards the fashion show and up on the stage where Gina, our host, had invited the girls up to take a bow. Each girl was speaking about how Gina and the fashion show experience had positively affected them. Abby stopped just before the edge of the stage and as I held my breath, stepped forward and was handed the microphone by Gina. "I HAVE A SOCIAL PHOBIA!" she announced, way too loud.

We were stunned. Was she embarrassed? Did we push her too hard or expect too much? No one seemed to know what to say. She stood there saying nothing for a good minute, then handing the microphone back to Gina, stepped down and went back to her position by the food line. She did not mention anything else about that moment, even when asked. We decided to leave it alone, deciding it may have been something she was gearing herself up to do and forced herself to follow through with it as a test of her bravery. She seemed satisfied. We were happy with her progress and proudly reported back to the county how we were faring.

As it turned out, we would be thankful the state insisted on the two-week grace period to monitor her behavior. Only days later she started to deteriorate. It appeared that success was frightening for her. All the positive attention she got for her vulnerable behavior appeared to trigger her fear, giving her drastic anxiety spikes. In retrospect we questioned whether it was in fact a very well-thought-out, long-term plan by her to extract herself from Southern Oaks. Giving everyone what they were looking for from her – good behavior, vulnerability, compliance with appointments and medication, and trusting others – in order to achieve her goal, fed by self-hatred about how life had discarded her. Abby planned her death.

A Tuesday morning began with her refusing to get out of bed. Her scheduled appointment with her DBT therapist loomed close. It had started with a conflict the night before between Abby and other girls in the house. Abby knew by refusing to get up, she would cause everyone to be late for school, enabling her to feel more in control and get revenge. Taking this stand sent her message loud and clear, and boxed Abby into needing to follow through, including missing her therapy appointment, in order to win this conflict. This was Abby's battle, fought with whatever ammunition she perceived she had.

While we pondered how to intervene, the overnight staff brought to our attention several disturbing journal entries Abby had written the night before. These entries confirmed our suspicions that she was indeed planning a suicide and had been doing so even during her placement at SOGS. Her detailed plan was very specific and achievable--the classic criteria professionals use to determine whether a threat of suicide is credible and imminent. Her note met all the criteria, including a high probability of her ability to complete the suicide. Abby's intelligence made her plan all the more achievable. We immediately put a safety plan in place at the group home. A staffer was sent to supervise Abby in her room, so she was in adult presence at all times from that moment forward. Southern Oaks was contacted by phone and put on alert that Abby was no longer appropriate for group home placement due to recent discoveries and behaviors. We made immediate plans for her removal.

Despite our attempts at mediating mental health placement, Southern Oaks insisted she be returned to them as she was still under state custody and their primary obligation was to protect the community. The Southern Oaks staff informed us they were immediately dispatching several officers to the group home to pick up Abby and return her. This presented a dilemma as the officers were currently over two hours away. By this time, Abby's behaviors were escalating to a harmful state.

She was verbally threatening others. She knew that we had found her journal and were aware of her suicidal intent, so there was no need for her to keep up her "good girl" façade. She spoke openly of her long-term plan to earn enough privileges to be able to follow through with her own suicide. It would be to no advantage to let Abby know she would soon be taken back into custody and returned to a secure facility.

The other girls were shuttled safely off to school and Abby had left her bed and moved to the main common room of the group home. ABC was located on a busy street and one of the plans she verbalized, to throw herself in front of a car, was easily accessible to her. As you can well imagine, staff were very hyper-vigilant to Abby's whereabouts in relation to the front door and access to leaving the group home. Reconstructing the event afterwards, we realized how Abby obtained her method. Earlier in the day, a seasoned staff person had taken all the girls down to the laundry room to change loads, keeping every-one in sight. The staff person believes Abby spied a shard of glass inadvertently left by a workman replacing a broken window. Later, Abby's mood lightened dramatically, and she became more animated. Shift change occurred, and though concerns about Abby were passed on, her current cooperation lessened the urgency of the matter for the new shift. At dinner prep time, Abby volunteered that she knew where a griddle was that the staff were trying to find. A newer staff person then took her back down to the basement. It was then we believe she somehow obtained and concealed the earlier spotted piece of glass from the cracked basement window.

After coming upstairs Abby concealed the glass in her cubby, a space allotted to each girl, which was located between the lower level and up-stairs staircase. The rest of the wait was uneventful. When the officers from Southern Oaks entered the building, Abby was sitting in the living room having very little contact or interaction with her peers or staff. She had her forefinger in her mouth, appearing like a little girl. When the Southern Oaks people arrived, she immediately said "Uh uh, my time is up, my time is up, I haven't done anything criminal, hurting yourself is not a crime... it didn't say anywhere that I can't hurt myself....my time is up, my time is up".

Abby started heading to the bathroom upstairs, pausing at her cubby and dashing rather quickly up the steps. Mary Kay quickly realized something was amiss and followed her upstairs. She arrived just in time to prevent the bathroom door from being closed. By this time Abby was distraught screaming,

"I ain't goin' back! I ain't goin' back! That's not the way it's supposed to work! "Don't touch me! Don't touch me!"

Through the cracked door Mary Kay was able to see blood. Using all her strength and adrenaline, she forced the door open into a night-marish scene of a glazed, frantic child. Somewhere in the midst of this drama, back-up was called to the upstairs level and the two officers from Southern Oaks made their way upstairs.

It was not a large bathroom and Abby fought wildly. Blood was covering a good portion of the walls and floor. Abby's arms, hands and clothing were also covered in blood. She was standing with her back against the window which led to a two-story drop, a rather precarious position. The toilet was on one side of her, and the cabinets lined the wall on the other side. CVC staff scrambled to don gloves as more staff arrived to help. Mary Kay attempted to deescalate Abby by talking to her while Southern Oaks staff got into position to restrain her. Abby read their moves and attempted to evade them, but there simply was not enough room in the bathroom and in a second all were on the floor falling forward towards the tub, but safely away from the window. Sliding in the blood, Mary Kay continued to yell for gloves. Abby flailed her limbs and kicked at the adults, maintaining possession of the 3-inch shard of glass that protruded through her fingers which she now used as a weapon against her perceived persecutors.

She was biting herself to the point that I thought she could have taken flesh. She was also screaming and asking to be shot.

"Please, please shoot me, I'll pay you, money is not an object, please, please shoot me, I told them all I would only go back there dead."

In the meantime, staff called 911 because she would not allow us to treat her cut and it was impossible for the four of us to remove her from the bathroom, as she would kick and flail whenever their restraint was lessened or removed. She also responded to threats of using mace or a taser with anticipation as she reported the last time she was maced, her "lung collapsed"... and the last time you "tazed me my heart stopped." She alternately begged to be maced or tasered. When the four squad cars, ambulance and fire truck arrived, I was replaced in the bathroom by a paramedic. Abby continued to beg them to shoot or mace her. After quite a while, she was transported by the ambulance to the hospital where they sedated her, treated her wound, and released her to the personnel from Southern Oaks to transport.

The struggle felt like it lasted forever, though in reality only a few minutes went by. The Southern Oaks officers secured the glass from Abby without any further injury beyond the ones Abby had self-inflicted. Certainly, all three professionals who had come in contact with the blood would need to be tested and cleared, but for now it was over...and sad as it was, Abby was on her way back to safety, having proven to everyone that no matter what her motivation, she was capable of functioning in society, at least for short periods of time.

Afterwards, we discovered several suicide notes she had written the night before in a folder she had been seen carrying around periodically that day. One was to her mother, one to her grandmother, and one to her county case worker.

Mary Kay

As the adrenaline subsided, cleanup began, and my aching muscles started to throb, I decided I might be too old for this. Reconstructing the scene in my head, I was strongly convinced that our original inklings and concerns about Abby prior to pre-screening had some definite merit. As we debriefed with staff members, we sadly wondered what would happen to that little girl, who had been institutionalized at such a young age. One thing we knew for sure – she would not be returning to CVC. One bloodbath per child is our limit. However, I don't believe either one of us regretted giving Abby a shot at making it. It was a good plan. And as my dear friend tries to tell me, you can't save them all. Unfortunately, Abby was one of the ones we couldn't.

Excerpts from an email I sent to her Case Worker speaks to our hindsight...

"Hi. Sorry I haven't been able to contact you until now. Friday held a pretty disastrous chain of events. I certainly believe that you made the right call in revoking her. I suspect now that Abby had been planning to suicide even prior to her release from [Southern Oaks]. Things that preceded the arrival of the [Southern Oaks] team (she had NO idea that they were coming) indicate she had a plan...

Her mood had been defensive and demanding off and on throughout the day; however she was completing work given to her that required her to take ownership for her behavior earlier. The work showed some insight into herself and her patterns.

Abby begged [the officers] to shoot her, mace her etc... She was removed by the ambulance to the hospital where they sedated her, treated her wound, and released her to the personnel from [Southern Oaks] to transport.

It became obvious to me that our level of care cannot keep Abby safe, and we regretfully will not be able to serve her in the future. I have suspicions that Abby's long-term plan, possibly even when she turned her behavior around at [Southern Oaks] was to suicide and if this unusual set of circumstances had not occurred, we could have very well found Abby after having successfully accomplished her goal.

In her folder...there were suicide notes to you, her Grandma, and her mother. In the struggle in the bathroom, she asked me to tell her family "it was not their fault...it was better this way and it was bound to happen."

If we could offer support to Abby in any way we would like to do that. The girls would like to write letters of support if you and the staff believe it would not interfere with her treatment. It's my thought that it could give closure on both ends. We enjoyed working with you and your county. I believe everyone involved did a good job planning and transitioning for Abby. We are regretful that it didn't work but satisfied that Abby had the best shot at this time in her life to make it. Hopefully we can work together at some point in the future. I will send the incident reports out today, but wanted you to have a complete picture, rather than the snapshots the police and incident reports would give.

-Sincerely, Mary Kay Lutzow, Director, Candlelight Vision Corp."

8

Safety First

Mary Kay

The bottom line at the group home was always safety. We preached this concept repeatedly to the girls beginning at their pre-screening interview. "We will do whatever we need to do to keep you safe, the other girls safe, and the community safe." In fact, we had turned placements down for the sole reason of not believing we could do an adequate job of keeping that particular girl safe.

One instance revolved around a young lady who was residing at a locked mental health facility. She had been there for approximately one week after stabbing herself in the throat with a shard of glass. At her pre-screening interview, we saw a petite young lady looking several years younger than her 14 years, constantly fingering a deep red, angry looking, very fresh scar about four inches long across her trachea. The interview went well on the outside, but our antennae were up as, despite what her counselors were telling us, it didn't look as if the feelings that drove her to harming herself severely enough to land her in ICU, and then on a locked unit, had been adequately resolved. The timing just appeared too soon and the young lady's stated motivations for ceasing to harm herself seemed a little too well-rehearsed.

We ended up discussing our concerns with the mental health facility staff who understood. We ultimately turned the placement down as we were simply not confident that we could keep her safe from herself.

Another instance in which we declined a placement was before we even interviewed her. A call came in from a county who frequently placed clients with us about a young lady who was the subject of stalking by a much older former boyfriend who was considered dangerous by the police. He had, so far, yet to be caught or charged with any crime. The authorities were "keeping an eye on him." The Case Worker was looking for a placement for her that would keep her identity secret (which we always did) far beyond what we felt was capable. She would have to be registered in school. We did go out locally in public on outings. We recommended a placement outside the county for her own safety as we couldn't guarantee her safety, and a dangerous situation could end up affecting the other girls' and the staff's safety as well.

For the most part, however, we felt comfortable enough with the measures we had in place to accept even moderate-risk placements. One of the most common safety risks we encountered was runaways. Girls that ran away from home or from us put themselves at risk by relying on friends, acquaintances, or strangers to provide them with food, clothing, and shelter. Almost every girl who has run away will proclaim that she knows "how to take care of myself." Yet, those same girls will tell you stories of providing sexual favors, money, or drugs in exchange for basic needs. Even the toughest girls were in danger of being victimized in some way when they were on the run.

Since it would be unrealistic to turn down girls for placement simply because they had a history of running away from home and were likely to run away again, we developed some proactive interventions to discourage running away, fitting within our philosophy of safety.

Girls with a history of running away or who had stated they would run away if placed at a group home were told upon intake that we were concerned about that possibility, as it would put them in danger.

"We are dedicated to keeping everyone safe," we told them. One way we do this is by providing pajamas for residents to wear if they are worried about running away or if we are worried about them running away.

The pajamas we provided were meant to be worn inside the group home only. They were not ugly but were obviously not regular street clothing. Most were pastel and flannel, though we had a number of lighter options since spring and summer were our most busy seasons for "itchy feet." The pajamas were an option the client could request if she felt as if she were in danger of taking off during an argument or another heated moment. We encouraged girls to use this option to self-intervene and provide themselves with a physical reminder of making a good choice to stay put. Many girls did request pajamas as a self-intervention and successfully thwarted their own urges to leave a situation they were having trouble dealing with. This success fed itself and we saw more successes build once they had some confidence in conquering their fears of confronting a problem rather than running from it.

If a client was not at the point where she could request the pajamas for herself, the staff could make the decision that the girl we were concerned about would need to wear the pajamas until we felt the danger had passed. In these cases, the girl's clothing was kept in the office, so she did not have unrestricted access to it, and her shoes were confiscated. The pajamas really served two purposes. First, it was a physical reminder to the girls to help them pause to make better choices. Secondly, when they did run away - and this happened, pajamas or not - they would be easier for the police to spot, therefore bringing them back quicker and reducing the likelihood of danger to the client. The police were well aware of our "anti-runaway" intervention and knew to look for pajamas and bare feet.

It wasn't only the police who knew about the pajamas and what it meant if someone was wearing them. Our volunteer mentors who worked one on one with the girls were well versed in this intervention, as usually, if a client was "in pajamas" she was only able to visit with her mentor on the grounds of the group home. Though this sometimes threw a wrench into their plans, the mentors showed amazing flexibility as they too, were completely invested in their match's safety.

It happened one day, in the middle of a sunny afternoon, that one of our mentors, Kristen, was driving down a main thoroughfare in the city when she spotted a teenage girl walking along the sidewalk on a bridge. She didn't recognize this girl, but what caught her eye was her clothing. She was in pajamas. Now, Kristen knew what this might mean and although she couldn't identify the girl specifically as being from the group home, she decided she just couldn't let this go unchecked. She immediately turned her car to keep this girl in sight and dialed the group home's number.

"Do you have one of the girls missing? she asked. "I think I see her." Getting enough of a description to feel as if she had the right person, Kristen miraculously spotted a police car turning in front of her. She waved down the police car and explained what was going on with the teenager on the bridge. The girl, who had been on the run for a total of 35 minutes, was safely returned to the group home. Debriefing with the mentor and the police afterwards it was noted the efficient teamwork that happened to bring this girl back safely.

We used pajamas as an effective intervention and prevention measure for over eight years until the state licensing standards changed to disallow this way to deter runaways. As we packed up the pajamas, we reflected on the many times they had been helpful to the clients and us and really, may have saved lives.

-A resident showing off the mural at TLC2

9

More on Safety

Mary Kay

Self-harm was not uncommon at the group home. To an outsider it is hard to fathom someone deliberately causing herself pain or watching herself bleed. Nevertheless, to our population, it made perfect sense. There are more ways than the average person can imagine to harm yourself. We think we may have seen it all. There are the girls who picked scabs, the girls who pulled their hair out until they were close to bald. We had clients who banged their heads against the wall, and those who rubbed their skin away with washcloths and erasers. One young woman even stuck wires and needles under her skin until they disappeared. Piercings and self-inflicted tattoos are another kind of self-harm. However, by far, the most common way that we saw clients hurt themselves was cutting themselves with some object.

To us, as staff, we took any self-harm seriously. We did learn to evaluate how lethal their attempts were – in other words, how likely they were to die from their wounds - to assist in determining the intervention. Our assessment included looking at the motivation behind the attempt.

The most worrisome self-harmer was the child who had no desire to live, or believed they had nothing to live for. One such young lady crossed our path early in ABC's history. June had chronic addiction issues. Her addiction served to protect her in some way from the pain that reality had to offer. Sexual and physical abuse pervaded her child-hood, with a mother unable to protect her due to her own mental illness. June had no desire to be sober or free from drugs. She was one of those quiet young women who just nodded and agreed with whatever staff suggested. She was not a behavior problem and rarely stood out in a group. Her shoulder length brown stringy hair, gaunt sunken eyes, and her lifeless expression helped her fade into the background. She did not appear to express any emotion, no matter how intense, outwardly.

Though she initially presented as a girl who would self-harm occa-sionally, it became clear after a very short time, this was a child who was determined to die. Staff was meticulous in removing any sharp object or other material she could harm herself with. Glass was removed from pictures frames, she was not allowed spiral notebooks, pens were forbid-den. Tacks, staples, nails – all sought out and removed from her grasp.

One afternoon, June asked if she could change her shirt. She came out of her room with a black T-shirt on, with some childish inscription on the front. We were always very careful about writing and logos, but on this occasion, it was the color we needed to pay attention to. It turned out June had gone into the bathroom, broken a light bulb, and cut herself deeply on her stomach and chest. She threw away the glass and picked up the light bulb to leave no evidence. June had rounded out her plan by deliberately picking a dark colored T-shirt so no one would notice she was bleeding. This is an example of an actively suicidal adolescent. She was not appropriate for the group home level of care and had to be quickly removed to a psychiatric hospital.

Not quite as lethal as the serious suicide attempt, is the "self-punisher." This girl generally accepts responsibility for the bad things that have happened to her and others in her life, even though she isn't to blame. This is not unusual in the case of sexual abuse victims who often feel they are at fault for their abuser's hurtful actions. If they can-not get past this stage, they continue to feel as if they deserve to be hurt.

They are looking for a level of suffering that would eventually relieve their guilt over their abuse.

One such girl that we worked with had been raised primarily in institutions after rampant family incest was discovered and the family was separated. Despite her very young age, she accepted responsibility not only for the abuse, but also for the demise of the family and separation of her siblings. Sandi was resourceful and staff again had to be thorough and vigilant in sweeping the environment for potential instruments of self-harm. At one point, Sandi had used parts from her glasses to cut her arm and hands. After they were taken away, it was discovered she had kept the miniature screws that held the frame together to further self-harm. When this attempt was foiled, she appropriated the inside workings of her curtain rod to create a sharp enough tool to damage her skin. Sandi was not above carving designs in the skin of her hands.

Her arms and legs were covered in scars showing a long history of her self-destructive actions. Sandi didn't have a zest for life, but she also did not have a quest for death. She was simply attempting to find some resolution to the unthinkable things that had happened to her and the overwhelming responsibility she felt for the ruin of everyone she loved. Sandi truly believed it when her perpetrator told her it was her fault.

"Self-punishers" needed a more nurturing and gentle approach. They need to know they are worth caring about and that people do believe in them and their value as a person. This nurturing can take the place of the parenting she had lacked. One intervention that worked well with Sandi was giving her a permanent red marker. For some reason the word "permanent" meant a lot to Sandi. We solicited her agreement to use the marker in place of sharp objects when she felt the urge to cut herself. The attempt was for her to get the same relief when drawing on her skin with the red marker that she felt when seeing her own blood flow down her arm. This obviously was a much safer practice, though it did hamper our ability to take her out in public in short sleeves. Our goal was to wean her from cutting to drawing to eventually other more socially acceptable means of dealing with her feelings. Once Sandi felt ready, she graduated from drawing on her flesh to expressing her intense emotions by using the red marker on large sheets of paper.

Another category cutters fell into was the "relief cutter." These young ladies experience internal suffering and emotions that they have no skills to express or control. Over time, they discover that physical pain is preferable to the emotional pain they live with. In addition, something they can control and care for afterwards.

These girls often repress and deny the reality of their past abuse. When feelings come, they will stuff them back down to avoid such unpleasantness. This feeds the pressure cooker and they come to a point where something must give. The cutting comes when this level of emotion reaches the breaking point. It serves to let out enough "steam" to make things more manageable for them. To this end, cutting is performing a valuable service and in and of itself can become an addictive behavior, much like alcohol or drugs can relieve the same kind of emotional pressure.

Lucy was a pretty young lady, only thirteen when she came to us. She had been a victim of sexual abuse by a number of her mother's transient boyfriends. That lifestyle was the only one she knew. Her mother was also raised in a similar environment. Although she wanted to protect her child, she really did not know how to make things different. After all, no one protected her.

In this particular family, the mother was open to treatment and education, which led to the mother and Lucy learning together for an ultimately better outcome for Lucy and the family system.

In Lucy's case, and others like her, staff would reinforce the necessity of keeping her wounds clean by giving her a first aid kit and expecting her to clean and dress the cuts to prevent infection. The emphasis was put upon exploring feelings and precipitating events that led to or triggered the cutting in the first place, with the goal of them eventually being able to talk to staff prior to the cutting.

Then there is "the scratcher." This client might look like she has been in a fight with a cat. Several scratches, only barely breaking the surface of the skin are noticeable in these cases. These young women are generally looking for attention, showing off their new wounds with abandon in a skimpy tank top for all to see. They relished the reaction of others' responses. These young women really didn't cause us much concern. They needed either to be redirected to a drama class or find healthier ways to be noticed. Our general reaction to "the scratcher" was to not react at all, or possibly redirect them to more weather appropriate clothing, and encourage them to talk.

Inevitably, when you had any of the above self-harmers in the population and in close quarters with drama-seeking adolescents who often were looking for new ways to act out, a certain phenomenon appeared - the "copycat cutter." Contagious cutting emerged and would run through the house like a flu virus, and we could only hope it was the twenty-four-hour variety.

It made sense. Someone else was getting attention, be it negative or positive, for a behavior they, themselves, had yet to try. Even "the scratcher" could send teachers and parents into panic mode proving it to be an effective way to garner a corner of adult concern.

Our general approach with a girl who had never cut before, but suddenly decided it was a terrific idea, was to choose between two approaches. One approach was ignoring the behavior completely in hopes that it would simply disappear without attention. The other approaches were to heap burning coals of kindness upon their heads, and give them an extra (and sometimes annoying) dose of attention, i.e. "Oh, I don't think you can go to that school dance, honey. You aren't safe or stable enough to be without a staff member next to you." "How about you sleep on the couch so we can keep an eye on you and make sure you are safe." "Oh, no, you can't stay here; you need to come along with me, so I know you are safe."

Somehow, these kind consequences usually healed them rather quickly, unless we misjudged their stamina. Some continued to up the ante and graduated to another self-harm category, which then required another, more intense intervention.

10

Introduction Group

Mary Kay

--Jill--

Jill was placed in August. Her history was wrought with conflict. There were charges of battery and assault peppered through her paperwork. Her behaviors indicated a very low frustration tolerance as well as a highly impulsive reaction to situations outside of her comfort zone. Jill was well defended and projected an aura that would discourage her peers from challenging or confronting her.

At the group homes, safety for the girls was always reinforced as the heart of our program. Candlelight Vision would be a safe place for all to heal. It was going to be important that we leveled the playing field with her peers to preserve the therapeutic environment. Our first opportunity to do that would be in the Introduction Group. In the this group each resident shared a condensed version of their story including where they were from, how long they had been there, the charges that brought them to Candlelight Vision, what they were working on, what they had learned about themselves, and words of wisdom for the new client. It would be important for Jill to understand that in the scheme of things she was not as big and bad as she was attempting to project.

We began with one of our clients from Milwaukee who had come to us following a lengthy stay at Southern Oaks Girls School. All girls were cuffed and shackled at Southern Oaks and their disciplinary menu included isolation. There was little tolerance for infractions of the rules. Although Jill saw herself as hard and tough, she was really just a puppy on the porch. The sooner she came to that realization the better chance she had.

Her peer from Milwaukee had been working hard on her programming and recovery. The initial history she revealed did not match the young lady who sat with us on Jill's first day. Coming out of generational familial gang involvement, the things she shared of her family's legal history and experiences were indeed eye opening for a girl who had no concept of big city life in the 'hood.

This client concluded with her words of wisdom to Jill, "Just be yourself; you don't have to pretend to be tough. They see right through that anyway. You will only make it really hard for yourself." We continued around the circle with the other clients sharing their stories of abuse, assault, and incarceration. Jill was pretty wide-eyed as the other girls shared where they had been and where they were today. The words of wisdom that they had imparted included, "be honest," "give it a chance," "don't run away... their pajamas are really ugly."

Then it was Jill's turn to share. Staff anxiously waited to see how she would present to the group. Was she going to be hostile and defensive or receptive and open to feedback?

Jill began by announcing, "This was not my idea. I'm not sure if I'm going to stay. You all seem pretty cool, but I am not promising!"

There was a stifled chuckle from the group as they welcomed her and confided they had felt the same way coming in. Some of them shared they still struggle on hard days. It appeared the Introduction Group had succeeded in at least engaging Jill in the process, but time would tell.

--Stevanna--

A referral came one afternoon. As we looked over the information, I immediately recognized the name of the young lady. This was a child I had worked with in previous employment. A glut of mixed emotions came flooding back, memories of a heart-wrenching situation. Memories of extreme powerlessness, of a young lady I visited in jail, just a baby herself, with chronic addiction issues. Her drug of choice was alcohol, but anything else would do. I spent a good deal of time interviewing this young lady years ago when she was about 13 or 14, assessing her dependency issues.

Many people were invested in this young lady's care. Her home environment was not stable or dependable. Her siblings had similar issues. There were few family resources to draw upon. Many of the professional people involved wanted her to remain local to stay connected to the resources she had developed. At that time, I had recommended an out of state treatment center, precisely because of the local "resources" she had developed.

This young lady ended up in an outpatient program that I facilitated and continued to drink. The risk became more complex when she became pregnant. Many attempts were made to intervene on the baby's behalf. Personally, I attempted to call upon the courts, citing a newly instated law allowing pregnant women to be incarcerated for the protection of their child, to be applied in this case. It was denied because she was a juvenile. She continued to drink as her pregnancy progressed. She had a history of running and staying on the run long-term, and I lost track of her in the course of one of these runs. Now her name, Stevanna, was staring at me on the fax just received at Candlelight Vision.

She was a tough kid, I knew. She had a lot of unhealthy connections that would encourage her continued illegal mobility, not to mention her likely toxic effect on our fragile community at the group home we had. In continuing to read the referral information sent by her social worker, I discovered she had a two-year-old daughter that was currently in foster care. I wondered about the baby's cognitive functioning, knowing what her first trimester of life was like. Did she have Fetal Alcohol Syndrome? Had she been abused or neglected?

The referral reported that Stevanna was anxious and motivated to raise her daughter and be a good mom. Motivated, I was sure. Capable...I wondered, knowing the history, and the familial gang ties. If Stevanna was ever going to be equipped to nurture and love this baby, she was going to need to be nurtured and loved herself; THAT was something we were good at: nurturing, loving, and giving accountability. The foster family lived in the vicinity. Setting up visitation and teaching parenting skills was something we could do.

The biggest hurdle we could see would be the life changes we would ask her to make. Basically, she would be rejecting the lifestyle she had been taught and grew up thinking was okay. Her friends, her family, her behavior and thinking patterns – all would need to be overhauled. No longer was Stevanna changing only for herself. Another life was at stake. If it wasn't going to happen, we knew there was a family who could give the baby what she needed to survive and deserved in her foster family. They had shown a significant investment in the baby so far and the word was, they were willing and ready to adopt her if Stevanna could or would not make the necessary changes for the baby to be safe. Stevanna would have to decide and stick to it. It was sink-or-swim time. We believed we had a shot at providing the life jacket--whether she put it on or not would be her choice.

After reviewing our recommendations and discussing logistics (and hitting a few rummage sales for baby items), we decided it was a go. The only other nagging concern in our minds was the fact that she came as a package deal with her county social worker, a woman we had found difficult to work with in the past. She was often enabling of the girls we worked with, not allowing them to feel the consequences of their own choices and giving into demands easily. In the field, we called this rescuing. It set our clients back in their treatment and did not allow them to be empowered to change their behaviors for the better.

Stevanna was set to arrive and visitation for Angelena, her baby, was set up on a weekly basis, to be increased as the treatment team and the foster parents agreed. Everyone braced themselves for her arrival. The social worker delivered Stevanna with a great ta-da, as she swaggered her way through the dining room with the crotch of her pants sagging, dressed in red and black, tattoos dotting her arms, and a baseball cap cocked to one side. She essentially came in claiming and making no secret of her gang involvement and affiliation, lest any of her peers had a question. Her round and frightened face gave her away, but her garb and swagger were the Stevanna I remembered. She walked in the door as I stood in the doorway of the office. Her eyes hit mine and her head dropped.

I said, "Hi, Stevie. Nice outfit!" She lifted her head and smiled at me, and I thought to myself, "Well, I hope that establishes our bottom line here regarding her dress."

I asked her for her hat, holding my hand out, which she willingly surrendered with a half-cocked smile. Despite this promising start, Stevanna did not know how to "do" powerless or deal with authority figures. She was simply programmed to challenge and rebel. She immediately began testing the waters during her intake meeting where the rules of the group home were explained. She had no family to sign her papers, only her social worker, who was very interested in making this work for Stevanna. Since Stevanna was a ward of the state, her social worker signed all the needed papers and consents. We immediately talked about colors that she was and was not allowed to wear. Obviously, the combination of red and black was off the list, which she feigned confusion about. Let's just make it concise and say we had a "rubber hit the road" intake, with no discussion encouraged and no debate accepted. The alternative of the door was offered several times much to the horror of the social worker.

Stevanna eventually realized we were serious about her compliance and since she hadn't lined up any way to leave at the moment, she decided her best course of action, at least for the time being, was to make a show of compliance. To her credit, when we did talk about her child, Angelena – what Angelena deserved and what she needed from a mother — Stevanna did show genuine remorse and desire. As we said earlier, motivation was not the question. Whether or not Stevanna could delay her gratification and overcome the obstacles that lay before her to give Angelena what she needed was the challenge that lay before all of us.

Right after intake we sorted through her clothes and found her something to wear that didn't indicate that she was in a gang, although everything she had was three sizes too big. When you stripped away all the gruffness and swagger, you saw a hurting, guilt-ridden little girl who was in over her head and knew it. She, like us, didn't know whether she was going to be able to do this or not. All her energy was put into maintaining her façade and preventing others from seeing her pain and her fear.

Once the other girls were home from school, that picture of a vulnerable little girl disappeared and we had gruff and swagger one more time. It was going to be important for staff to establish her place in the pecking order because her peers were not going to be strong enough to do it themselves.

Typically, when each new client enters the group home, the girls begin to re-assess and evaluate their milieu and how well the new girl will fit into the crowd. Generally, there are girls with more power than others in the home. A new girl coming in can be a threat to this power as the girls scramble to rearrange themselves in a hierarchy of sorts. Trust that has been built among the existing clients is temporarily traumatized and must go through a rebuilding process. The internal process started with realization that no one knows...

- who the new girl is,
- what her connections are to the outside world,
- whether she will stay or not,
- whether she will keep confidentiality or not,

• whether they are safe or not.

The new girls coming in were generally well-defended and not used to being open or taking risks by being vulnerable, which is exactly what we ask them to do. It's a time of hyper-alertness and vigilant observation. Things are heightened when the new client presents as tough as Stevanna. Staff watched carefully what was happening.

As we said, the first step in a new client's orientation process was a "Introduction Group." The point of the Introduction Group was to put everyone in a position of having to take small to moderate risks, therefore beginning the therapeutic process. Hopefully, the clients that had been there longer would go deeper with the risks, setting an example for the newer clients. Each girl was asked to share their information with the new client going last. This is where staff was going to be able to help establish the pecking order with Stevanna by delving deeper with our questions and exposing to the group some of Stevanna's vulnerabilities, in a gentle and non-shaming way. We were looking to put a few small holes in her wall of defenses, allowing the other clients' a glimpse of the similarities of Stevanna's issues to theirs. This would be a difficult group for Stevanna. She would need to be nurtured and challenged, a delicate balance, a challenge for even the most seasoned staff members. I decided I would stay for this group, hoping that our previous connection would give her a sense of safety as we navigated these waters.

Although Stevanna struggled during this group as we knew she most surely would, she seemed to give it her best effort, most likely motivated by the upcoming visit with Angelena that she knew had already been arranged. With her established in the milieu the best way we could, Stevanna began her journey at A Better Choice Group Home. The other girls went through their typical pecking order process and were somewhat intimidated by Stevanna, but we seemed to have been fairly successful in the initial group, assimilating her issues with theirs.

The first visit with Angelena was stressful for Stevanna. She had not seen her in a long time and it was obviously stressful for the foster parents as well. They arrived on time with Angelena. As the staff opened the door to greet them, everyone was struck by the beauty of those big brown eyes, beautiful black braided hair, and tiny body bundled up in her little pink snowsuit. Angelena was walking and quite active. Stevanna had been out to rummage sales with staff that let her pick up some toys so she could play with Angelena. The foster parents sat on a loveseat in the window area and quietly watched as Stevanna attempted to engage Angelena. It was obvious how emotionally overwhelmed Stevanna was at the sight of her daughter and how lost she was with what to do with her. Stevanna continued to call Angelena, asking her to "Come to Mama," and seemed quite disheartened that Angelena did not run to her in recognition and joy. Stevanna sat on the floor with the toys, continuing to attempt to engage Angelena. It was obvious by Stevanna's attempts to have Angelena come to her rather than her going to Angelena that she had not a clue of where to begin. After observing this interaction for a period of time, staff went in and sat on the floor by Angelena, inviting Stevanna to bring some toys in order to model appropriate interaction.

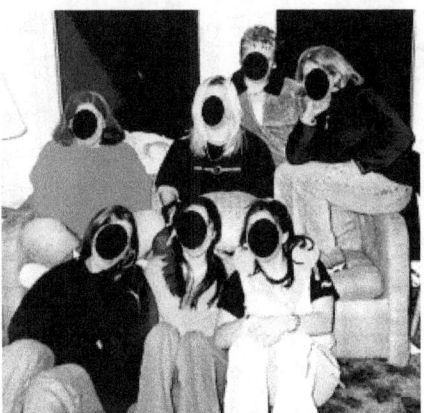

~ a group of girls hanging out at ABC

11

An Unusual Intake

Mary Kay

Some things you just must see to believe. Even after many, many years, we could still be shocked. We received a phone call one afternoon asking if we could take an emergency placement of a young lady on a Chapter 51 hold. This is a legal mental health commitment, meaning this just-turned 13-year-old young lady had been determined to be a danger to herself or others to the point that she was under a commitment order which would determine where she was placed in order to preserve her and others' safety. In this particular case, the young lady's mother was on a mental health hold open, which meant that she, too, was experiencing severe mental health issues but was determined by the court to be able to manage on her own under the supervision of medical and psychiatric personnel as long as she followed the rules set out for her by the court and her mental health providers. In a hold open situation, if the identified patient violates this agreement set forth in court, he or she may be revoked and hospitalized against their will, but in their best interest. Hold opens generally have a determined time frame, such as 60 or 90 days.

Obviously, this young lady was having some difficulties and her mother was unable to provide the structure that she needed. The case worker indicated that the mother reinforced some of the negative behavior of her child. For example, how she wore her makeup, how she dressed, and generally how she presented herself to the community. Her mother appeared to be more a peer to Sydney than a parental figure who was able to set appropriate limits and boundaries. Sydney's mother and father were divorced. The father was fearful of her mother's long-standing stalking-type behaviors towards him. He lived with different relatives to avoid having his residence known to her. He had very strong feelings about the relationship and lack of boundaries between Sydney and her mother, but did not appear strong enough to effectively be able to confront this unhealthy dynamic.

Sydney was admitted to CVC on a short-term respite placement meant to be fifteen days, allowing the county to complete the court hearings necessary to determine her placement. Mother was contesting placement at our facility. Both parents sounded very rational during our phone contact with them prior to her placement. Both referenced Sydney's makeup, referring to it as "heavy eye makeup."

It was during lunchtime at the group home that we expected our new placement to arrive. The girls were sitting at the table as a big buzz arose, whooping and hooting comments burst through the structured lunch time routine. As we tried to settle them down and ascertain the source of the hoopla, I froze in my tracks. I lost my breath and stood frozen in the middle of the dining room. Now, in over twenty years in the field, there really isn't much that surprised me anymore. But OH MY GOD! Ozzy Osbourne was walking up our driveway in a young girl's body. With everything you could imagine pierced. "Heavy" didn't begin to describe the makeup she was wearing. Everything was black from head to toe – her hair, her clothes, her mesh gloves, her fingernails, her combat boots, and HALF OF HER FACE, from her forehead to her collarbone. The other half was completely painted stark white with a lightning bolt drawn down the middle of her nose, her lip, her chin, and her neck, to her collarbone. This was more than heavy eye makeup!

As I tried to gather my wits about me, I prayed she had no bat in her pocket that she planned to sacrifice. When I recovered, I told the staff to take the other children next door while I did the intake. My second thought was "Oh my God, the neighbor's young children were playing in the front yard."

'Okay, deep breath! Here we go,' I told myself.

"Hey kiddo, welcome. You must be Mom – come on in." The intake process started.

The first battle came quickly. The piercings were the issue. I assured her we were not going to force her to remove her piercings – that was totally up to her. She simply would not be able to participate in any activities until she had turned them in. Sharing that it was her free expression and her right, but that it certainly would not be fair to the other kids that she would be allowed hers when they did not have the same privilege. Sydney was very understanding and she took the envelope I offered her indicating she would consider the request. Her mother, however, was quite vocal in her disagreement and mentioned legalities, lawyers, and her intent to contact Sydney's lawyer because she was quite sure that Sydney should be able to wear the jewelry. After all, she had just spent two hundred dollars paying for those piercings because it was what Sydney wanted and it made her happy. Many un-successful attempts to redirect her mother quickly indicated to us that, although Sydney was the identified client, the real problem would be driving out of the driveway today.

Shortly after her mother left, the clients returned to meet their new housemate. They greeted her openly as they would any other peer. I think they might have had a little pep talk from the staff before they returned, but even so, I was proud of them. The staff and I had a quick huddle in the office, identified that we were not going to get into power struggles; We were not going to address her makeup. The piercings were the first issue we were addressing, and that she would need to wash her face at some point. This young lady obviously needed the safety of her thick garish makeup and outlandish clothing to feel somewhat in control of herself and her life. To strip her of too much too quickly would be devastating and leave her too vulnerable. It would, I explained to the staff on duty, expose her powerlessness and wounds too early, leaving us no way to engage her as she fought for power and control over her life once again. We would force her into a power struggle that we would most definitely lose. We elected to attempt to engage her in a non-threatening way and help her feel safe in her new, albeit temporary, environment.

Sydney responded more quickly than we thought to the request that she turn in her piercings, by simply placing them in the envelope and handing it to staff before her first bedtime. Sydney, it appeared, was proving more rational than her outward appearance might indicate. Her rationality was short-lived though, when the next morning she discovered we would not be providing her a fresh supply of her accustomed stage paint. Having slept in her makeup, yesterday's supply was beginning to fade. Initially, Sydney refused to get out of bed or leave her room. This was accommodated by bringing her breakfast to her room. Normally, breakfast in bed was not on the agenda for a resistant client. However, this one needed some nurturing and some reassurance, and we did individualize their treatment planning.

While she devoured her breakfast, we acknowledged that we understood it was scary for her and that her makeup provided some comfort that helped keep her safe. She angrily dismissed everything we had to say as the kind of drivel adults usually came up with. After all, anyone over twenty-five had no idea what they were talking about. In leaving her room, we reassured her we cared about her, and we understood, but we did expect her to come out of her room and participate in programming...requests we would be making numerous times during her stay.

Sydney did not exit her room until the girls came home from school that afternoon. Even that was a big risk for her as her makeup by now was truly fading. Her long, stringy dyed gothic black hair hung in her face to disguise her disappearing makeup. It was really a blessing that we had a good group of girls at this point. They went on about their day, including Sydney as if there was nothing unusual. They made it clear she was accepted as part of the group. Sydney absorbed that unconditional acceptance like a sponge. Included in this peer group who was so accepting and nurturing was a drug addict who had almost died twice from overdoses, a middle-schooler who had tried to kill a younger child, and a chronic runaway unable to deal with a parent who would never be able to meet her needs. Another young lady whose mother was dying from a chronic illness, was dealing with not knowing if she had the same illness. All took a role in helping Sydney adjust to her new home.

12

In Search of a Perfect Roommate

Mary Kay

Mattress moving: One of the most dreaded times that staff encountered in their experience at the group home involved therapeutic room changes. These occurred for numerous different reasons. Regardless of why, it was always a time of turmoil and chaos for both staff and clients alike. Sometimes room changes had the goal of separating clients, and sometimes the goal of finding a good match for them. With eight beds at A Better Choice, we had no single rooms to work with unless we were at less than full capacity. TLC^2, our transitional living house for older, more stable girls, sported one single room that we usually used, not as a privilege, but for a client who posed theft or hygiene complaints when mixed with others.

The room change process usually began at the Thursday afternoon staff meeting, when all staff members were together to compare notes. We would often resort to drawing pictures representing the rooms and plug the names of the clients in (in pencil) until a satisfactory combination appeared, or at least the one we thought would cause the least trouble. A typical conversation at these staffing meetings might have sounded like this:

Mary Kay: We need to talk about bed changes.

All staff: collective groan

Staff 1: Susie needs to get away from Mandy. They are plotting their next run.

Staff 2: Okay, but Susie can't be with Julie either or on the first floor or she'll go out the window again.

Staff 3: Well, that leaves her with Roxanne on the second floor where we can't supervise them as closely...and remember when they backed up the toilet?

Staff 1: Don't forget, Mandy needs to stay in the big upstairs bedroom - she's a door slammer and that door's already broken. We agreed to keep all the slammers in that room, at least till the door was fixed.

Staff 2: What about moving Roxanne into Sandy's room?

Staff 3: No way – I think they are starting a relationship – remember the love notes we found in the nightly journals?

Staff 1: Well, we are back to square one. I guess Susie will need to be on the first floor, and we will have to increase room checks. Now, what about Mandy?

Staff 4: No one can stand rooming with Mandy. She doesn't use soap when she showers and her closet smells like a locker room. We also found used tampons in the ceiling tiles last week.

Mary Kay: At least she didn't flush them!

...And on and on it went. At this point, someone usually requested a break, and we would finish up, doing the best job we could coming up with a workable arrangement for both clients and staff.

After school, the announcement would be made, and the complaining would commence. We understood that many of the girls felt territorial about their rooms, as they had invested time and energy into decorating them to make themselves feel as at home as possible. They had typically had a lot of moves in their lives, and these room changes could trigger thoughts of other difficult changes in their lives. We knew we were asking them to deal with a lot during these necessary moves. Thus, they were called therapeutic room changes and the resulting emotions and reactions could help us address some relationship and treatment issues.

One young lady who had a bent for interior design was most displeased when her name came up for a room change. Massive amounts of tears and tantruming quickly ensued after the announcement was made. Surprised by her over-reaction, the staff soon became aware of the root of her meltdown...It seems that she had spent a good deal of the weekend re-decorating her room. This exercise in interior design included appropriating an end table from the hallway to place beside her bed, and the nicest touch of all was the new red curtains that cast a rosy shadow in her pink bedroom. Since all the bedrooms had the same bedding and curtains, this was a literal red flag. We quickly discovered her white curtains were now in the red-accented living room. Though we appreciated her talent in decorating, her move included returning curtains to their rightful place, with assurances that she could creatively decorate her new bedroom using her assigned bedding and curtains.

Mattress moving took up most of the evening. They didn't always move their mattresses per say, but there were a few that would refuse to sleep on someone else's mattress and haul the whole thing down the hall, bumping down the stairs, clearing the path to their new room. There were also cases when staff decided the entire mattress would move. Enuresis, or wetting at night, can be an issue in sexually abused children. In this case, the plastic covered mattress followed the client for each room change, without any attention called to the issue. Each room had the same furniture. So, to expedite and simplify things, only the dresser drawers were swapped, and staff would help bag up their belongings, and then await the day when this circus would happen all over again.

A prevalent issue that came up during room changes was determining who would sleep on the top bunk. Size, of course, played a role in this decision. Seniority or turf issues could dictate this as well. Top bunk was considered the least favorable spot. Girls generally started there and worked their way to a bottom bunk or, even better, a single bed. Some girls were so vehement about not sleeping on the top bunk that they actually moved their mattress to the floor. Choosing not to have power struggles, we just insisted that they move the mattress back to the top bunk each morning and make their bed. Usually, they soon got tired of all this exercise and we avoided an argument.

Then there were the young ladies who refused to leave their beloved mattress in the early mornings, feeling they needed more beauty sleep than the group home's schedule allowed. Again, trying to avoid the power-struggle, staff would patiently wait for the client's urgent need for the bathroom and take that opportunity to remove the mattress to an unavailable location. This still allowed the client the choice to continue sleeping, albeit uncomfortably, or to join the waking world and her obligations.

In one extreme instance, a client, Alli, pressed us into making a creative move to address her persistent refusal to leave her mattress.

Alli, a dowdy, rather sullen-looking adolescent, had perfected the teenage scowl and eye roll. Her long blonde hair usually hung down over her face, hiding her eyes. Alli came to be known as the queen of passive-aggressive behavior at the group home, and could outwait the most patient of the staff. Unfortunately, she also appeared to be immune to the morning call of nature. Repeatedly, Alli would refuse to get out of bed, either making the whole group late for school, or forcing them to walk the two miles to school so staff could remain to supervise her. After weeks of this, drastic measures were needed, as both staff and clients were at peak frustration level.

The first step of our plan was to move Alli's mattress into the back office area on the first floor. This would still afford her a measure of privacy since the offices were not used at night. Our hope was that when the staff came in to use the office in the morning, the hustle and bustle would make it difficult to continue sleeping. Alli's ability to sleep through our "hustle and bustle" equaled her ability to avoid nature's call, and staff soon tired of stepping over Alli to perform their duties.

On to Plan B!

The common area of ABC, where the clients gathered and ate their meals, was located directly between the kitchen and the front office, which was equipped with a double set of glass French doors for the sake of supervision. Still attempting to give Alli choices, and not falling into her covert power struggle she seemed to thrive upon, we were empathetic towards her attachment to her mattress. We told her the mattress was no longer welcome in the back office as it was too disruptive to staff. She was to sleep in her room at night with her roommates, and if she so desired to stay in bed after wake-up call, she may move her mattress to the common area and sleep till her heart's content under staff supervision.

The constant flow of clients, staff, and visitors finally appeared to drive a compromise with Alli. If she rose as expected in the morning and complete her responsibilities like the other clients, we would consider moving her into a smaller bedroom with only one other roommate. This appeared to appeal to Alli, as she complied and held up her end of this bargain, and the mattress dilemma resolved, leaving us to move on to more pressing issues.

–Flowers in the Attic–

In a house where eight adolescents lived, and at least two staff members were on duty during waking hours, space was at a premium. At ABC, there were three bedrooms – two triples and one double. ABC was an older, more spacious house, and these were bigger bedrooms, for sure. However, for struggling teenage girls, bunking together with another girl who struggled often puts the girls' limited social and conflict resolution skills to the test. These conflicts were excellent real-life learning experiences, and since they were inevitable, we tried to use them to the best of our abilities to teach and reinforce the skills the ladies would need to get along with others.

Sometimes conflicts began innocently enough. Someone was using too much of the closet space, or leaving their books on the floor to

MARY KAY LUTZOW & DANEL BURCHBY

be tripped on. Sometimes, the scuffles were more of the sibling variety. "Don't touch my stuff," or a disagreement over when the lights were going to be turned off at night.

However, the issues that we paid most attention to were those that escalated beyond the first level of disagreement, and into a full-blown conflict that affected the rest of the house. With the memories of elephants, the girls could stretch these arguments on for days. Snippy comments would pervade the house; sarcasm reigned; subtle, button-pushing maneuvers were carried out.

"Sorry you need the curling iron...I already have it and won't be done till the bus leaves."

"I heard Tommy is going to break up with you."

Before we could blink, it seemed, lines were drawn, and the other girls in the house could get pulled into the mix, choosing sides and throwing the house into an uproar.

Allissa and Linda were a prime example. Allissa was a lanky girl with a short brown bob and thick glasses. She tried desperately to fit in, but lacked basic social skills and often would end up irritating her peers. Unfortunately, Allissa was bright enough to know this, and often used this trait purposefully to get under her peers' skins. Allissa also had a violent side, necessitating temporary removal on two previous occasions from the group home after trying to hurt staff members.

She threatened to run away regularly, and did so several times, once even running away to the police station. We had grown tired of her threats and responded to her latest threat to run away by drawing her a map to the local police station so it would save the police the trouble of looking for her. She followed the map diligently and was promptly returned to the group home.

Allissa was on the bad side of the majority of her peers, but her roommate Linda had had quite enough. Linda was a much more so-cially adept young lady and was part of the "cool" crowd. She wore her short hair stylishly and knew about such things as makeup and talking to boys. Linda was less overt in her acting-out than Allissa, but caused staff just as much grief overall. Due to her more adept social skills, Linda could send Allissa into a froth with simply a word or two; then stand back, and watch the flames ignite. Often Allissa ended up with the consequence when Linda was behind the outburst.

What started as small nit-picky complaints turned into a full-blown house war. As staff saw the rest of the girls lining up to take sides, we decided one of our more extreme roommate consequences was in order – Flowers in the Attic.

Author V.C. Andrews, popular in the 1980s, gave us the name for this consequence. The book features four children who were locked away in the attic by their mother, in hopes of gaining the approval of her own mother. Meant to be temporary, the children languished in the attic for years. The crux of the novel is seeing the children become closer than normal siblings and creating their own family.

While only having a fleeting resemblance to the original story, the nickname stuck. We decided to implement "Flowers in the Attic" for Allissa and Linda. The concept was simple, really...the girls were to stay in their room together for as long as it took to see some resolution (or at least some improvement) in their relationship. We knew, however, that they probably couldn't do this without some help. They were sent in with an assignment: Each was given a series of questions to ask each other to facilitate a level of social intimacy and find some common ground. There were questions that pertained to their beliefs or attitudes, how they grew up, their goals, and what some of their favorite things were. We monitored them with a baby monitor, so they knew we were listening to them and making sure they were completing the assignment. After the first phase of the consequence, they received some conflict resolution homework to do together, including role-plays. Again, staff monitored how they interacted remotely. In the end, Linda and Allissa spent the majority of the day in their room for about 1 ½ days. They weren't best friends when they rejoined the rest of the girls, but the tension had dropped and truthfully, they may have just run out of things to fight about.

They had done good work. Each had managed to find something they had in common with the other, and now had more tools to use to relate to others in a more positive, assertive way. Yes, it would have been easier to just switch one of them to a different room. In the end, though, it would not have solved anything except to give the staff less headaches. Most likely, though, the girls would have carried their mal-adaptive social skills into another roommate relationship, and we would have repeated the same pattern, teaching them nothing but to run away from problems, or that they weren't responsible for solving them.

The moral of the story was, it's worth a little headache and effort on the part of the staff and girls to help create a healthier pattern of relating.

~Marn, one of the Founding Mothers

13

The Mentor Program

Danel

Mentoring was a buzz word in the early 2000s. Colin Powell, the president, and numerous sports heroes got on board with the concept of providing guidance to at-risk youth by way of an adult friend. The adult could remain free from the obligations of parenting, yet give advice, suggestions, and actually model the skills that the young person could emulate in a way that might be more well received than if a therapist or parent were providing this same information. The mentor was seen as a combination of confidant, role model, and friend.

There were numerous mentoring agencies in our area – Best Friends, Big Brothers/Big Sisters, and County Mentoring programs. Enamored with this idea, I began doing some research to see which of the agencies in our area could provide the best fit for our girls. I gathered information about each program and what they offered and found that not unlike most mentoring agencies nationally, they were overburdened and had waiting lists of children without mentors. In fact, the average wait at one agency was close to two years. Being somewhat naïve to this problem, I was shocked.

Nonetheless, our girls needed mentors. I was sure of it. With the poor social and relationship skills our girls came to us with, an outside person who could model the skills needed to create and maintain a friendship from the beginning and throughout their time with us could help them tremendously. It could also let us focus on treatment needs more than social skills development.

A waiting list was unacceptable for our needs. We often only had the girls for six to nine months. We needed someone there from the beginning to follow them through their courses of treatment, be there for those two months or two years. I wondered if we could tailor make a program that could fit our needs, that we could be responsible for implementing specific to our population. Back to information gathering. I again called each mentoring agency in the area and explained my intent and asked for their help. They were more than accommodating and gave me copies of their policies, applications, and other information I needed to have a realistic understanding of what was involved in creating a mentorship program.

As I sat with all this information, I noted the most important areas that I needed to consider. First, all of our mentors would need to be female; we would need to screen them for safety, get permission from the parents, and provide training and ongoing supervision. This was doable, I thought. I drew up some guidelines for the mentors and the mentees as well as permission slips for the parents. One of the crucial decisions we made was to make the mentorship program mandatory, a part of every girl's treatment plan.

Once we had all the necessary paperwork, I created an orientation for mentors to go through before they could begin spending time with their match. Crucial to this effort was stressing boundaries, common manipulative behaviors, expectations, how to react to uncomfortable situations, education on self-harm and suicidal behaviors, and ideas for spending time together. Everything was presented to the State licensing agent for approval, even getting an exception to the licensing guidelines that volunteers never work alone with clients. Our licensing agent really went to bat for us here, knowing the concept of a mentor would be lost if they were shadowed by a staff member during their time together.

"All ready," I thought. "Now, I need people." I embarked on my first efforts at recruiting. Notices went out to universities, church bulletins, the local newspapers, and of course I hit up my friends who I thought would do an excellent job. After several weeks, I had two mentors in, trained, and ready to go. Thus started our pilot program of Mentoring. The first two clients were eager to be matched and we encountered very few problem areas during these matches. As we continued recruiting and advertising, as well as using word of mouth, we created an overflow. Yes, more mentors than we could use! The other agencies were astounded. They continued to have waiting lists. We were able to match our girls within two weeks of them coming into the group home. We wanted the girls to get through the group home orientation period before they could be matched. "So I know you are sticking around," I told them.

Most were eager to be matched and once they found out I oversaw the program, asked me continuously when they would get a mentor. This may have had more to do with seeing the other girls come and go with their mentors and doing fun things than the desire for a real relationship, but we took what we could get. I believe, for most of the matches I made, the relationship turned out to be one of the most effective components of their treatment, if not to simply reinforce how to build a relationship. Of course, there were exceptions. Not everyone wanted to be matched. Some had had a bad experience with a previous mentor; some just felt they didn't want to learn to get along with another person. Underlying most resistance was fear. In accordance with our policy, we simply told them it was part of the program they were expected to comply with. I took time to find them a mentor with some experience who had thick skin and an understanding that any behaviors meant to sabotage the relationship had nothing to do with her. Nine times out of ten, the relationship flourished despite the initial pushback.

Parent resistance was another issue we encountered at times. We did take the time to explain that the mentors were part of their daughter's treatment, and they were specifically trained to understand their role, and not meant to replace a parent. Despite this effort, some parents were jealous or threatened about the relationship developing between their daughter and the mentor. Some had a hard time understanding why, when on a sanction, their daughter could not have visits with them, but could go out with their mentor. Some were so threatened that they sabotaged the relationship. Such was the case with Stacey.

–Stacey–

Stacey was a young lady from several counties away. She was matched with one of our most experienced mentors who also happened to be an AODA counselor named Kelly. Kelly had a good head on her shoulders and was able to not personalize some of the negative things that came her way. In recovery herself, Kelly had a knack for engaging kids on a genuine level, challenging their negative beliefs and values, while never judging them. She'd had several successful matches under her belt prior to being matched with Stacey.

Stacey was a quiet girl, who had a history of using alcohol and drugs, mostly to deal with her mother's untreated mental illness. Her mother and her adoptive father had just recently separated. Her relationship with her mother deteriorated and their fights became worse and worse. The police were called to one fight and Stacey ended up being charged with Battery and Disorderly Conduct after she admitted to pushing her mother and pulling her hair. She was fifteen years old. Her drinking and stealing escalated, and Stacey was eventually placed out of her home at ABC Group Home.

Stacey was unique in that, early on, she was able to show an impressive amount of insight into her family's unhealthy patterns. It was obvious she was a very bright girl. However, when it came to her mother, Connie, Stacey reverted back to a little girl again. She was unable to stand up for herself in her mother's presence and became a very passive, sometimes frightened child. Stacey's mother was threatened by the fact that Stacey was in a group home and believed that others were judging her because of this. Despite our effort to engage her, Connie appeared to deteriorate during Stacey's stay until she became verbally combative with the staff and refused to engage in meaningful family sessions. One of the areas in which Connie was especially resistant to was Stacey having a mentor. Several months into her match Stacey was quite comfortable with Kelly and seemed to feel she had a confidant and friend in her. She looked to her for guidance and appeared to be getting quite a lot out of the relationship.

Connie became angry at the staff for confronting her on bringing a scale for Stacey (she was concerned about her weight gain). Having a scale would have been devastating for Stacey's fragile self-esteem. Connie launched her attack, picking Kelly as the target. Behind the scenes, she persisted with Stacey about how she didn't need a mentor and how she was being disloyal to her, her mother, by having fun with Kelly. She subtly and not so subtly implied her love was conditional upon Stacey getting out of this relationship and if she didn't, that meant Stacey did not love her.

Despite her knowledge and insight, Stacey simply could not hold up to this intense pressure and began to avoid Kelly and be sullen on their visits to drive Kelly away. Though Kelly understood what was happening and we all worked together to salvage the relationship, in the end, Stacey was simply not strong enough at that point to do anything that she thought would risk her mother's love.

–Mya–

Tara was a local social worker who found us through a mention in the paper. She had not heard of the group home before and once she researched us, she found she lived only a few blocks away. Tara worked professionally with at-risk boys, the counterpart to our population. She thought this would make a nice venture that was different enough from her work to stave off burn-out, but similar enough to help her feel confident. Extremely personable, Tara was excited to be a part of our mentor program. As is often the case, the mentors that are most "qualified" or appear as if they will be a strong positive influence often end up matched with the toughest girls: the girls who resist the mentorship experience, or have very powerful patterns of negativity that will be difficult to break.

Tara was definitely qualified. I matched her with a Native American young lady who typically presented as stoic and un-emotive, carrying her feelings deep within her and trusting no one. Mya had family ties to criminal behavior and saw her time at Candlelight as "doing time," an attitude of just getting through the experience without being interested in bettering herself.

Despite her initial resistance to all things suggested to her, Mya soon found herself enjoying spending time with Tara. Not wanting to acknowledge this small inroad with her, I stood back and enjoyed watching the relationship grow. Mya became almost possessive of Tara. "MY mentor takes me to the roller rink," she would brag to the other girls. "MY mentor is coming tonight so I don't have to hang out here." Mya felt the need to own this relationship as her idea, lest it be a victory for the staff. Nevertheless, Mya showed positive changes due to the relationship. She showed cracks in her wall of defenses and let us peek at her feelings once in a while. She begrudgingly undertook treatment work assigned to her. Most of all, we saw her smile more often.

The relationship had been building over several months by the time Tara got engaged. She happily included Mya in her wedding planning, and they spent hours trying on dresses and looking at flower arrangements. After several more months, Tara approached me about asking Mya to attend the wedding. This presented a bit of a dilemma as there would be alcohol present. Tara obviously could not supervise her during the ceremony and reception, which were to be held out of town. She would also need permission from her parents and her County worker.

Despite the obstacles, we felt it was important to attempt to arrange this as we saw such a difference in Mya's demeanor and attitude. After getting permission from her parents and County, a staff volunteered to attend with Mya to provide supervision. Mya found a dress in our Clothes Closet (donated clothing) to wear and modeled it proudly before the group.

The week before the wedding was to happen, a heartbreaking turn of events played out. Mya ran away. She walked away from the group home and disappeared. The requisite calls were made, and then we waited. Tara was beside herself and unsure of what was happening. We spent more than a few minutes discussing how behaviors can reflect a lot of things, most often not related to the very people they hurt. It was a difficult time. Mya was not found before the wedding, and Tara went on to be a beautiful bride. After two weeks, Mya was officially discharged and her bed was released by the county.

Several weeks later, Mya turned up. We were never sure where she had been. She returned with her previous sullen attitude and took a length of time before she showed any signs of communicating on a meaningful level with us. Tara, bless her heart, was willing to mentor her again and they resumed their relationship, albeit a slightly changed one. Mya never fully recovered to the level of healthiness she had been moving towards and after only a month or so we lost her to a run again, this time for good. Though we processed through what happened and Tara heard over and over again that nothing Mya did reflected on her, it was difficult, and she grieved. We did not get her back as a mentor again. Our loss.

Can we predict these things? Should we only match up girls who are willing to have a mentor? Should we discontinue the program to prevent such heartbreak? We couldn't help asking ourselves these questions. The answer we discovered was a resounding "no" to all. The purpose of the mentorship program was to build relationships and to use that process to model the creation and maintenance of relationships. This was the one common denominator all our girls had: they were deficient in genuine relational skills, without want or gain, but with compromise, nurture and empathy. The rewards were simply so much greater than the risks of heartbreak, which is a natural occurrence in life as well. We worked hard for our mentors to understand that: This selfless act they were pursuing could have consequences for them. It could be terrifically rewarding or terribly hurtful. Luckily, we were blessed with so many people willing to take this risk to positively impact a hurting child. We salute Tara and the others that came before and after her.

–Kendra–

Kendra came to us lost. She bore the physical scars of curling irons, electric cords, and broomsticks; with broken teeth and a tough "don't even think about messing with me" attitude. She had a shiny round chocolate colored face, deep dimples, and a wide smile. She was a mixture of contradictions. The dirt under her fingernails spoke of a life spent scrambling, though she liked nice clothes and wore tight fitting, preferably luminescent, outfits to "look good." She had survived in her father's home by learning to steal, by taking rather than asking, and earning her own keep. She was a survivor who started young. After Kendra's mother left her and her three sisters with their father who preferred the company of cocaine to his growing daughters, Kendra hustled as best she could, made her own rules, and convinced herself she didn't care about the rest. A child of an overburdened urban Bureau of Child Welfare, she was placed quickly after spending several nights in juvenile detention and deemed "out of control." Kendra was 13 years old. The intake process was a culture shock – mostly white staff and peers, roommates, rules, staff watching over her at all hours, adults worrying about her safety, small town USA vs. inner city. She was at a complete loss when she came to ABC.

We watched Kendra closely the first few weeks. Her survival skills were prevalent. A girl with a sweet smile, Kendra could usually get the other girls to do what she wanted. The staff fell in love with her. Her father didn't call. The Case Worker was "looking into" when he would be able to visit.

Part of her first four weeks included the mandatory bio-psych-social interview with me. It was immediately apparent Kendra had huge gaps to be filled, educationally, socially, and with relationships.

"Why you gots to axe me that?" Kendra complained when I asked her what school she attended. "Too many to count, I don't know," she finally answered be-grudgingly, her happy face clouded over and her eyes slammed down to the floor. When she was asked what jobs she held in the past during her initial interview she answered "dancing," later revealing that she meant lap dancing for much older men for money.

"I would never have sex with them. That's nasty!" Kendra insisted, appalled I might think such a thing. She, unashamed, bared her arms and legs, showing me scars from abuse and accidents. Her eyes were empty.

Continually needing and craving nurturing, yet terrified to receive any, Kendra was in a holding pattern. Extremely bright, she had picked up on the concepts of Barriers in Thinking and other educational material easily. Relationships were a different matter. As is often the case with children who feel as if their life is out of control, Kendra had a hard time differentiating between having personal control over her actions, and taking control of a situation and/or other people around her. Having little to no power her whole life, Kendra could focus in on a possibility to grab power like a laser. One evening Kendra entertained herself by privately telling each and every girl in the house that another peer was "talkin' smack" about her and calling her a "ho." Staff were so busy that night diffusing conflict, bickering, and outright verbal fights between the offended residents, that no one noticed Kendra watching the drama unfold while sitting quietly in the corner.

At other times (in fact most of the time) Kendra ate up attention and nurturing as if she were famished for it. Kendra relished the bed-time story routine, snuggling up next to staff and closing her eyes to listen to the tale. During a slumber party in the living room one summer weekend night, Kendra purposefully counted and took note of each resident that wanted to position their sleeping bag next to hers, lapping up the positive feedback, almost hoarding it. Kendra's fear that it may be fleeting, leave and never return, or perhaps she had just imagined it to be so was apparent. So fragile were her good feelings, Kendra could sense a perceived slight far before it happened and would often shun the offender before it could become a reality for her. Her behavior served to give her more control in her depleted life.

Kendra was an inner city Black teen who had been thrust into a small northern town with mostly white staff and peers. Knowing how out of place Kendra must feel and how important it was for her to keep a connection to and feel proud of her culture and heritage, I felt it was important to give Kendra a connection and relationship with a strong Black woman. Despite my search, none were to be found after several weeks. At this point, I was feeling that Kendra's need for a friend who could model relationship skills and love her unconditionally outside of a professional relationship was paramount. Jennifer, an angel, walked in the door to ABC and into Kendra's life.

Jennifer was the epitome of unconditional love and embraced Kendra without question from day one. As the process goes, I call the mentor before making the match to give the mentor information about the resident, answer any questions, and generally try to put the mentor at ease about the role they are about to play in the child's life. Jennifer listened quietly and asked only one question, "When do I get to meet her?"

Gaps in Kendra's life were large. At one point, the group home was the recipient of a generous donation of several new bikes. No less than fifteen times did Kendra ask to ride bikes that day.

"When can we? I'm gonna get the red one," claimed Kendra pouncing on a new feeling of ownership even though the bikes were meant for the house.

"Izit time?"

"Yes, Kendra, it's time now."

"Finally! You staff gots too much to do, and no time for what I want."

Tact not being her strong suit, Kendra rushed ahead of the staff and the other girls to assert the newly beloved red bike as hers for the evening. After several minutes of attempting to carefully steady herself on the bike, it became obvious to all that Kendra had not ridden a bike before. Uncharacteristically unashamed of her inadequacies, Kendra allowed a staff member to assist her to get her balance and wobbled down the driveway on her maiden voyage. Kendra's round featured face broke into a smile showing all her teeth. Giggling like a toddler, she moved to head on down the sidewalk.

Loudly proclaiming her new talents and passion to the others, "Imma gonna get a new red bike like this when I'm old like you, (staff name)," "Can you see me? I got it!" "Look at me, look at me!!"

Long after the others tired of riding bikes, Kendra remained. Staff allowed her to remain outside after everyone else went in and often checked back with her to find her happily riding circles in the driveway, a glimpse of the childhood Kendra had never been allowed.

So many times, we see this happen; childhood stops at a certain age when adults fail to or are unable to protect, provide for, or nurture their children. The children remain ignorant to or sometimes are agonizingly aware of what they lack or need, and end up normalizing their experiences and ultimately passing them on to their own children, which oftentimes come much too early. Simple childhood experiences like bike riding, finger-painting, or sleepovers are not privileges or extras. They add up to a childhood. Kids like Kendra ended up having adult experiences and familiarity with things that aren't healthy even for adults; leaving them with the belief that adult experiences are okay, expected, or ideal regardless of how they feel. Everything is experienced much earlier: sex, alcohol, drugs, making choices without supervision. Like a baby who learns to walk at seven months instead of at a more developmentally appropriate age, Kendra had the ability, but lacked the judgment, to make healthy choices for herself.

As Kendra gained confidence in herself as a young woman, she began to show maturity in relationships, and trust within the house. We once again began to focus on her need to be somehow connected to her culture. Contacting the agencies in the area that were owned, managed, or founded by African American men and women, I sought an experience different from the mentorship role, yet one that would continue to focus on pride, acceptance, and self-worth. My search led me to an area church that offered a step-dancing program, "Step it Up," for youth and was coached by an African American pastor. Kendra loved the idea immediately. Flashing her trademark smile, Kendra quickly made friends at the mixed-race practices, drawing envy from her peers at the group home.

Never was her smile bigger than on stage performing for anyone she could get to come, including peers, staff, her mentor, and even other girls' mentors.

Jennifer and Kendra's time together soon became special events. With her nose pressed against the window, Kendra announced to all that "MY mentor always comes every week." "I'm gonna get outta here tonight." "Whatever. I'm gonna have Burger King, not tuna fish like you guys." Then the coup: "She gonna bring me sumthin'."

Having nothing of note to her name, possessions were a never-ending ambition. To possess was to be acknowledged, to possess was to matter, and to possess was to impress. Therefore, receiving gifts had the effect of bolstering her tenuous self-confidence. Though used to earning her possessions by sometimes unsavory means, Kendra also embodied an air of entitlement.

Being cute, flashing her dimples, and talking in a little girl voice often brought results from well-meaning people. However, when that failed to satisfy her, other tactics surfaced. On a crisp fall day, the first few weeks of school complete, the leaves were just edging toward color, but the temperature had dipped below sixty degrees early. Jennifer returned Kendra from a visit and asked to speak with staff in the office privately. Kendra turned and without a word, eyes cast downward, joined the other girls who were gossiping rather than cutting vegetables for the night's dinner in the group home's kitchen. A slight smirk adorned her face and her eyes flitted to the windowed office door more than a few times, trying to take in the scene.

"I'm a little worried about Kendra," began Jennifer. "It's starting to get chilly, and she was cold tonight in her windbreaker. I was wondering if I could buy her a winter coat."

Jennifer went on to describe Kendra's refusal to go to the park with her as planned because she was too cold outside in her light coat. Instead, they ended up watching a movie in Jennifer's living room. Jennifer's face went from shocked to confused to dismayed when she was told that Kendra had been told to dress for the weather before her visit, how she had refused to wear anything other than her windbreaker, and finally, how she had a perfectly good, though donated, coat hanging on the hooks that lined the back hallway.

"But she didn't *ask* for a coat," uttered Jennifer, trying to take in all that had just transpired. "She just said she wished she had a warmer coat so we could do outside activities."

This was not a trait limited to Kendra. Conniving, manipulating, and outright stealing were sometimes employed by the residents to get what they wanted. Sometimes *stuff* fills a hole, an empty space in their lives. Sometimes it was a way to get revenge on someone who had crossed them. Sometimes it was the thrill of getting away with something. Sometimes it was a way to express feelings when it was too painful to feel them.

14

In the Mentor's Words

Danel

The following are accounts of mentoring from the mentors themselves. The beauty of volunteering this way is not only did our mentors give, they also received and many talked about how they benefited from the relationship with their match themselves. We were blessed to have some of the best mentors we could ask for during the tenure of CVC. These are a few of their stories.

–Lorynn–

It all started with our blue couch. We had bought a new couch and I had convinced the moving guys to move our old gently used blue one to Candlelight Vision Corp.

On the day of the delivery, I found myself inside the group home. Teen girls who were sitting around a large table, stopped eating and stared at me. The girls quickly asked who I was and what I was doing there. I was surprised to see a girl I met at juvenile detention. As a Christian mom, I visit the jail to lead a Sunday Teen Church Service. I knew of CVC because many of the girls in jail were court-ordered to reside at CVC. Life can be surprising and have unexpected developments. Little did I know that my work with teens would expand from jail ministry to mentoring at CVC.

It is important to think about making a mentoring commitment. I decided to mentor only when I had enough time, space, and energy to do so. Maintaining a high-quality friendship with a teen needs focus. I personally decided I would be loyal and not drop the girls, since I do not drop my own friends. I wanted to be a helpful, fun, positive influence and connect them to our community.

My CVC experience was a time where I became a more generous person. Even if I was mentoring one girl, I would try and think of all the girls and staff at the group home. I donated clothes from my daughters, books, art supplies, soda, snacks, and holiday decorations. Once, the CVC van ran out of gas by the high school. It was fun bringing a gas can to them with their cheers and thank yous as I drove away.

I learned that being in a group home filled with females can be challenging. Many of the girls were homesick and came from distant cities. I quickly became aware of the CVC rules, level system, rewards, and wonderful staff that guided them. I had excellent training and workshops to better understand the teens. I observed how the structure of the schedule helped them absorb their losses and gain more discipline. If they wanted money, they were encouraged to go out into the community and find part-time work. Mentors helped the girls by adding fun events and one-on-one time that they craved.

My own attitude changed. I realized "I" was also being mentored by the girls and staff. I appreciated my own childhood, parents, and memories of role models that changed my life. My actions and words of encouragement made a difference. I worked to maintain a standard of excellence, as the girls observed how I handled situations and people. The following is a brief description of three teen girls I had the privilege to know.

Kay was the first teen I mentored at Candlelight Vision. We had actually met previously when she was in jail, and I was given the nickname "church lady" by her. Kay was from a neighboring town, and we connected through knowledge of that city. My relatives lived near some of her family, too. At that time, the judge decided to send Kay to Southern Oaks Girls School. I mentioned to Kay that if I were going to Southern Oaks, I would make the most of it, get her high school diploma. We became pen pals. One day her social worker invited me to Kay's high school graduation party. Inside the walls of SOGS, I saw the joy of Kay completing a goal. I was so amazed that she did what I suggested! After SOGS, Kay was placed at Candlelight Vision's ABC group home. I went through mentor training and was motivated to be her mentor. Our first outing was to Dairy Queen where we ate ice cream cones together. We both cried into our ice cream because we were finally free from the tight monitoring of the jails.

Kay became part of the family. We went hiking, strawberry picking, saw movies, and talked on our porch a lot. I saw Kay work hard to transform her life in positive ways. After some questionable boyfriends, Kay met a great guy from a stable family. Later, I was at their wedding as Kay's Matron of Honor. She is happily married and has a daughter with my name as her daughter's middle name. Kay is a hard worker and has moved up from a factory position to an office administrative position. She attends my book club and is loved by the members. The ladies do not know of my and Kay's background together; They only know and see our special relationship.

My next match, Coral, was presented to me as a girl who needed special attention. Coral did not have trouble with the law but struggled with mental health issues. Coral liked coming to our home to cook, do homework, and do her laundry. Coral experienced difficulties at the group home and eventually was placed at a mental health center in a neighboring city. I went knowing the locked world of jails to learning the locked world of mental health institutions. Coral challenged me and forced me to set strong boundaries with her. Coral was very needy, depressed, and struggled with addictions. I learned to be assertive and strongly say "no" to her many demands. I continue now to see Coral on her birthday and Christmas. We have kept up our mentoring ritual of shopping and having lunch together. Coral saved every card and letter I have sent her through the years. She has our mentoring memories in a scrapbook.

After Coral left the group home, Tina, another girl from the group home, quickly called me and asked me to be *her* mentor. Tina has a personality that "jumps right into life." Upon coming to our home, she walked our dog, borrowed make-up, ate snacks, and quickly adapted to napping on our couch.

We were all surprised by Tina's energy and endless questions. After leaving Candlelight Vision, Tina became pregnant, and I have the honor of being her daughter's Godmother. Participating in Tina's daughter's baptism was a beautiful moment in my life. I continue to be a part of Tina's family and she is part of our family too.

I have always loved being a mother and raising our three children. I have loved being a youth minister in jails and an art teacher. Yet, it has been mentoring, for me, that has pushed me out of my comfort zone. Our entire family has grown from sharing our home, time, and possessions with Candlelight Vision's teens. The mentoring helped me become a better person, a more patient listener to teens, and to stay young! I always encourage adults to get to know teens and their delightful ways. Thank you, Candlelight for the adventures and influence you have had in my life.

–Lisa–

When I was sitting in church, I saw the ad for a teen mentor. I wondered what was involved and spoke to Danel. After hearing more about the opportunity, I felt strongly that I could be a mentor and show someone that even when life throws you lots of lemons, you still can make darn good lemonade and go on with life. I have always had a soft spot for kids in my heart and wished to boost someone's self-esteem.

I was a little nervous knowing that the girls have issues with wanting things their way. I hoped to be accepted by my match and her to like being around me, even if it meant just being at my home talking, cooking, or running errands. When I would meet a match for the first time, I would take them out to eat to talk to them in a casual way without my family present. If they said something that seemed to indicate they hoped for a reaction out of me, it wouldn't happen. I would process the information and ask a counselor at the group home about what was said.

I had previously given talks to the group home girls on what it is like being a parent to a special needs child. I did everything right during my pregnancy and still had a child with many needs. I wanted to let the girls know you don't know how things will turn out during a pregnancy and ask them to reflect on whether they are capable of handling a child with special needs. It is time consuming mentally and physically. I had been a mentor to one girl early on, and she had run away. I was scared for that girl and even got in my car to drive around the group home to see if I could see her and convince her to go back to the group home.

After one of my talks, I gave at the group home I got a call indicating one of the girls wanted me to be her mentor. I was honored, surprised, and touched that someone wanted to be matched with me. I believe Sara was starting to make changes during her time at the group home. She had a little brother with special needs so she knew I would understand some of her feelings about her home life. I had fun with Sara. She enjoyed going to church with me for an advent craft night. Sara loved art projects. I think one of the most important things I learned from Sara was not to let things get you down. She was frustrated at times with her mom and eventually went to be with her dad.

I still have a Christmas ornament she made for our family, and a picture she made for my daughter still hangs on her bedroom wall. My older boys also enjoyed hanging out with Sara. We all attended her graduation and got to talk about how special our relationship with Sara was. It was a touching ceremony, and I felt a little sad that she was moving on. I think of her often, especially when I look at the painting she made for my daughter, and I wonder how life is treating her and what she is doing. Did she go on to higher learning? Does she have a good job? Is she dating anyone or even married? I hope she is happy.

Amelia was my challenge. By the time I got matched with her, I had some experience with mentoring under my belt as well as the experience at my job dealing with elementary school children with behavior issues. My heart went out to Amelia, and I so wanted her to be able to learn to live independently as she was going to be 18 years old soon. Amelia was going to be adopted by another family. Unfortunately, I felt I was in competition with the family for Amelia's attention. I enjoyed being with her, but when issues arose and things became difficult, I didn't want to show my frustration with her. I would try to be patient and talk out my feelings with someone on the staff. I felt like Amelia was playing a game of wanting to ruin the mentor relationship so she could be with her soon-to-be adopted family. I truly felt she wanted to be a part of a family so badly that she would shut others out, even others that were helping her. Amelia loved music and was a good singer. She would put her heart and soul in music and would rather sing than do her school-work. What I thought were fun things such as going to a soccer game or spending a weekend away complete with campfires, and playing ghost in the graveyard, she balked at. These were childhood games and activities that my kids enjoyed and wanted to share with her.

Finally, I sat down with Mary Kay and Danel and talked with Amelia about my feelings and how her words and actions hurt me. Amelia continues to be in the back of my mind when I work with younger kids on the playground and know their family life isn't great. I try to reach out to them early on to let them know someone cares for them. I learned how to be a stronger role model to a child and give them high expectations in life, praise, and support. I wasn't there for Amelia's graduation. I'm not even sure she graduated from the program. Amelia needed love and support earlier in her life, not just starting at 17. I was relieved in some ways when my time ended with her. The roller coaster ride ended, and I could move on with my family. I was saddened when I heard the group home eventually closed. There needs to be someone out there for these girls. Someone that says we care and love you. To give them the tools to go out in life and work through issues.

I loved getting together with the other mentors and hearing their stories. Being a mentor taught me to be there even if it is for one child to make a difference: A hug, being a cheerleader, just letting someone know that they are important. I always felt God was speaking to me that day when I saw the notice in our church bulletin. Because of the group home I am working with a little girl today in the school district to make a difference early on so she doesn't wind up making poor choices in the next couple of years.

Thank you for allowing me to be a part of the mentor program. It taught me a lot.

–Julie–

I'd been sensing that I was supposed to be ministering to kids some- how, somewhere. I could have done that easily at my church, but that just did not seem to be the spot. Then one Sunday on the Lifestyle page of the newspaper was a picture and story of two women who once a month were volunteering to create a special night at Candlelight Vision, a local group home. A taco party, nail painting, Easter treats, etc. The last line of the article said "to be a mentor to one of the girls, contact us." So, I did. I went for the interview process and was matched with my first girl. I was very excited to meet her. All told, I had two matches, each for about a year.

Holly was a waif of a girl, one of the youngest ever placed at this home for girls. She was sweet and eager to please. Of course, that may have been part of her "situation." We spent time together doing things that a much younger child would enjoy, so it made for easy planning with Holly. She never seemed interested in going to my house. Instead, we often would go for walks or to the park to play. Holly wanted to be with me as much as possible.

Sophie was my second match. She was older, and much older looking than her age. Sophie always wanted to be doing something that involved spending money so that she could bring something back to show off to the other girls in the house. When we had her birthday dinner at Red Lobster, she ordered a full meal and dessert. She saved almost her entire lobster tail, uneaten, so she could not only show it to those at the house but take it to school the next day!

I did manage to get Sophie to appreciate going to the grocery store and picking up one simple treat. Then we would go to the park along the lake and sit with our food, binoculars, books, puzzle games like Sudoku.

Sophie had the ability to be pleasant and charming, unless you were not doing things her way or making her the most important person in the room. I did not allow her to do this with me, but it was evident as I saw how she interacted with others.

I learned patience with both girls. I gave my time and small things occasionally - a coloring book, a flower, birthday dinner, maybe a coffee outing for both of us, and occasionally a Dollar Tree trip. I purposefully never made my outings with the girls about doing expensive things. My gift to them was me, my heart to love them, my ears to listen to them (although cracking through that was hard - their trust was slow to come), and my promise to see them every week.

The fondness I took away from those two years included the possible impact I had on Jo. Jo was another girl in the house that for some reason took a liking and interest in me each time I came to the house. Perhaps it was my shaved head? I remember she asked me once in the summer when I was tanned and often dressed in flowing skirts and sandals if I was from a different country.

I also was pleased to do a Bible Study with the girls who chose to come. There'd be two or three or four. I know it often was just so they could get out of doing something else. But I'd like to think someday they may remember something we talked about. I tried to reach them through simple lessons with captivating pictures, and popular Christian music. A few of the girls were allowed to go to church with me. Jo was one of those.

Holly had gone to church to get out of the house. Jo went to learn more about God. I have no doubt in my mind that Jo truly accepted God into her heart. Being asked to Jo's graduation ceremony was very special to me. After she left the group home, she did not have anyone supporting her in her new lifestyle though I did see Jo occasionally at church off and on for several months.

All three of these girls knew they could always track me down through my church. I hope someday to hear from one!

My youngest daughter blessed me so much when I started mentoring. The Mother's Day card she gave me the first year, shortly after I started, said "Happy Mother's Day - You have a new daughter." She was referring to me being matched for the first time at Candlelight. It makes me cry even as I think about it. My daughter also gave me a large sterling silver cross one year with about 12-14 tiny ribbons and tiny little crosses hanging off each one, representing all the girls at Candlelight. I treasure it still even years after Candlelight closed.

Being a mentor to those girls was often a pain in the butt, feeling unappreciated, taken advantage of, and used. It was also joyful, fulfilling, and a time of learning for me for which I will ever be grateful. It was two years that I will never forget nor regret.

–Jennifer–

I believe that one of the most important purposes in life is to gain new perspectives. My mind was jolted into a fresh viewpoint the day I met Kendra. I was going through a period of personal growth and change, so I felt compelled to respond to an ad in the paper looking for mentors for at-risk teenage girls. The teenage years were a difficult time for me, yet I had a stable family life and home. I couldn't imagine the challenge that it must be for girls without support from family. I wanted to make a difference in another person's life, and I felt this would be a great avenue to do just that.

Our first meeting was fueled by a fear of silence. I chatted on nervously, asking question after question that were met with either a blunt yes or no. Kendra sang, chanted, rapped, danced, and drummed her way through that evening. I left feeling a little overwhelmed, but I knew that I couldn't wait to see her again.

Over the months, we experienced many adventures together. We forged an unlikely friendship because we respected each other enough to go outside of our comfort zones for the sake of the other. That was evident the day she climbed up on the back of a camel, screaming and yelling the whole time letting me know that she wasn't doing it for her entertainment. Or the day we ventured in the woods to camp, and she constantly glanced in fear at the dark, horrified at what lay outside of the ring of light from the campfire. I did the same for her the day I strapped on roller skates and anxiously crept my way around the roller rink while kids zoomed recklessly around me. I endured because as I looked at that teenaged face, I saw a small child, broken but hopeful, that longed to go skating and never had gotten the chance. I saw delight, determination, and a sense of belonging in her that I had not seen before.

In many ways I felt like a temporary replacement for her parents, which was a benefit to both of us. She had a person to bring school projects home to. One day she presented me with a shelf made in woodworking class. Believe me, that work of art was something only a mother could appreciate! As a parent would, I praised her victories and took every opportunity to tell her that I loved her. I also remember the shock and disappointment I felt the first time I went to the group home and was told she couldn't leave with me due to her poor behavior. I found it hard to believe that my "perfect angel" would misbehave, forgetting why she was there to begin with! But all the time spent together helped me draw upon the patience, unfaltering love, and acceptance that I would need later when I became a parent myself.

The day eventually came when Kendra's father decided he wanted her to come back home. Kendra seemed enthusiastic to return home to more familiar surroundings. I was terrified for her. Although she had always painted an elaborate picture of a near perfect home life, I knew the opposite to be true. I had been told that she came from one of the worst situations that the group home staff had seen. Early on in our relationship, I was offended that she didn't share the truth about her family with me, but over time, I learned it was her way of creating a better reality by voicing a dream in the present tense in hopes that it would come to pass in the future.

The night of her graduation from the group home was quite an intense emotional experience. At the ceremony, we shared our hopes and fears. There were many tears, smiles, and hugs. Afterwards, as the final hours ticked away, Kendra, my husband-to-be, and I headed back to my apartment for a final visit. As we had many times in the past, we fired up the Karaoke machine and sang, laughed, and acted goofy together for the last time. I would have loved to stow Kendra away with me, but realistically, I knew she had to go.

My view of life was forever impacted by my friendship with Kendra. Every time I see a bag of Flamin' Hot Cheetos or hear a song by Nelly, I am reminded of that brave girl, who despite feeling like she was stuck on an island, as she had once told me, had the courage to greet this life mostly with smiles. It really amazes me how much I benefited when I thought I was the one helping her!

15

Creative Interventions

Mary Kay

When we as a staff looked at giving a consequence to one of the clients for an indiscretion, we had to look at what was available to us and if we could be creative in tailoring the response to "fit the crime" as it were. In other words, we wanted as natural of a consequence as we could get. Cataloging our options, we usually ran through what level of response was necessary to adequately address the behavior. Some behaviors were addressed on the spot with a low level of consequence called an Incident. In these cases (often a swearing violation, poor attitude, sassing, or being unprepared for a group), the client was asked to fill out an incident form immediately. The form asked questions designed to have her rethink her behavior and get back on track as soon as possible. In other words, interrupt that cycle of negative thinking, feelings, and behavior and remind themselves of their tools they could use to handle things positively and respectfully.

In-house we had several options besides the incident form. The next level of consequence was called "Stop the World." This intervention does just what it says for the client – everything stops, at least all her privileges. The client was given notice of her standing and given work to complete before she is finished with the consequence. For example, she might be given a ripple chart in order to think about how her behaviors had affected other people, or be assigned extra chores or to make amends to someone she victimized. This allowed us to individualize each client's treatment within a consistent structure. Because Stop the World is meant to be a twenty-four hour consequence, it is reserved for more significant offenses than an incident might call for. Skipping a class at school, being in another peer's room, smoking, refusing a group, or accumulating three incidents in one day may all be grounds for Stop the World.

At the most extreme end of the spectrum of interventions staff could hand out was "Jeopardy Track." Jeopardy Track had a length of at least seven days and was designed to give a strong message to the client that her behaviors were placing her in jeopardy of returning to criminal and hurtful patterns. A formal packet of work was given to the client, including ownership and apology letters to everyone involved, a ripple chart, a study of the barriers in thinking they used and a plan for change. After the work is completed, (and hopefully new insights are gained) the client could petition off this consequence in front of her peers and staff. She would speak about the sincerity of the work that she completed and her plan for change. As a staff, we tried to use this consequence sparingly and for the worst offenses, such as illegal behavior, theft, running away, threats, or violence. With adequate warning, a client who is refusing to do or lagging behind on her Stop the World work could find herself on Jeopardy Track as well.

Once we have exhausted all our in-house options for consequences and the same patterns of behaviors continue to occur, we often look for creative and/or outside consequences to send the message that the behaviors are not acceptable and will not be tolerated.

We had a few options for outside consequences depending on co-operation from other individuals. We have asked police officers to give tickets for smoking to our clients. We have had clients make an appointment with the fire station to find out the consequences of smoking in bed or smoking through a dryer sheet to hide the smell.

Our most dramatic consequence we use outside the group home is juvenile detention, otherwise known as jail. Not a lot of people think of minors being in jail. Yet every county has a juvenile unit at the jail or can arrange for a bed at another county's jail for a juvenile. Juveniles are housed separately than adults and attend school (inside the detention facility), but nonetheless are placed in cells overnight, shackled when taken to court or into custody and given scrubs to wear. We, as the staff, did not have the power to put a client in jail. However, we work closely with the county case worker who has the power to put their clients who were placed at the group home under a delinquency petition in jail for 72 hours to investigate negative or potentially illegal behaviors.

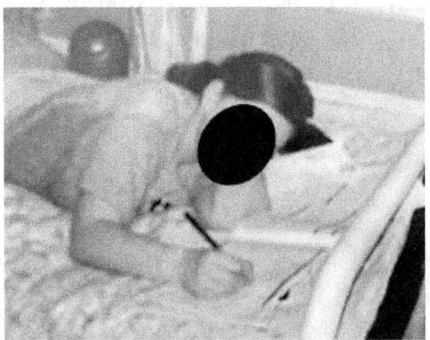

~ an ABC client completing an
assignment

Now, since the majority of clients we had were placed on delinquency petitions, we could work with the case worker and communicate the recommendation that the client be placed in jail to address her behaviors when our list of consequences had been utilized without effect. Now, for the few that were placed on Child in Need of Protective Services (CHIPS) Petitions or Juvenile in Need of Protective Services (JIPS) Petitions, or on Chapter 51 Mental Health Holds, this is not an option. A Delinquency Petition means that the clients had broken the law and been charged and adjudicated (convicted) in a juvenile court. A juvenile sentence is usually one year on supervision, which means being assigned a Case Worker and determining if an out of home placement is necessary.

We have worked with case workers successfully in using jail as an effective intervention. Since jail is not meant to be fun, it can be used as a deterrent. It can also be used as a time out from extreme feelings that are escalating at the group home and time to think about what payoffs that person is getting from her behaviors. We hoped the client would determine that the payoffs were fewer than the pain of the consequence. There have been times where a client has simply decided they are tired of the revolving door of the jail and that was motivation enough to change her behaviors.

Now, admittedly, it can be rather frustrating when a client has extremely negative behaviors, repeated patterns of victimizing others, and is not eligible for a stay in jail due to their legal status. It is often the case that the clients placed on JIPS or CHIPS petitions have nearly the same types of behaviors as the clients placed on Delinquency Petitions, but just haven't been through the court system to be adjudicated. When we ran out of consequences in-house with these kids, it tested our creativity to the max. We will detail some of the more creative interventions we used throughout the years, and some of the most successful.

–"Jail"–

One intervention we used a few times involved an "as-realistic-as-we-could-get-it" stay in jail. In other words, since we could not send the client to jail, we decided to bring the jail to the group home. Now, we could not and would not want to literally lock up a client. What we did do is tape off a corner of a common room to signify a jail cell. We placed a desk and all the client's work in it. She would be allowed to leave the area for meals and to use the bathroom and would sleep in her own bed at night. However, at other times, she would remain in her "cell." The hope was that the experience would signify that this was where her behaviors were leading her – to jail. It always amazed us that the client who would not follow directions or group home rules consistently would stay in her "cell" during the times she was assigned to. As in the real detention center, the fake jail cell often did have the effect of removing the client from her emotions of the immediate situation and allow time to think carefully about how her behaviors were impacting her and others.

—Power Balls—

Danel

One of the barriers in thinking we taught at CVC was called power thrusting. Power and control were common themes of treatment for the girls. Often the girls experience either too much power or not enough. In many cases, the power quotient tips violently from one end of the continuum to the other. First, when a child is abused or neglected, she has too little power and no control over her life. Victimization often leads to anger and resentment, which leads to negative behaviors and acting out, giving the child too much power, such as when she runs away or threatens her mother with suicide to get what she wants. This inconsistency is damaging for a girl's well-being and healthy development.

Power is a concept we teach from the very beginning. Personal power over our own behaviors is appropriate and healthy. Taking power from and making decisions for others is not. Often this is a new concept for the girls, and some have trouble understanding how and when they "give their power away."

Giving your power away is when a person chooses to let another person decide how she herself will act. A common example is "She made me so mad that I hit her." As I explained to the clients, "You gave her the power to make you mad and get you in trouble by hitting her. If you had confronted *her* behavior appropriately, she would be the one in trouble, not you. You gave her the power to get you in trouble." Sometimes the girls are so comfortable being victims that they don't realize that no one has power over their behaviors but them. Taking responsibility for their own behaviors is sometimes a foreign concept and requires that they have some self-awareness of what is happening. Our goal of empowering them to be strong young women would be lost without strongly emphasizing this point, that they can choose how they act no matter what.

There are cases where clients consistently give their power away to their peers over and over and then consistently complain about it. Sometimes it is clear that one or two peers hold a lot of power in the house by their posturing, subtle intimidation, or outright threats. In either of these cases, we have discovered that a hands-on experiential intervention can do wonders to open the girls' eyes to what is happening.

During a scheduled evening Issues Group, we addressed this topic and explained our concerns and our goal – everyone deserves to have personal power. If you choose to give it away, that is your choice, but there are consequences. If you choose to take power from others, that is also your choice, but there are consequences for that as well. You alone get to decide if you are going to give someone your power – no one can take it without permission. This last concept was shocking to the girls yet reinforced a sense of personal power. After the discussion during the group, the girls were given an equal number of balls – we called them Power Balls. They were neither very heavy nor very light. The amount they were given, usually five, represented their personal power. To carry around five, the girls felt a little weight, just enough to remind them that they had power in their lives, but not so much to be a burden.

The girls were instructed to go about their evening, and if a staff member saw them giving away their power or taking someone's power, they would instruct the appropriate transfer of a power ball. Over time, it would become apparent who had patterns of overpowering others and who tended to give away their personal power to others. In a typical timeframe of this intervention (usually several days), inevitably most of the power balls were transferred to one to two of the girls and the rest were left with very few. Remember, for a girl to take someone's power ball, the girl whose ball was taken had to actively give it away. This was an extremely eye-opening experience for most girls and appropriate treatment goals could be garnered from the results of this intervention, typically assertiveness training and empathy for others.

—Rotten Potatoes—

Mary Kay

Even though our clients were young girls, children really, who had only begun their journey in life, we often saw them enter CVC with the anger and cynicism of someone much older. Many came from situations in which they were thrust into an adult role much sooner than they could handle, where they learned survival skills that were not necessarily helpful to them as they got older. All this bred anger that covered up their hurt, sadness, and abandonment.

With nowhere to turn to process these feelings or seeing themselves as weak for even having these feelings, the anger, over time festered, often unleashing at unsuspecting people or paradoxically at people to whom they felt the most attachment. Unresolved anger turned into resentments. These buried feelings were one of the most difficult things to engage the clients to talk about. To open up these wounds was often unpalatable, if not downright scary. To not do so, though, caused continued pain for themselves and others.

To address the most severe of these cases, we turned to an experiential intervention intended to raise the client's awareness about how exactly these unresolved feelings were affecting her. Lidya was a clear example of this in action.

Lidya was a beautiful girl with dark, curly hair that hung down past her shoulder blades. She was adjudicated delinquent at the age of 15 for Possession of a Narcotic, and continued to have drug and alcohol related offenses and violations which culminated in a charge of stealing her mother's credit card after a family fight and ultimately led to her being placed at ABC group home. Lidya came from a two-parent family who appeared to be devoted to her, though had rescued her from consequences at times. Lidya had one sibling whom she identified as the "golden child," the one who could do no wrong. Lidya described a family pattern of her father intimidating and physically abusing her, then her mother rescuing her from the situation and trying to keep the peace between the two of them. Additionally, Lidya's grandfather had a lot of power in the family and dictated to the family what the family secrets and rules were. Lidya felt the whole family was intimidated by him and acquiesced to his wishes.

Lidya presented herself as haughty, arrogant, and generally unbothered by any consequence she earned, confident she could outlast us. She had buried her anger about her family issues and hurt underneath a seemingly impenetrable wall. Her emotions came out, however, in her behaviors, especially towards her mother. She saw her mother as unfailingly there for her, always in her corner and loyal. In Lidya's way of thinking, no matter how much she vented her anger and attitude on her mother, she would not abandon her. She could not say that about other members of her family. Consequently, Lidya was almost continually abusive to her mother and ordered her to meet her every need, emotionally blackmailing her if her mother showed any signs of not complying.

Despite our best efforts to make a connection for Lidya between her unresolved hurts and her current behavior, Lidya continued to insist she was "fine" and did not need to change any behaviors. Lidya was very bright and staff members suspected she did, indeed, make the connection but would not reveal this to staff as she was afraid of losing face and being vulnerable. A more rigorous intervention was called for.

Lidya was to wear a backpack during the time she was at the group home (not in the community). Before she donned the pack, staff sat down with her and listed all of her resentments on pieces of paper, from feeling as if her sister was favored, to being slapped in the face by her father, to feeling like her family was ashamed of her. Lidya was quite cooperative, almost intrigued by where this was going and readily listed all of the things she thought were "unfair" or "sucked" about her past.

When that exercise was over, Lidya's eyes widened as another staff member heavily sat down a 20-pound bag of potatoes on the table in front of her. Lidya and the staff member then worked together to rubber band each piece of paper (and there were plenty) to a potato and place it in the backpack. The pack was filled about three quarters of the way full when the last potato was tossed inside. Lidya was now to wear the backpack and record her insights in a journal at the end of each night. Confused but dropping back into her "nothing is going to get to me" demeanor, Lidya complied, mumbling under her breath.

Each night Lidya recorded the trials and tribulations of her hefty pack, citing comments from peers and the weight being a burden on her. Staff processed her thoughts and experience with her daily until a theme emerged. Lidya was starting to acknowledge and compare the weight of the potatoes to the weight of her anger and feelings she had been carrying around with her. Slowly she talked more and more about her feelings of neglect, abandonment, and fear. She began to acknowledge the pain she had and, in turn, the pain she caused.

After about a week, Lidya noticed the potatoes starting to smell and get rotten. This was the turning point for her. She processed with staff about the resentments she had, ultimately hurting herself and making part of her feel "rotten" like the potatoes. With this insight and Lidya's experiential exercise with getting to know her anger up close and personal, the exercise ended. Lidya was not miraculously cured of her negative behaviors, but we did notice a slight improvement in her interactions with her mother and a more empathetic approach to others in general. Lidya became much more open to processing her feelings without shame and began to lose the need to put on her "tough girl" attitude. The potatoes in the backpack netted similar results for others during the first ten years of CVC and became a favorite intervention of staff members.

—Give Me My Space—

Mary Kay

Boundaries are an unfailingly common problem at the group home. Close quarters, adolescent moods, and heightened emotions mixed in with a history of family and intimate relationships that fell short of modeling healthy boundaries made for many instances of overstepping and opportunities for teaching "where you end and the other person begins." This blurry distinction was apparent in several forms that took shape over the years at ABC.

Jerri, a sturdy girl from a city just south of where CVC was located, lived with her grandmother since the age of four and hadn't seen either parent in five years. Jerri's first police contact was when she was in kindergarten after calling 911 and hanging up. She had had regular contact since then for fighting, stealing, and running away. She was the youngest of ten children, all of whom had served time in jail or prison. Jerri simply didn't see any other way of life as a viable option for herself. The familial patterns went back generations and, in a way, is what was expected of her as well. Jerri's grandmother did the best she could, but was unable to prevent Jerri's behaviors from worsening to the point where the county stepped in and placed Jerri with us to attempt to instill some hope for some prosocial behaviors.

Jerri was used to getting her way by intimidating those around her. She was big for her age and carried herself with the authority of one who had no fear of being hurt in a fight and would just as soon smack you as greet you. Jerri stood close to people. Towering over them, she exuded the message that she was stronger and there would be consequences for refusing her. Jerri often put her hands on the person she was talking to and made gestures that encroached on the other person's personal space.

Numerous attempts to redirect her, model the appropriate behaviors, and bring to her attention to the inappropriateness of her lack of boundaries were met with resistance. Jerri could not understand why this was an inappropriate way of getting what she wanted. Eventually, Jerri was assigned the hula-hoop as an intervention.

The hula-hoop was an experiential intervention meant to concretely model for Jerri how close she was to others and where a more suitable distance lay. This intervention was used only within the confines of the group home, so as not to embarrass or shame the client. Jerri was given a hula- hoop that had a couple of pieces of rope tied on it mimicking suspenders. She was expected to wear the hula-hoop and not be any closer to another person than the hoop allowed. Jerri would wear the hula-hoop until she voiced and displayed an understanding of what was expected of her. Now we understood Jerri could still intimidate others without being on top of them. However, this was Jerri's standard operating procedure and we felt if we could break this pattern, we would be making headway with Jerri asking for her needs and wants rather than demanding them with her intimidating body language.

Jerri progressed during the next few days and ended up wearing the hoop for a little over a week, at which time, she indicated she had gotten a good deal out of the experience and was ready to try things a different way. Fortunately, Jerri had peers who supported her and encouraged her with positive feedback that they were less afraid of her now that she was behaving differently towards them, and were more likely to respond positively to her now than with her prior behaviors.

Another example of when the hula-hoop was used to address a boundary issue was with Carla. Carla was a 14-year-old young lady who was slightly cognitively delayed. She lacked social skills and struggled to make even a few friends. Carla's mother also suffered mental challenges and could not model or teach Carla the necessary skills to function around her peers or others in general. On her own a good deal of the time when she was living at home, Carla was extremely needy when she was admitted to ABC group home. From the first day forward, Carla offered and asked for hugs constantly from staff, peers, volunteers, and sometimes even strangers. Carla was extremely open with her history, and it would not be unusual for her to recite her entire story, including sexual abuse and other very personal anecdotes in front of people she had just met. Carla craved the attention and others' interest to validate her own self-worth.

As this behavior had been and could continue to place Carla at risk for further victimization, we went about attempting to curb her attention-seeking behaviors by ignoring them, scheduling physical contact, giving her positive attention for appropriate behaviors, and social skills education. Carla responded slightly to these interventions but continued to "put herself out there" for others as an open book, emotionally and physically. We decided the hula-hoop would be an apt intervention to try, as Carla learned very concretely.

Carla quickly understood what was expected of her and worked hard not to get any closer to others than the hoop would allow. She was quick to point out her success. Of course, we still needed to make sure she was given the attention she needed. Our goal was not to take attention away from Carla but redirect how she asked for it and increase her self-worth so the vast amount of outside validation became less necessary. As Carla experienced some success with the hula-hoop, we did, indeed, see these things happen. Although Carla did have difficulty transferring this lesson to her lack of verbal boundaries and continued to over-share, we were happy with our progress and retired the hoop with the promise that we would reinstate it if she should forget what she learned.

—You were where, now?—

Mary Kay

One of the most frustrating things for staff to deal with is manipulation by the girls. One extremely common form of manipulation is lying. Lying to avoid consequences, lying to get what they want, lying to gain power over another person, lying to see if they can get away with it, or simply lying to watch another person's reaction were seen repeatedly at the group home.

The two main goals each of the girls has during their stay with us are respect and responsibility. Obviously lying, for whatever reason, violates both basic tenets we are trying to teach. Sometimes it is observable when a half-truth or blatant mistruth is being told. Lack of eye contact, nervous gestures, or easily confirmed lies would often give the client away in a matter of moments. In some of these cases our regular progressive discipline structure (Incident, Stop the World, Jeopardy Track) was sufficient to "cure"' the girl of trying again. In others, however, being caught could challenge them to up the ante, motivate them to "get better" at lying to avoid detection rather than give up the practice. Putting a population of troubled girls together can have an effect that is not desirable at times. Simply put, the girls can refine their negative behaviors by sharing notes and techniques with each other.

Other girls, more skilled at dishonesty, made it very difficult to detect their lies and staff could find themselves buying in to the stories and not being able to hold that girl accountable. One example is a young lady, 14-years-old and in her last year of middle school. Cooper was slightly cognitively impaired, as were her parents, though she certainly had the capacity to know right from wrong. She was often un-groomed and struggled mightily with social skills. She seemed to enjoy chaos and gossip, often finding herself on the outs with her peers as she told one story too many.

Cooper was with us for many months and her habits appeared to be making a turn for the better. We saw fewer negative behaviors and more of an effort to get along with others. We praised her heartily as she seemed to thrive on positive reinforcement. We were all thrilled and believed Cooper might have picked up some positive habits she could maintain despite the difficult and chaotic home life she would be returning to.

The other shoe dropped one day when we received a call from the police liaison officer from the middle school she attended. Did we know

Cooper was hanging out on the football field smoking with a question-able crowd forty-five minutes after school ended? No, we most certainly did not!

Several weeks earlier, Cooper had come to staff to ask if she could join the Drama Club, an after-school program. While we encouraged extra-curricular activities for the clients, we were also aware that they were struggling with deep, debilitating life issues that needed their focus on treatment in order to overcome. We reviewed every request for an outside activity closely. Considerations of how it may affect that girl's progress, sobriety, and recovery during treatment were factors. At the time Cooper made the request, we had been so happy with her progress and new efforts towards healthy interaction and pro-social behavior that we agreed to her request, thinking that her dramatic tendencies could perhaps be put to good use in an organized activity.

What we failed to do was confirm with the Drama teacher her inclu-sion in the club and her attendance. We drove to the middle school each day to pick her up at the conclusion of the Drama Club and she was waiting for us dutifully each time with stories and enthusiasm about her activities there. She continued to do well at the group home.

After the officer's call, we arrived to pick her up and her demeanor and attitude had made a 180-degree turn. She arrived at the van door sulky, eyes downcast and mumbling. She had been busted. Not only had she not been going to Drama Club, but she had been associating with other kids who had been smoking marijuana and generally causing trouble on school grounds for weeks.

What a lesson for us. No longer did we allow an extra-curricular event to take place without extra checks in place to ensure that is exactly where the client would be. Thus, the intervention of Confirmation Tickets.

Confirmation Tickets were an intervention we designed to use with girls who consistently lied or were un-truthful about many different areas in their lives to the extent that it was causing a significant detrimental effect on their treatment. We understood, as teenagers, we could expect some limit pushing. We understood that some of this was developmentally normal. What we could not tolerate was the anti-social, continued dishonesty that flew in the face of the respect and responsibility values we were teaching.

Any girl who was assigned the Confirmation Tickets was given a stack of tickets that asked her to write out whatever she was telling us and to get it signed by another person who could verify what she was saying.

"You did your chore last night? Fine, fill out a Confirmation Ticket and have the staff that was on last night sign it, THEN we will count it as done."

"You don't have any homework tonight. Please have your teacher sign your Confirmation Ticket for us."

The idea was to encourage truthful behavior by letting them know it will be more difficult to pull off a lie when everyone is communicating. This can build the foundation for breaking the habit of lying, but also begin the process of forming a behavioral pattern that can be built upon to develop a moral pattern creating the value of honesty within themselves. Normally, girls did not need the Confirmation Tickets longer than a couple of weeks before it became more trouble to do the tickets than to figure out ways to get away with things.

— Poop Cake, Anyone? —

Mary Kay

Sixteen-year-old Bree had been at the group home for ten months, though the average is closer to six. Several times now she had made her way through the levels to earn more privileges for herself only to regress and sabotage her progress, violating rules that sent her back to a no-privilege status for a time. Bree stood at least 5 foot 9 inches, a mature looking young woman who wore her dyed blonde hair short and close to her head, wore glasses and held herself with confidence, though would often have trouble meeting your eyes unless she was angry.

Staff was at their wit's end with Bree, and truthfully, her mother too. It was the general consensus that Bree's mother was behind some of the behaviors and lack of effort we were seeing with Bree. Covertly and even blatantly sending messages to Bree that the group home was brainwashing her and no good could come of following the rules, the mother's mood provided a roller coaster of a template for Bree to follow. Bree was certainly intelligent and understood the concept of thinking for herself, yet there was a pull, a force so great, called Mom that she could not seem to resist. Bree took to believing staff and the group home, not to mention her Case Worker and the judge, were conspiring and would never let her return home. Fueled by her mother's input, Bree regressed to a point that staff ceased to see her putting forth the effort to gain privileges she once loved: walking outside alone, computer time, and staying up late. Feeling sorry for herself and her predicament became a full-time pursuit for Bree and staff watched in horror as her once high grades plummeted.

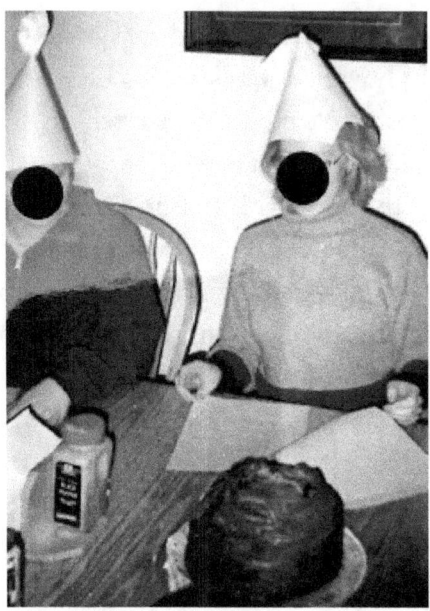

~ The Pity Party, complete with Poop
Cake

Convinced drastic measures needed to be taken, an intervention was crafted to hopefully open Bree's eyes to the reality of the situation. That she had the power to create different and better things for herself rather than feeling victimized by the system; that indeed, her personal power was in jeopardy due to her actions and it was eating away at her self-esteem and confidence. We planned a Pity Party, with all of the trimmings, food, and entertainment. All the residents and staff were invited. So as not to ambush her, Bree was told of this intervention prior and was guarded, but willing to see what was planned.

In surprise party fashion, Bree was sent upstairs until the festivities began. In time, she was called down and entered down the front staircase warily. A giant face with a turned down mouth was drawn on poster board and hung on the door. Pin the Tear on the Eye challenged the sign. Staff were nearby with blindfolds for the partygoers. Sad music was played. Each girl read a prepared statement to Bree about how worried they were for her, how they feared she would return to her

MARY KAY LUTZOW & DANEL BURCHBY

self- destructive ways if she continued to fight against her treatment program, and lastly, how Bree was affecting each of them. By acting in this way, they had lost a role model. Bree listened with her face towards the floor. She did not reply, but it was obvious she was listening. She thanked the girls with an uncharacteristic deference. After several tears were shed, the culmination of the party was brought out – a poop cake. That's right, a chocolate cake shaped like a giant cow-pie, complete with plastic flies adorning the dark brown frosting. Party hats were adorned and, as practiced, staff and girls alike belted out the party's theme song:

> *Happy Pity Party to you,*
> *You don't have a clue,*
> *When you give up like thi-is,*
> *You will always have poo.*

Repeat several times until the girls dissolved in laughter. Bree's face sported a tentative smile and she thanked everyone for her party, not elaborating. All but a few ate the poop cake, and the party quietly wrapped up. I'd like to say this intervention cured Bree of her self-pity or that she was able to block out her mother's negative messages after that. She still struggled and had setbacks, but the seed was planted and she rarely complained about how she was being victimized after the party, lest she would be in for an even more bizarre display. Bree was able to find some strength by the end of her stay at CVC and was doing what was best for her, refuting her mother's negative ideas without feeling like she would lose her mother's love and support. Bree made significant progress and eventually returned home to her mother.

—Therapeutic Retreats—

Mary Kay

Sometimes the day-to-day reality of the world just proved to be too much for our girls. At these times we noticed the milieu of the home was fractured with conflicts abounding and constant crises fueled by unresolved issues. The lack of trust and unity in the house prevented any therapeutic movement forward. We then struggled with their willingness to go beyond the superficial in highly complex treatment issues. It was at these times we needed to pull from our experiences and skill sets and move to create an effective intervention.

In these types of situations – pulling back from the outside world, creating a smaller, safer environment to process the crises and create mutual understanding and empathy towards their peers – we used The Retreat. A retreat consisted of five to seven days of intense therapeutic focus within the group home. The girls were limited in their contact with the outside world to create safety and trust within the group. No family or mentor passes would occur; no outside recreational activities or community services were scheduled. Retreats were held during the summer or on school breaks to ensure a stretch of uninterrupted therapeutic time.

Each part of their day was carefully planned to provide learning and insight into their individual unresolved issues, and how collectively those issues affected their relationships within the group, their families, and their peers. Intensive group and experiential activities were balanced with time for personal reflection and journaling. Provocative and relevant movies were shown to stimulate insight and personal awareness.

Susie was one such client who participated in a retreat during her stay with us. Her day began with reflection and goal setting at breakfast time. Susie would only talk when she was participating in a retreat activity, otherwise was expected to be silent in reflection (unless speaking with staff). Susie wrote in her journal throughout the day to process her thoughts and feelings. Silence prevented the normal bickering and chatting among teenage girls that would distract from the purpose of this exercise. After breakfast, the marathon group began. Facilitated by staff and focused on how their feelings connected to their behaviors, and how those behaviors ultimately affected those around them, these groups necessitated extended time frames to allow the circular flow for patterns to surface.

Susie discovered through a marathon group session that she had feelings of abandonment relating to a childhood event in which she was injured by her mother's neglect, resulting in her long- term hospitalization. During this time, Susie's family did not visit or interact with her on a consistent basis.

Susie told staff that this time in her life didn't bother her and she had forgotten all about it. "Why do you keep talking about this?" "That was a long time ago...it was no big deal!" Susie saw this as a closed issue since she had been in counseling in which she talked about and felt she resolved issues of her mother's neglect. However, staff continued to see anger, her inability to connect and trust others, an inability to ask for help, and a continued strained relationship with her family. Susie was also refusing visits from her family... "It's just easier if they don't come."

Her behaviors reflected these internal conflicts. Susie had a history of running away and it continued at the group home. She returned sullen and uncommunicative each time. Susie was unable to connect with another girl in the group, Megan who had been adopted and was grieving the loss of her biological family. During the time immediately before the retreat, staff had seen conflict between Susie and Megan escalate and not respond to typical behavioral interventions. During the marathon group, Susie was able to identify her feelings of abandonment and anger towards her mother and hear the same emotions coming from Megan when she spoke of being "dropped off" at social services to be placed for adoption. Because of Susie's newly found insight, Megan was also able to identify her strong feelings of abandonment relating to the adoption. This did not happen in minutes. Marathon groups allowed time to get beyond denial, time that was not available during an hour long after school group. This type of increased awareness was typical and the intended goal of the retreat. Now, this didn't always stop the behaviors that resulted, but it gave the staff and the clients something to work with when those behaviors erupted again. Once the denial had been stripped, the real issue could be addressed much more efficiently.

Susie journaled after this group to specifically selected music, recording her thoughts and feelings on paper. Strains of "Concrete Angel," and "Lean On Me" reverberated throughout the silent room while all of the girls found a private spot to write.

Realizing her conflict with her peer was much deeper than she realized, Susie broke down in tears. Staff observed Susie crying while writing.

"It looks like this group was really hard for you, Susie," said one staff member. Susie then sobbed and leaned into the staff for comfort, though she couldn't talk at that time. Later Susie sought out that staff to show her the journal entry:

"I hate these FUCKING groups...hate hate hate. What do they think they are trying to do????? I'm not like Megan...WTF????? I don't steal from anyone. I just want to go home. Even my bitch of a mother is better than this. I'm calling my fucking social worker to get me out of here before I flip out on someone. Why are they picking on me and making me talk about something so long ago. My mom is still here – she came last weekend. It's not like she's gone like Megan's mom that would suck to be adopted. Even though it sucked to be alone in the hospital, at least my mom came back. I don't think I could handle it if she just forgot about me or dumped me with someone else. Even though I worry sometimes when mom goes out she's not coming back or will realize she doesn't want a kid who's so fucked up. That what[sic] I thought when she left me here. How can you do that to your own kid? You can't even pee without asking permission!!! F'ed UP! Maybe that's why Megan ran away from her parents – to look for her real family. I feel sorry for her...I'd totally do the same thing. Holy Shit, I do the same thing. But I run away to get away from these rules....stupid rules. Besides, my mom worries about me and will talk to me while I'm gone. I can't stand not talking to her. Even though I don't remember much, it did suck not talking to her when

I was hurt. I do remember being afraid – no one loved me anymore or I wouldn't get visitors like the girl next door. I know the nurse felt sorry for me, but really it wasn't a big deal – so long ago."

Susie and the staff were able to process this journal entry and all the repressed feelings she had about her mom and Megan. Susie was just at the beginning, but it was a start and better than what we had to work with before. This would be continually addressed during the retreat and in her individual treatment plan.

Megan, too, was able to identify similar feelings of anger and sadness about her adoption. Developing this empathy and the realization that even though their circumstances may be different, they were both affected in a similar fashion.

Lunch followed journal time. We knew that by the end of this emotional time, the girls might be ready to comfort themselves and those feelings with food. While we wanted to accommodate their need for comfort, we knew to be aware of serving size and not allowing the girls to overeat as a way to cope. As the girls maintained their silence, the staff read from Wally Lamb's "She's Come Undone," a story about a fictional young lady that reflects many of the same issues and feelings of a traumatized adolescent. This was designed to normalize their experiences and resulting emotions.

Many of the girls felt so alone in their struggles that they naturally acted out to avoid dealing with them. They were able to relate to the characters in this book and feel more accepting of themselves and their circumstances, especially the experiences that were beyond their control.

After lunch, Susie, along with the other clients, received a suitcase. This suitcase represented the baggage that staff identified her having accumulated throughout her life. Each suitcase was chosen carefully and filled with different objects that represented a past issue. In Susie's suitcase was:

- a broken doll representing her injury as a child,
- a book entitled "Trust No One,"
- a nurse figure,
- a broken watch to represent that Susie had never let that time in her life go,
- a map to represent her many moves,
- a poster of missing children representing the danger of her runaways,
- a blanket to represent the comfort she needed,
- a mask to represent how she covered up what she really felt,
- and a piece of plastic food to represent how she comforted her feelings by eating rather than in a healthy way.

Susie was given time to look through her items and figure out the significance of them. She would be carrying this suitcase with her wherever she went during the retreat, symbolizing the weight she carried with her by hanging on to these issues rather than working through them. Later in the week, Susie would use these items to help her identify her resentments and make a list of things she did not wish to be part of her life anymore.

There were always deeply held secrets that had not been revealed thus far in treatment until this list was drawn up. Her case manager reviewed Susie's list and gave her an opportunity to name and prioritize these resentments by choosing from a twenty-pound bag of potatoes – a potato for each resentment. A big resentment equaled a big potato; a minor one received only a tiny spud. These potatoes were added to their suitcase as extra weight they would be carrying. Susie reviewed the contents of her suitcase regularly. If an issue met some level of resolution, she could remove it from the suitcase. Issues that remained continued to weigh down her bag. By the end of the retreat, it could get pretty ripe as some potatoes were beginning to rot (another successful symbolism opportunity for us). The list of resentments, however, would remain a part of their suitcase until the final day of retreat.

To break up the intensity of self-discovery, Susie participated in an experiential activity with her peers. A rope was placed outside on the lawn with a flag tied in the middle. Susie was assigned to a team that manned one end of the rope. Having strategically placed Megan on the other end of the rope, instructions were given, "The goal of this exercise is to get the flag over your line."

Immediately Susie dug in her heels along with her peers and gave it her best effort to pull the rope towards their own line in order to WIN.

"Wait, wait, wait!" called the staff facilitating the exercise. "Remind me again, the goal of this exercise?" she would ask the group.

Cries of "To win, "To beat them," "To get the flag over here" rang out as the girls tried to figure out why the game had been stopped. Each time the game was paused, the flag was put back in the middle and the girls given the exact same instructions. This proved very frustrating for the team who thought they were winning usually then pointing out how the losing team had to look to staff to help them. Before the exercise was restarted each time, the teams were given the opportunity to strategize, discuss the goal, and create their game plan. This went on for quite some time. Susie's energy and enthusiasm was flagging.

Eventually, both teams concluded that they could all win if they cooperatively walked the flag over both team's lines, one after the other. After all, the instructions did not say anything about being first or even about winning.

After processing this, Susie was uncharacteristically talkative about this new concept of not having to have a winner and a loser. Susie was able to see even her runaways as a way she set up herself as a winner and her mother as a loser. Staff was impressed with Susie's insight, and they saw some latent leadership qualities emerging. During later groups, staff noticed Susie asking a peer, "How could you have both been winners?"

After expending all this energy outdoors with the rope, it was snack time. Susie led the troops to the table where a snack was already set out. In the spirit of the retreat, snacks were designed to be therapeutic, in an indirect and often fun way. Today's snack was graham crackers, peanut butter, gumdrops, and pretzels. Before eating, the girls were given directions: "Create the house you grew up in with only the ingredients you are given."

Without talking, the girls got to work with music playing in the background: "Go Light your Candle," and "Daddy Don't Leave." Before eating, girls took a turn explaining what they had built and the meaning behind it. Susie described the home that she had lived in the longest, almost one year. For Susie, these were good memories because Mom was living with a man who was not abusive and favored Susie over her siblings. She was secure and attended the same school for her entire sixth grade. While identifying positive memories, it also elicited memories of continuous moves, Mom's unsavory taste in men, and other issues listed on her resentment list that she carried just a few feet away in her suitcase. After each girl had a turn, they finally could eat their creation.

Other snacks throughout the week would include:

- Oreo cookies, which prompted discussion about seeing issues in an absolute (or black and white) way;
- Crackers and a can of squirt cheese to discuss making mountains out of molehills; and
- Raisins or "ants" stuck on a celery stick or "log" by peanut butter, which focused on how they would allow others to "bug" them and how they could "unstick" themselves from those situations.

After snack time, Susie, with her suitcase, retrieved a comforter and settled in the living room to watch a carefully chosen movie. That night "The Prince of Tides" was showing, featuring Nick Nolte and Barbara Streisand. The main character was attempting to overcome a dysfunctional childhood. The next night, "Parenthood" would be shown, a lighthearted movie that carried the message that all families struggled in one way or another.

Suppertime led the girls back to the table, where staff would return to the book that was read aloud at lunchtime. After supper, with quiet and relaxing music playing, Susie and her peers journaled about their day.

> *"Thank God the staff finally stopped comparing me to Megan she is cooler than I thought, I guess. Too bad we were on opposite sides in the rope game. Man, I couldn't believe that snack – I was SOOOOOO hungry and we had to wait to eat. I haven't thought about Charlie in forever!!! I miss him. He was the only one who ever treated me good[sic]. I wish my mom stayed with him; maybe I wouldn't be so f'ed up. The other losers she picked hated me – or only wanted me for a toy, for sex. I bet Don was happy I got hurt and was in the hospital – what a loser!*
> *What's up with mom leaving me there to be with him...geez- I wish she knew how it felt! It's not fair I have to suffer! She should suffer too. Now I feel like running away just when things were going well and I was actually getting into this retreat-thing. Maybe I'll take off tonight. I don't know if I can handle a whole week of this!!!"*

Staff noticed Susie becoming agitated while writing and approached her afterwards to touch base. Susie shared her journal entry with the staff and together they decided Susie could turn her shoes into the office and wear the house pajamas the next day to help her with the decision not to run.

Staff tried to make connections with her about how she punished her mother by running away to "get back" at her for leaving her in the hospital. Susie balked at this discussion and reverted to some old patterns, "Why do you keep talking about this...nothing's wrong!!" Susie ran to her room and staff allowed her time to regroup.

This "two steps forward, three steps back" progress was typical, and these deep-rooted issues were not going to be solved overnight. Susie was making terrific progress and needed some nurturing as she dealt with her realities.

A half-hour before bedtime, staff retrieved Susie from her room for the final activity of the retreat for the night, bedtime stories. Allowed to snuggle up in comforters and pajamas, the girls crowded around the staff in the living room and listened to old childhood favorites such as "Goodnight Moon," "Love you Forever," and assorted fairy tales.

After bedtime stories, the girls retired to their bedrooms where staff (all female) would tuck them in individually in an attempt to provide a safe and nurturing environment after a long, hard day. This facilitated one of the goals for the retreat, to help the girls get in touch with their inner child and remember that they deserved to be nurtured and safe.

At the end of the week, all the activities performed, all the groups completed, all the snacks eaten, Susie and her peers gathered for a final review of their suitcases. By the end of the week, Susie was ready to release the broken doll, indicating her greater understanding of how this event shaped her life. She held the list of resentments in her hand as each of the girls reviewed and shared what they were willing to let go of.

The suitcases were not all empty, as there were some issues girls chose not to address yet. However, they were all much lighter. Many tears had been shed and the hope was that empathy had grown between the girls to create a more stable and trusting environment for them to heal. Susie was handed a helium balloon and when given the signal, she released the balloon, giving herself permission to move on with her life as she set her inner child free.

After the balloons were released, each of the girls were sent on a mission to gather kindling. It was significant that they each participated in the fire-building. Staff contributed the lighter fluid. Once the fire was lit in the Weber grill, Susie stepped forward and shared what the week meant to her, "I didn't want to do this...I thought it was really lame and stupid. But it was cooler than I thought it would be. I didn't know some of that stuff was still bugging me. Thanks for listening." Each girl shared and then set their resentment lists on fire. The group waited until the fire consumed each list. "Lean On Me" played as the group hugged. A truly powerful experience.

16

School Daze

Danel

Sometimes the most difficult time to contain and manage the client's behavior was during the school day. Unsurprisingly, not all of them were interested in their academic performance. Some of the girls saw it as an opportunity to be out from under our watchful eye; they were quite creative in devising their own extra-curricular activities, some of which included sex in the bathroom, stealing from the locker rooms, leaving for portions of the day undetected, and a variety of other mis-adventures.

Initially, when ABC opened, we had an agreement with the school district and employed our own teacher on site. The agreement allowed us to keep the girls at the group home upon arrival for up to thirty days. This allowed us an opportunity to stabilize their behavior, assess their patterns of behavior, and learn how they reacted to stress. In general, we coaxed them beyond their desire to run away from the group home. Hopefully, by the time they were to attend school, they were adequately engaged in our program.

Having a teacher on staff turned out to be a wise decision and a vital component to the success of transitioning the girls into the public school system. Although most of our clients were very bright and capa-ble, they didn't see themselves that way. Street smarts were cool; book smarts were for "nerds" and "preps." The sad and ironic thing is they all wanted to feel successful and smart. There were many factors that played into a poor school track record.

Some of the girls came from chaotic and disruptive homes where survival was much more important than homework. It is hard to do your homework when you are watching your mother get beat up by your father. Some of the girls came from very stable two parent families and needed to prove their power and independence. If your father is a teacher in the school district you attend, there's no better way to get even than to fail academically and be an embarrassing behavior problem. Sometimes their own addiction took higher priority. Fitting in with the in-crowd and finding their next fix can interfere with geometry. Some of the girls were masters at disguising a learning disorder by misdirecting the adults' attention to their ever-increasing inappropriate behaviors. Better to fail on their terms than to expose their weaknesses.

The other important part of the agreement with the school district was the ability to rein the girls back into the group home for untrustworthy or acting out behavior at school. The concept of school as a privilege was a difficult one for the girls and parents alike to understand. Our mantra regarding this was "school is mandatory, where you attend school is a privilege." After a few days at home with us, the girls were usually anxious to return to school and behave.

There were a few exceptions to this rule. If there came a point where the intervention of pulling them out of school failed, one of the staff members would be assigned or volunteer to attend school with the offending young lady. Mary Kay always enjoyed putting on her bunny slippers and toting her terribly out-of-style school bag and shadowing a client to history class. She took great delight in being able to answer some of the questions the teacher posed to the class. One such trip usually netted the result we were after and discouraged future offenses from the client herself and all the other residents.

We found great success in these measures. After all, desperate times call for desperate measures. The desperate situation we faced was working with these girls now before they ended up in corrections and lost any hope at a public school education. Others had come from corrections and were in danger of being sent back. We took pride in our creativity to intervene successfully, even if it did not win us friends with some of the school staff. Our girls had learned how, when, and with whom to turn on the tears and share their "poor me" story which oftentimes could find an audience at school.

We had one young lady who managed to engage a guidance counselor into "rescue" mode. Securing a contact with the State Advocacy for Children office, she managed to spend a lot of time out of class in the guidance office calling her advocate, rather than completing her homework and following the same rules as everyone else. This enabling move on the part of the guidance counselor was not well received by her social worker or her parole officer who were very accustomed to hearing her "poor me" stories and seeing her turning on the tears to take the heat off of her offending behavior. We never could convince that guidance counselor that we were acting in the girl's best interest by holding her accountable. This girl presented with a level of criminal thinking obviously not previously encountered by this school staff. You can always fool some of the people some of the time.

17

Suni's Journey

Mary Kay

Suni was born in the wrong era. At 16, she was a modern-day flower child with wispy, long, straight chocolate brown hair which she occasionally tried to grow into dreadlocks, wide brown eyes, a soft smile, and a waif-like build. Though Suni professed peace and love, she had a truck driver's mouth on her and chose skateboards as her preferred method of transportation, transforming herself into a punk-looking tomboy when she rode. Suni and her mother were at their wit's end with each other. Suni had been placed at CVC, her first out-of-home placement, on a JIPS petition for running away repeatedly, several times leaving the state, constituting a danger to herself.

One level of child welfare petition is a Juvenile in Need of Protection or JIPS petition. This kind of petition is usually filed when an adolescent is not committing criminal acts, but "offenses" that are harmful to herself such as dangerous sexual activity, running away, drug and alcohol use, self-mutilation, truancy, or the like. These types of "crimes" are called *status offenses*, only considered offenses because of the child's age. If she were an adult she could not "run away" because it would be legal for her to go where she wanted to.

Suni, since the age of thirteen, had been seeing her boyfriend, a twenty-year-old man named Logan. Oblivious to the inappropriateness of this, Suni turned belligerent, rebellious, and verbally abusive when not allowed to see him. At times, her mother described her banging her head against the wall shouting "LO-GAN! LO-GAN! LO-GAN!" at the top of her lungs for literally hours. Logical arguments, guilt trips, or threats could not deter Suni from believing Logan was her one true love and that her parents were persecuting her by not allowing the relationship. Repeatedly, she would run away to his apartment, leave town for several days with him, or simply meet him at the skateboard park without permission. For years, Suni and Logan kept their relationship alive with secret meetings.

Suni lived with her mother, stepfather, and younger stepbrother in a small town of less than 40,000 people. Her mother never thought she would be standing in the courthouse one day filing a restraining order on Suni's behalf against her 14-year-old daughter's adult boyfriend, yet that is where she found herself. A Harassment Restraining Order was issued based on her mother's written statement. Now the police could become involved. Her parents began calling her in as a runaway whenever she broke curfew, or they suspected she was with Logan. Logan was arrested several times in violation of the restraining order and jailed for several days, though never long term. He was also charged with sex with an underage child. He was not charged with this however, until Suni reached the age of 16, thereby reducing the penalty. He did not stay in jail long, though, and was soon back to figuring out how to work the system so he could be with Suni, and Suni was all too willing to go along.

The police were called to her home one afternoon when a verbal argument escalated into threats and a physical hair-pulling altercation between Suni and her mother. Suni's stepfather was also there that day but tended to be more soft spoken and drift to the side when arguments escalated, believing this was an issue between Suni and her mother. No one was charged that day, but after reviewing the numerous calls to the police and the repeated runaways, the officer suggested to Suni's mother that they file a JIPS petition at the local county courthouse.

Feeling like she had no other options to help lead her child back to a safe path, Suni's mother chose to pursue that option. Suni's case quickly moved through the court system. It involved a court date in which her parents had to verbalize Suni's need for protection and their inability to provide it in front of a judge. Suni was officially judged "out of control" that day. If anything, this seemed to fuel her resolve to be with who she called her one true love.

Out of home placement was not considered right away. It took several more runaways and another altercation with her mother for Suni to be brought back to court and be ordered to group home placement. Though a group home was available in Suni's home county, her case worker believed it was in Suni's best interest to be placed a distance away to separate her from the influence of Logan and the negative peer connections she had made in her own county, yet not so far away that her parents could not be actively involved in Suni's treatment.

Suni entered the group home her first day with a façade of arrogance. Only if you looked closely or somehow managed to catch her off guard did her cover crack. She was angry, sullen and did not hesitate to tell you she thought "this place is dumb" and never going to make her forget Logan. Looking up at the ceiling when she spoke to you was a sure sign she was close to weeping, and if you looked quick you could see her eyes shining with tears. As the days turned into weeks, Suni continued to resist the program and getting close to anyone at the group home. She openly complained about her roommates and declared herself better than her peers, talking down to them in a haughty tone of voice.

Suni spent over two months on the orientation phase, a phase designed to last only two weeks. Her refusal to acclimate to the rules, whether it was to follow staff directions, let us know where she was going in the house, or turn off her reading lamp at lights out time, staff could count on a battle of wills. Suni was never physically aggressive and eventually took to being compliant to win some privileges, always retaining a passive-aggressive manner to her rebellion. One day the group of girls might find themselves serving up Kool-Aid for a snack that Suni had made with hot water. Staff found pens disappearing from the office at an amazing rate, only to find a stash of them tossed in Suni's garbage can.

Though Suni was not openly defiant with staff, she did run away one time, a planned run in which she snuck out the back door of the group home and moved quickly down the residential streets, finding new clothing and a sleeping bag someone had hung out on their clothesline. Suni later told staff she had slept in the ditch in that sleeping bag before Logan came to pick her up. She spent the weekend with Logan until police found her, arrested Logan, and returned her to the group home.

Though Suni professed to have deeply enjoyed the time spent with Logan and that the consequences were worth the small amount of time they had together, her demeanor was different. She confided bits and pieces to staff hinting she was not treated in the way she had hoped by Logan. She alluded to verbal abuse, being ignored, and a general dissatisfaction with the relationship that was the antipathy of her earlier declarations. This was kept covert and Suni continued to profess her inclination to be with Logan forever despite what her parents said.

Suni's resistance was deeply entrenched in unresolved and unrecognized grief stemming from her parent's relationship and resulting divorce. Suni appeared to blame her mother and stepfather for the loss of a "normal" family system. The confusing part was, she really cared for her stepfather and his son. Mother made great efforts to protect Suni from her biological dad's drinking. Thus, the only person left to be angry with was Mom. Suni's doggedly hanging on to Logan was really her refusal to let Mom take yet another significant man away from her.

Mom, in the meantime, was struggling to protect and preserve her daughter's innocence, both relating to exposure to her father's unhealthy habits and early sexual activity. Ironically, the man Suni chose as a boyfriend and was determined to love was much like her biological father in terms of attitude, chemical use, and disregard for authority and social norms. Mother and Suni were unable to resolve the "come here, go away" pattern they had established.

One way Suni bucked conventional social norms was to declare early on that her placement was a win-lose situation and that she was heavily invested in winning. To Suni, her winning meant beating her mother. Suni was really a child of privilege. She was not denied any material things in her life either out of poverty or parental limitations, so the whole idea of being a flower child was a romantic ideal built in her head. Picking Logan, knowing her future with him would not be one of wealth or comfort, played into this fantasy. She took this to the extreme of asserting she planned on living in her car and working at the gas station as her future career plan, thus denying any need for the independent living skills curriculum provided by the group home, studying for school, or planning for any higher education. She would simply exist with her car and her boyfriend, using the facilities at the gas station for hygiene, and skateboarding in her free time, living on love. Every need she could think of would be satisfied. Suni continued to develop this fantasy until it began to become reality for her. Suni was getting to the age that the county was insisting on transitional living skills, and it would be detrimental to not address her unrealistic vision for herself.

Staff huddled and brainstormed during the weekly staffing meeting – this was a crisis. Since Suni had resisted bonding or allowing herself to trust any one staff member, this mission of re-education was made more difficult. One way we addressed this issue was to bring on board her mentor. Despite her resistance to buying into anything the group home had to offer, she was unable to resist bonding with her mentor, Beth.

Beth was divorced with a compassionate, yet realistic outlook on life. She worked at the local District Attorney's office as a paralegal, overcoming several life obstacles for herself. Beth's interest in mentoring adolescents was genuine and she was able to give Suni the support and listening ear she needed while reinforcing healthy choices. Beth showed her commitment to Suni by remaining nonjudgmental about her future living in a car. She addressed this revelation subtly by taking her out to eat at a fast-food restaurant and quietly commenting on the price. Beth went on to let Suni know how much she herself spent on groceries when she had a kitchen to cook things in. Suni took it all in and would later say that this conversation had a huge impact in her decision to renege on the unrealistic dream. Beth was able to connect where we were not simply because Suni viewed her as an outsider to the "system" that she had not allowed herself to trust. Beth was neutral ground, a safe place to process things where Suni did not have to create a win-lose situation.

Beth's intervention laid the groundwork and reinforced what we ultimately decided to be an appropriate intervention. Suni seemed to respond best with an experiential approach, learning hands-on rather than by worksheet or lecture. In a lucky coincidence, one of CVC's night staff had an older car that was experiencing serious engine difficulties and not able to start in the parking lot right on campus. After consulting with Suni's case worker and parents, this became Suni's new home for a certain period of the day. Of course, she was not allowed to sleep out in the car as her fantasy dictated. However, we felt a solid portion of her day spent "living" in the car would reinforce some realities that may have been missing in her fantasy. In addition, daily living activities would have to be negotiated. She was given a budget of play money based on a full-time gas station salary and expected to spend that on her meals, showers, and other needs and wants, budgeting in gas money and upkeep of her "home."

Staff introduced this idea to her after all prep work was completed. After her shock, Suni warmed to the idea and packed up a few days of clothing and headed out to her new home. At first, Suni relished the quietness away from her peers and staff (even though staff kept a good eye on her throughout the day). She laid back and stretched out to write letters to Logan, feeling confident she would show us just how comfortable she was with this arrangement. In true Suni-style, even when she was uncomfortable or unhappy with parts of this real-life skit, she was determined to make it work. Mealtimes were especially eye-opening for her as staff priced out what she had dished up on her plate. She found herself skipping showers to afford the types of meals she wanted. The mid-summer's heat blazed through the car, even with the windows open. We noticed Suni coming in to use the bathroom more frequently while soaking up the air conditioning during these brief reprieves.

All in all, the intervention lasted about a week. Though Suni did not verbally concede, she gradually moved her things back into the group home and seemed more willing to participate in groups. We noticed she spoke less, if at all, of that particular future for herself. That was how Suni operated.... never willing to admit what she saw as defeat. We were secure, however, in the knowledge that a message was sent and received. The matter of her relationship with Logan, however, took a more real-life experiment to open Suni's eyes.

Suni showed interest in developing age-appropriate relationships with boys while at the group home and dated other boys after completing CVC programming and moving into her own apartment locally. Nevertheless, Suni eventually moved back to her home county and when Logan was released from jail, not being able to resist the pull to revive her childhood fantasy. At age 18, Suni and Logan eventually married. Suni kept up communication with CVC, inviting staff members to her bridal shower and the wedding. Mom valiantly supported Suni and helped arrange the wedding, even throwing her a shower. Suni was, after all, an adult in the eyes of the law, able to make her own decisions she had so badly wanted to make all along. Within a year, staff received notice that Logan was unable to demonstrate the commitment that Suni had made to him and had cheated on her with an underage girl. Suni indicated she had filed a restraining order against Logan earlier that year prior to finding out he was unfaithful, for domestic abuse. Suni found empowerment in divorcing him and going on to live her life truly independently. Suni continued to keep in close contact with her mentor and would occasionally call or stop by CVC to see the staff for the next several years after her discharge.

18

Octoberfest...Taking the "fun" out of fundraiser

Mary Kay

CVC began as a business and turned non-profit early on. As with all non-profits, our budget exceeded our income. We were determined to fill the gap with fundraisers, the lifeblood of the non-profit. We were always looking for creative, new, and fun ways to raise money to fill the gaps in the budget that our fees didn't cover. While we occasionally wrote grants, we preferred more hands-on ways to raise money that the girls could get involved with. In the following chapter we will delve into one of our most successful efforts, *The Beauty Brigade Live*, measured by the involvement of the girls and the community, as well as the funds raised. Another successful effort brought a known presenter to host a professional continuing education training for social workers and other professionals in the field.

In contrast, this chapter will detail the Octoberfest fundraiser, a less successful venture. Though we successfully involved the clients in this effort, ultimately, it did not result in the funds we envisioned, but with costs both monetarily, in time, and with frustration. Still, we can look back now and laugh at the well-meaning effort that turned to chaos.

Our local community held an event each year in late September called Octoberfest, much like other communities, with vendors, bands, food and drinks. It is generally very well attended, filling multiple blocks with vendor booths, music stages, and drinking corrals. It is common for non-profit agencies to host a booth to fundraise amongst the bands and entertainment and is generally, weather-permitting, very well attended by the public. Now, we had participated in Octoberfest in the past with good results, selling lemonade at a booth. One specific staff member had taken on the entire responsibility of planning and staffing the booth, making it appear to be a simple adventure. This year, that staff member was no longer employed with us.

Though it was held in September, the direction the event went for us was reminiscent of a Halloween nightmare. When Octoberfest was again suggested by a staff member as a fundraising idea, it seemed like a great way to make a few bucks, get our name out there, and have fun in the process...emphasis on "seemed like."

Based on past experiences, we decided we needed to keep things as simple as possible. Different committees were established, reports were made at weekly staffing meetings regarding what we could sell, how much the clients would be involved, how much to charge, what the requirements of the city would be, and who would work at the event itself. Our research, we thought, was more than adequate and we felt prepared as the day of the event drew near. The girls would depart from their normal schedule to assist staff with getting supplies, be educated about the budget and income projections, as well as attend the event itself. We wanted to incorporate the girls into the community as much as possible and empower them to be engaged in activities that could impact them directly.

Due to the season, we decided that caramel apples would be a great seller. Our product committee even found an orchard willing to donate the apples, reducing our upfront costs – perfect, we thought. We would pair this with hot apple cider people could use to warm up if the weather was brisk, and cold water if the weather took a turn to hotter temperature. In the Midwest, one could never know what to expect in the fall for weather. Sprinkles, nuts, apples, caramel, beverages...our bases were covered. Volunteers, some willing, some drafted, were scheduled in shifts.

A few days before the fateful Saturday, the weather forecast predicted rain showers. We decided a tent was in order as a safety net. The only problem was our booth was placed on the street and there was no way to anchor the tent. It seemed reasonable to use five-gallon pails of concrete. Mixing concrete with adolescent girls was not a joyous experience, and lining the poles up in the middle of the concrete so the tent would stand evenly proved difficult. Eventually we accomplished the mission, and the girls were sent to take showers.

The following day, we went to pick up supplies. The orchard who indicated their willingness to donate the apples had a sudden change of heart which left us scrambling to replace this very crucial element to our plan. At the eleventh hour, an offer of donated apples did come through. The catch was the new orchard was located about an hour away, which required some creative logistics and travel time.

~ a staff member with a client

It appeared that we overestimated several supplies – the water, the caramel, and the sprinkles. If we sold out, we were going to be millionaires. With our crock pots and extension cords in hand, at 5:30am, we met at the group home and caravanned to the site assigned to us. While unloading, one of the five-gallon pails of concrete fell from the van, snapping the pole of the tent, leaving us tent-less with clouds approaching. The volunteers suddenly looked less enthused about their shift.

Tables and crockpots were set up, and the extension cords were wrapped in plastic. Minutes later, inspectors came through and informed us that some of our extension cords did not meet proper standards. Staff went off to replace the extension cords with ones that were up to code. It was a good day for Menards. The remaining early morning shift began the caramel melting process with our diminished supplies in the newly arrived drizzle. The caramel was hardening on every available surface. We had to keep the crock pots covered so it didn't get too watery. In general, this was turning out to be a much higher-maintenance project than we expected. We were getting quite a bit of practice using the skills we taught the girls on how to handle stressful, anger-provoking situations. Staff worked hard to model managing their own frustration and try to be upbeat and positive despite the circumstance.

Caramel apples were a popular item that year. We noted several other booths selling the same. As staff returned with the new, up-to-code extension cords, yet a different inspector came through, identifying the remaining extension cords as unacceptable as well. No amount of rational discussion with this individual could convince him that we had already been inspected and passed muster. Out came the checkbook and back to Menards we went.

Meanwhile, sales were slow. The rain had obviously deterred a good number of people from attending Octoberfest this year. The darling straw hats we bought to get into the fall spirit were now wilting around the heads of the first shift, with two more shifts to go. Morale was declining. We anxiously awaited a new day shift with a fresher attitude.

As we were bemoaning how much applesauce we would have to make back at the group home to use up the apples left over, a bright spot in the afternoon appeared; a gentleman appeared and asked to buy a good portion of our remaining apples. Our initial relief at getting rid of the apples soon turned to despair when we realized he was from a competing caramel apple booth further up the street that was obviously doing better than us. We were now approximately six hours into a nine-hour day, part way through the last shift, when the thunderclouds again rolled in. We decided to cut our losses and call it quits for the day. Whatever caramel was left was dipped and set out free for the taking (suddenly we had more customers than the completing booths). We took our soggy sprinkles, staff, and teenagers back to the group home.

The next day, we served free caramel apples at the local churches, made batches of applesauce, and had caramel apples and water at every event for the rest of the year. We did learn that lots of planning does not necessarily mean well-planned. We did not choose to be a part of that event again, opting for other, simpler, indoor opportunities to raise funds. Despite the obstacles in execution and poor outcome, the lessons learned by the clients were immeasurable, from understanding the need to be flexible when unexpected barriers come up, to not giving up when things get hard, AND knowing when to give up to preserve their sanity. The girls watched the staff put in a strong effort outside of their normal job duties as an investment in them and the program and that sent a powerful message of worth to them.

19

The Beauty Brigade Live!

Gina, Case Manager

The dream began in a fitting room at *Empty Your Closet* Consignment Store in a nearby town. I was immensely pleased to find so many cute outfits that fit into my "non-profit staff" budget. The feeling of satisfaction while trying on fashionable clothes triggered my memories of doing fashion shows as a teenager.

I didn't feel very pretty as a young adolescent and seemed to have a hard time finding my niche in the beginning of junior high. When my mom asked me if I wanted to audition for a local fashion show, I jumped at the chance. I was both shocked and proud to find out that I made it. It was such an awesome experience the night of the big show to be walking on the stage in the spotlight, with hip clothing and my hair and make-up professionally done. I'll never forget how proud I was when I saw the pictures after the show. I remember feeling more confident when the next school year rolled around, and I could hardly wait for the next opportunity to do a fashion show. I had several more opportunities for fashion shows, and my confidence grew and grew.

Here I was, an adult - still loving clothes, but working for a non-profit agency. My paychecks weren't exactly conducive to long trips to the mall! Thankfully, I had been introduced to the art of consignment shopping.

As usual, on my days off, I was thinking about the girls at Candle-light. As I thought about the fashion shows I had been in, I wanted the girls to experience those feelings of pride and beauty. I wanted them to be able to step out on a stage and to believe in themselves – which, to me, is true beauty.

I had come to know the manager and owner at *Empty Your Closet* from my frequent shopping trips. I approached them about my vision for a fashion show where the girls from Candlelight Vision could model. They understood our vision right away! I was also excited to share my vision with Mary Kay. I just knew she would embrace it – and she did. Mary Kay is a woman who believes in the power of women and is always up for a new adventure.

We searched high and low for just the right venue – we approached banquet halls to donate dinners, but that didn't happen. We settled on renting a church basement and having a local pasta company cater. Some of the staff seemed to catch on to the vision and excitedly gathered donations for the show – we were especially excited when one of the staff obtained a matching grant from a business for the entire fashion show!

As the planning progressed, it was easy to think of a name for the show. Let me fill you in on a bit of history first. For a while, we had a short gray & maroon school bus as one of our company vehicles. This machine had all of the perks of a bus – windows that you had to pinch the corners of to move up and down, a handle that only the driver could use to open the door, and no radio – which meant lots of singing from the girls – you know the fun camp songs, "The ABC song," "God's Got the Whole World in His Hands," and, of course, everyone's favorite while riding on the bus..."The Wheels on the Bus Go Round and Round." Naturally, the teenage girls HATED being seen on this bus! They would sputter and complain if staff made the heinous decision to pick them up from school with the bus. One of the louder girls with a fun sense of humor used to say that they were the "Beauty Brigade" riding around in the bus. So, it just seemed natural to name the fashion show *The Beauty Brigade Live!*

As the time got closer to the show, it was my task to get a list of sizes from the girls to take to *Empty Your Closet* so Marcia, Bonnie, and their team could pick out clothes in advance. A unique aspect of modeling for a consignment store is that they don't have a variety of sizes in each outfit.

As stereotypical as it seems, women aren't usually too fond of sharing their sizes and the girls at ABC were no exception. I sought to assure the girls that only Marcia at *Empty Your Closet* and I would see their sizes, and that it was important to be honest so that Marcia could pick out clothes that would fit them well, before they came in for their fitting. Well, it seemed a little strange when almost everyone reported being a size three, so I had to ask the girls to find a pair of jeans that fit them really nicely so I could look at the label and write down that size "since different clothes run differently!" The next year, I got a little savvier and just looked at their clothing inventory for their sizes.

Danel arranged for the local newspaper to do a feature story about Candlelight Vision that was published the day before our debut show. The timing could not have been better. Our phones were ringing with people wanting to buy tickets and we even hand-delivered some of them because it was starting to look like there would be none available at the door. It was exciting, but I can't say it was necessarily surprising - many of us had a strong faith and had been praying about the show. I remember telling one of the girl's mom, who was also committed to praying about the show, that I was praying for 100 guests to come. She asked me why I stopped at 100. Evidently nobody else stopped at 100 because we surely had more than 100 guests at the show!

Finally, the big day arrived. Mary Kay had been up much of the previous night making her to-die-for lemon bars for dessert, only to find out that tickets kept selling and selling and selling. She was frantically cutting them in half and placing them on more plates in the kitchen as we continued seating more and more guests. Meanwhile, a special volunteer had come to the group home to do hair and make-up for the girls. Haley was a dedicated and creative long-term volunteer. Having four children of her own, and enrolled in school, she lovingly found time to help our girls. Her mother, Bonnie, was the manager at *Empty your Closet*. I had shared with Bonnie that I was disappointed when a local salon was no longer able to donate their time to do the girls' hair and make-up, and she mentioned that her daughter Haley was good with hair and had a heart for working with teenagers. Bonnie connected us and Haley showed up armed with curling irons, foundation, eye make-up, compacts, sparkles, and the grace of an angel. I had a young cousin who played the piano and was eager to share her talent as dinner entertainment.

The girls' eyes sparkled as they walked into that church basement, their hair full of twists, sparkles, and bobby pins, their hearts pounding with anticipation. They shined in their outfits – they wore everything from jeans to dresses – and we'll never forget how their eyes shone as they pranced down the center aisle that we had created between the tables.

One young lady didn't want to be in the show but spent hours crocheting beautiful handbags for the silent auction we decided would accompany the show. She seemed to be a leader amongst her peers and inspired some of them to make handbags and bracelets as well. In fact, I still have a beautiful hot pink crocheted bag that I purchased at that silent auction, and I get compliments every time I use it. It was gracious of *Empty Your Closet* to allow that young lady to also wear a special outfit for the evening. She looked beautiful, and you could see her pride as she sported a pantsuit and gingerly went up to the microphone to say that she enjoyed being a part of the evening.

The silent auction grew each year in subsequent fashion shows to over a hundred community members and businesses donating items to support Candlelight Vision Corp.

Our venue changed after the first show when we partnered with a different church. St. Mark's Church hosted the fashion shows after year one – they have a beautiful, carpeted fellowship hall that they allowed us to use free of charge – and their building engineer put together a stage for us. With the stage, it was especially fun to see the girls grow in confidence between the night of rehearsal and the night of the show. *The Beauty Brigade Live* was not just about outward beauty but instead about imparting self worth and being proud of oneself, challenging anxiety, feeling connected to the community, and feeling a sense of accomplishment.

To literally put the frosting on the cake, Mary Kay cooked elegant meals to serve our guests in years two through five – ranging from beef tips to lasagna rolls. No more sticky pasta from the caterer. After my cousin had moved on to college, we had several local artists share their talents during dinner and after the show – everything from rocking guitar to vocals and jazz piano were entertainment at the dinners throughout the years. We also eventually found a beauty salon to donate their time and talent to give the girls special hairdos and make-up.

One year, a staff member donned clothing from *Empty your Closet* the night of the show in hopes of convincing a resident with a kindred-tomboy spirit to step up to the stage. The young lady preferred to be an attendant, helping her peers make their grand entrance; but the staff team rolled in laughter as they saw their tomboyish co-worker up on stage in dress shoes and a skirt.

Staff, volunteers, and residents pulled together to pull off each of the shows. As our show gained recognition in the area, community members came through with everything from manicures to flowers to cleaning up the kitchen after the dinner. We felt truly blessed. I couldn't agree more with Sophia Loren, "Beauty is how you feel inside, and it reflects in your eyes. It is not something physical."

It brings tears to our eyes to think about one of the girls, Josie, who had had a spree of running away and sneaking off with a shady young man. Two days after the fashion show, he had been pressuring her to leave school with him and Josie refused. I distinctly remember her standing in the back office with tears in her eyes saying, "I just couldn't do that after the fashion show. That night I realized I AM special and deserve more than that." I cried with her. That realization was a long time coming for her, and despite anything that has happened no one could take that from her.

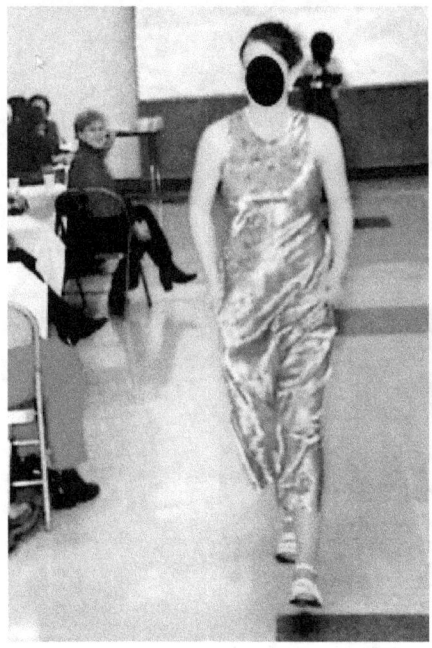

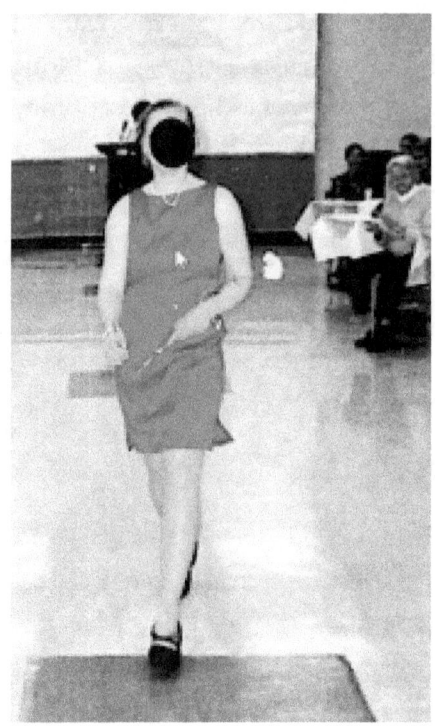

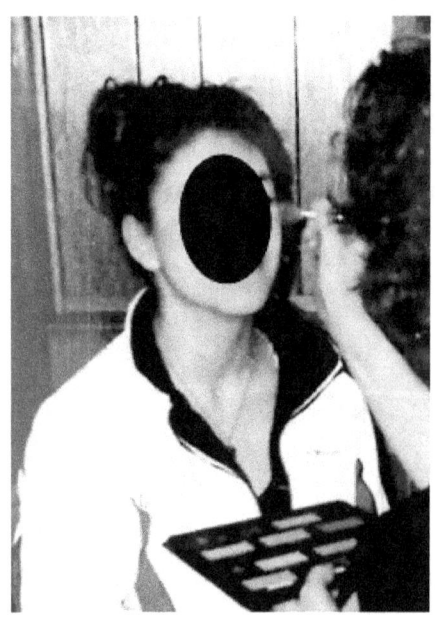

20

Sorry Ladies...

Mary Kay

One of the most surprising rules that the girls encounter when they are first placed at one of CVC's group homes is the rule prohibiting tampon use.

"What?" They demand. "That's bogus! I'm not wearing any diapers."

But sanitary napkins or pads had been all that was allowed while they resided at the group home. It wasn't always this way. In the beginning it made sense to offer both options to the girls who were becoming young women in our household. As these things tend to do, a multitude of young women living together on the same schedule, their cycles usually end up somewhat synchronized and we can expect one week of crabbiness and another week of girls lined up at the office door asking for supplies to maintain good hygiene.

The former week was sometimes referred to as Hell Week or PMS Week by the staff, who had taken to marking the calendar to prepare themselves for an onslaught of moodiness and sniping beyond what was normal for our population. This, of course, was done out of earshot of the residents.

We would, however, take the time to individually look at monthly patterns with girls we felt were legitimately unduly affected by the surge in hormones to help them identify times in which they might have to work harder to maintain a healthy attitude and respectful behaviors towards others. This was a tool that some found extremely helpful and empowering to look at - how they could self-intervene if they knew what was coming.

Identifying patterns is one of the key factors in CVC's programming. Patterns of behaviors, patterns of feelings, patterns of thoughts, patterns of family interactions, and so on. Patterns show up all over in our daily lives without us giving much thought to why we do what we do. Identifying these patterns is crucial for our girls so they can work to change destructive behaviors and replace them with new patterns of healthy and pro-social interactions. For example, a resident might identify that every time she feels inadequate, she lashes out in anger. This is a destructive pattern. Prior to treatment, this girl might say to herself, "My friends make me so mad when they make plans without me." By identifying her pattern of reacting in anger when she really feels inadequate, she can feel empowered to change her behaviors and now say to herself, "It doesn't mean there is something wrong with me just because I wasn't consulted on these plans." A new healthy pattern is beginning to be established. This is true, in a small way, for menstrual cycles. Though they are largely unavoidable, a girl can at least feel some control over the process if she can predict what may happen.

The week after Hell Week brought sometimes hourly requests for tampons and pads and time and time again, despite the creative signs, the lectures at the house meetings, or the loss of privileges, the toilets at the group home became clogged. Being an older house, the pipes were not as forgiving as we would have liked and several times, the basement became flooded with sewage, necessitating a call to the plumber to fish out mountains of used tampons from the pipes, a process that took numerous hours and was extremely costly, not mention disgusting. When all interventions failed to elicit any changes in the girls' tendency to flush their used feminine products rather than throw them in the provided container, an executive decision was made to cease buying tampons and only provide sanitary napkins for the girls.

As could be expected, this brought forth a surge of complaints from girls (and some of the staff). We held firm, though, and the plumber bills gradually got paid off. An unexpected result of this moratorium emerged as tampons quickly became a hot item on the underground market of CVC. The girls were adept at finding ways to obtain and sneak in this new "contraband." Several discovered that simply asking the school nurse could net them several each day. Some snuck them into the house after bringing them back from home visits and one girl, we found out later, stole them from a neighborhood convenience store.

Despite all these creative ways to get around CVC's new rule, for the most part, the pipes remained free of new blockages. Every month or two, the issue would be brought up at a house meeting and the girls would, collectively, ask for their tampon privileges back. This gave the staff a chance to cite the ripple effect our negative behaviors often have on other people. For example, if a teenager shoplifts, the store might make a policy that prohibits any teenager from being in the store unaccompanied. In this case, the behavior of the residents that came before them had affected their privileges. Hopefully, it was a lesson in empathy. However, it mostly elicited cries of "unfair."

We urged them to be proactive problem solvers, rather than reactive complainers. So, together, the girls came up with a proposal for staff to consider that addressed our concerns. They put it in writing and presented it to us to consider at our weekly staff meeting.

> *"We, the girls living in ABC Group Home, promise to never flush our tampons and always use the trash. We agree to get consequences if we do like Stop the World or Jeopardy Track or even extra chores. We will sell bead bracelets at the Fashion Show to raise money to pay the plumber if we don't follow this."*
>
> *Signed [all the girls at ABC]*

Apparently, they saw the upcoming Beauty Brigade Fashion Show as the perfect opportunity to sell the craft items they had been working on and now had a purpose for the money they might earn. Impressed by the creativeness and the ingenuity of this idea, we agreed to try. The girls busily prepared numerous bracelets and set up a nice-looking stand for the Fashion Show patrons to peruse. We did discourage them from announcing what the funds were being raised for, not sure if this was an appropriate topic to broadcast to the general public. The girls did reach the amount needed for the "plumber deposit" through this valiant effort. Sadly, several months later, after a number of new residents were admitted to the group home, disaster struck the decades-old pipes again. The deposit was spent after discovering tampons were causing the obstruction, and pads became the permanent rule in the house. The girls won the battle but lost the war. It appeared we were just not able to carry over the motivation and learning from one group of residents to another. We will forever remember the tampon fundraiser.

21

The Great Outdoors

Mary Kay

The positive, bonding moments we found on regular outdoor treks to the north wilderness encouraged us to add yet another outdoor adventure to our therapeutic summer schedule.

We discussed this idea, weighing the pros and cons in numerous staffings, before the decision was made. We understood this was to be a big undertaking, not only for the recreational value but the personal challenge of managing many different personalities without the structure or routine of the group home. We did not want either the kids or the staff on duty, to "burn out" by becoming more overwhelmed by the trip than any fun they were getting out of it. For staff particularly, this was a concern as at the group home and even during the traditional annual trip up north, staff was scheduled on a rotating basis. That would not be the case on this trip. We had specific staff experienced with adventure programs that were anxious to reproduce such an experience. We would have staff sleeping at night rather than awake staff to supervise the kids. We would not have a quick response time for on-call staff or law enforcement if needed. The campsite picked was a good distance away from home base.

Despite these concerns, we felt we had a solid plan, and the staff were excited to lead this adventure, picturing bonding moments by the campfire, trust exercises, and providing lessons in responsibility for the kids by having them set up and take down their own tents and help prepare their own meals.

~ The lake "up north"

Unfortunately, we belatedly realized we had not consulted or checked in with the clients on what they envisioned for this trip. As we soon realized, these two visions could not have been further apart. The girls had in mind a quiet, relaxing time at the beach with no responsibilities.

Adding to the pending mutiny was the fact that this particular group of clients was probably one of the most difficult blends of personalities and had many problematic issues requiring constant vigilance even at the group home to keep on top of their antics. Nevertheless, we were excited, envisioning a turning point for them. Based on the activities planned, the enthusiasm of the staff, and the possibilities for genuine insight and growth, we were cautiously optimistic. We should have had some indication by the lack of effort the girls were willing to put into packing the van, but staff was so excited to go, they weren't at all put out by getting things organized with the minimal help they received from the girls. Van packed – check, food organized – check, route mapped – check, girls in the van – check. Off we went.

Granted, neither Danel nor myself was present on the trip. We know what was reported. We know it didn't end well. Soon we would know we didn't plan nearly enough. We certainly would come to know we severely underestimated the need to have a comprehensive Plan B. Two and half hours after the van pulled into the campsite, money was discovered missing from a staff member's purse. This prelude to what was to become a challenging weekend came before anyone even left the van. We should have seen it coming.

Nevertheless, the staff persevered with what was going to be a good wilderness experience come hell or high water. Soon after this confrontation, a client magically found a twenty-dollar bill floating in the lake. This, of course, raised many an eyebrow and a good deal of suspicion. With the money found, they trooped back to the campground to pitch the tents. The girls, however, would have preferred to stay at the beach. While the staff didn't mind packing the van, pitching the tents without help did not fit with their vision of lessons of responsibility and independence they had on the schedule. The first of many battles ensued.

~ fun on the water

To show their independence and outrage at any expectation of them, a spontaneous protest was held involving a march, showing off their colorful vocabulary (which cleared the neighboring sites of families with children), and a general decibel level that let everyone at the campsite know they were unhappy. Still determined to turn this around into a positive experience, the embarrassed staff placed the girls strategically separating the powerhouses from the followers, indicating their willingness to either wait until they were willing to set up the tents or sleep outside. After a lengthy wait and a few mosquito bites, the girls decided it was in their best interest to erect the tents. Still using flowery language not appreciated by the surrounding campsites, the tents found their way upright as the night wound down.

The campfire experience is one of the oldest traditions and the one most looked forward to by many campers. The staff members were no exception. The fire ablaze and supper served, the group huddled comfortably around the fire to chat. The tension from the previous few hours, however, proved to still be high between the staff and the girls. Staff's attempted to engage them once again in their vision for the trip were unsuccessful and they chose to withdraw from the campfire to their tents where they could still supervise, yet leave them to hopefully deescalate without being physically present as a reminder of the conflict. While the overt conflict with staff lessened, it did not result in either positive attitudes or conversations between the clients. Staff gleaned a lot of information as they monitored the situation from inside the tent. The sun set and the girls did comply with directions to retire for the night. We are sure prayers were said for a better day when the sun rose.

More conflict emerged with breakfast – pancakes or cereal? Conflict continued throughout the day as staff doggedly pursued their vision. They eventually were forced to lower their expectations, as the girls remained deeply entrenched in stomping out what little was left of the staff's determination. Thus, set in the burnout we were initially concerned about. Sunday morning came only with the wish to pack up and return, which did not go without incident. A last-ditch attempt at salvaging the weekend resulted in pulling together a group to process what happened. Surprise – the group did not go well nor did the packing. The girls staged a sit-in (their political advocacy skills were being honed on this trip) requiring the staff, one more time, to outwait their power move.

Many valuable lessons were learned that weekend. The staff's determination was admirable. A more seasoned or less tolerant staff might have turned the van around and returned after the missing twenty dollars. In hindsight and after many hours of debriefing, despite the enthusiasm and possibilities for the trip, the group of girls we had was not conducive to the vision we had planned or for offsite behavior management for that length of time. Plan Bs are important. Fresh staff is important. Knowing your limits is important. Knowing when to throw in the towel is important lest you be abused for three days.

Despite this growth opportunity, we look back on the many positive outdoor weekends that were part of the standard summer curriculum for years with fond and sometimes amusing memories. Our annual camping trips took place in a small town an hour north of the group home, at a family trailer on a wide expanse of land and near a local county campground sporting swimming, trails, cliff diving, and a natural waterslide in the river.

During these trips, staff were required to work their regular shifts, only at the campground. Separate sleeping accommodations were arranged. Staffing for this weekend was never a problem because the staff enjoyed the time there as much as the kids. Staff would often stay longer than their shift required, enjoying the camaraderie with kids and other staff members. Although there were therapeutic exercises woven in, it was generally a low stress recreational experience with jet skis and fishing, an end of the summer reward before the grind of school started again. It was meant to show the girls that recreation was a necessary part of recovery.

One very new staff member was unsure about this whole camping thing. She didn't know what to do with her purse on the trip. She was so new, she hadn't really developed a trusting relationship with the girls or the staff, so she chose to carry it with her wherever she went. It looked a bit silly with her swimming suit and posed a real dilemma when she wanted to go out on the Jet Ski. As time wore on, the purpose of the weekend, which was bonding and trust, was evident even for staff. The rookie staff person was eventually able to leave her purse in a safe location without fear.

~ a client getting a ride on the Jet Ski
with a staff member

One of my more vivid memories is getting up early in the morning and sitting on the deck, being joined by another very new staff person. While we were on the deck, a bear crossed through the back of the property. She began talking about seeing bears in her hometown. I was surprised as that was in the area where my mother grew up. As we continued to talk, we discovered that her grandmother was my mother's sister. It was a real kind of spiritual moment and brought awareness on that early morning of just how small this world really is. That opened the door to a relationship with that part of my mother's family that had long since closed after my mother's death.

The spiritual side of the camping experience was brought out in more than that one instance. For a while we had been offering a voluntary spirituality group facilitated by one of our most seasoned staff members called Forward in Spiritual Health. It was well-attended by the clients and as it grew, the staff member volunteered her time to take interested girls to church services as well. They had been studying biblical baptism and what it meant in the group. Three of those girls approached this staff person during one of the campouts, asking her to baptize them. It was a very private and special time for the four of them and was a significant turning point in their recovery.

Of course, everything was not all smooth sailing and over the years there were several incidents. Some years, some girls were not allowed to attend the trip due to previous dangerous behaviors. Some girls on the trip needed to return to the group home because their negative behaviors were impacting the rest of the clients. On one occasion we were informed by the park director that one of our girls was "casing" cars. It turned out we were close to this girl's hometown, and she was looking for a car with keys in it to return there surreptitiously. On yet another occasion, one hot headed young lady brandished a butter knife to show her displeasure and needed to be restrained while the police searched for the remote location of the trailer. She was removed without a glitch in the weekend plans. But over all the years, the memories of those weekends were held with a deep fondness by staff and clients alike.

Closing ceremonies at the end of the camping trips always ended with a campfire. After their last trip to the beach, they would return to the trailer, each client would be asked to go out into the woods and find something that represented them and their weekend experience. They were asked to bring it to the closing campfire that evening. Campfires earlier in the weekend had included goofy songs and s'mores until your belly hurt. This one would be different, more serious.

The ceremony began with staff feedback to each girl about growth that was seen over the weekend. Then each of the girls would present the item she chose to represent her and talk about how and why she chose this item. It was a very moving and insightful time. One young lady brought what appeared to be a dead limb from a tree with a vibrantly green leaf growing out the other end, explaining that she was once dead, but now felt alive because she was able to feel and enjoy life again. Another young lady brought a flower that was growing up from a rock and talked about how this experience had helped her to flower through hard times. Yet another girl brought a rock covered in moss and talked about how she had covered herself and pretended to be something she wasn't, how she was hard and bitter, pretending to be attractive, sobbing about wanting to be real. One client brought mushrooms and explained how she had allowed mushrooms (drugs) to steal her life from her and how this weekend reminded her about how life was worth living, that she didn't want the drugs in her life anymore. One girl brought a dead bird and told us how drugs and alcohol had taken her song and her life, but this weekend had taught her that she still had a song and if she wanted a life, she could have it. She was choosing life.

With these revelations and insights, as well as three days of restful camaraderie, the girls and staff headed back to the group home, back to the routine. School started shortly thereafter, and new adventures awaited.

~ a group of clients relaxing at the beach

22

Christmas Stories

Mary Kay

Christmas is always a season of mixed emotions at the group home. The big anticipatory question begins early: "Who is going home for the holiday?" Once each girl has that question answered for herself, things settle down a little bit. Though there is still an air of sadness, excitement, regret and anger that permeates the air, making it crackle with unspoken tensions that could let loose at any minor infraction. Playing a big part in Candlelight's mission is teaching the girls to give back to the community and the holiday time is a time of many opportunities to do this. From making cards for nursing home residents to shoveling sidewalks, the staff planned many activities designed to empower the girls to help those less fortunate than themselves.

During December of 2000, the girls were allowed to pick a giving opportunities they most wished to do. Having heard the commercials on the radio, the girls conferred and chose the Christian Christmas Shoebox drive as their charity. This involved working with the local Christian radio station to get a list of names and ages of children in the program. The girls would be filling a shoebox for each child with goodies and small gifts. Occasionally, CVC was chosen by other groups as the recipient of such shoeboxes for the residents, and it seemed very appropriate that they give back in the same way. The decision of the girls was unanimously approved by the staff and they were given an allotment of money to spend (supervised) on gifts for the children, as well as being expected to either spend a small amount of their own money, hand-make an item, or donate an item they owned to the cause so they had a bit of personal investment in the donation. It is easy to be generous with someone else's money and the lesson would have been lost had we left it at that. Excitement grew as the girls visited the dollar store and other shops gathering gifts for "their kids." The large square coffee table became the receptacle for the items, and it accumulated there throughout the weeks leading up to Christmas – pens, stickers, candy, hair bows, journals, headphones, body lotions in all scents, and handmade cards and beaded bracelets (no gang colors allowed).

The activities of stuffing and wrapping the shoeboxes were reserved for the girls who would not be going home that Christmas as a way to help fill the day and distract from the building emotions that inevitably blew up in some fashion. The wrapping party began. Staff supervised while the girls laid out each child's box and then chose items that were appropriate for their age and gender. Some girls even put pictures of themselves in the shoeboxes, warming to the idea of making a difference for someone else. The girls were genuinely feeling good about this effort.

Later in the day, after the wrapping paper was picked up off the carpet and the extra tape scraped off the table, staff gathered the shoeboxes and stacked them in an oversized cardboard printer box to be delivered to the radio station the next day. After a treatment group session, the girls were allowed time for themselves in the common area of the lower level of the house. A staff member noticed a journal being used by one of the younger residents that looked quite a bit like the journal that had been sitting on the table waiting for a shoebox the day before. Come to think of it, it was the exact journal. Doing a little investigative work, the staff member searched the group home garbage cans and found candy wrappers matching the donated candy. It was apparent there was at least one girl who had yielded to her emotions of envy, anger, and resentment that Christmas and took what she thought she should have to compensate for her lack of home visit.

Staff conferred and a community group was quickly called. As it turned out, the culprits quickly confessed. Not one, but three of the residents had taken items from the shoeboxes. Once accountability happened, the group centered on feelings, rather than the items. Tears flowed as the girls finally spoke of their feelings of abandonment, hurt, and resentment. Why should they be at the group home while others went home? Staff gently guided them to their reality – some had behaviors that weren't safe for others that kept them from being home. Some simply didn't have homes available or safe for them. From there the staff moved toward empathy.

"Who are you hurting?" challenged one staff member. She then pulled out the list of the Christian Children's shoebox recipients they had been assigned and read each name and age one by one. Silence filled the air as that information settled in. Not one had thought about who they were taking from, only what they ended up with.

"You are hurting, so you hurt others. Has that ever happened any other time in your life?" The group moved towards three hours as the girls tearfully recounted times in which they had hurt others in their lives - running away and not letting their parents know they were safe, using drugs and alcohol, stealing, physically assaulting family members, failing school – in response to their hurts.

Another Christmas misstep occurred during another giving opportunity – ringing bells for the Salvation Army. Due to the often-harsh winters we suffer through, complaints rang out just as often as the tin bells during this mission. We were assigned to a department store just down the street from the group home, an "outside the doors" location that was frequented often by shoppers. Settling in for the shift were three girls and a staff member. Having dug out Santa hats for the occasion, spirits were high even though it was chilly. Staff led the girls in carols, and they watched as the passersby plunked in their change. As the end of the shift neared, the girls were tired, cold, and hungry, keen to get back. One girl, Thea, though, was eager to return to the bells, and let staff know she was willing to volunteer for any other shifts.

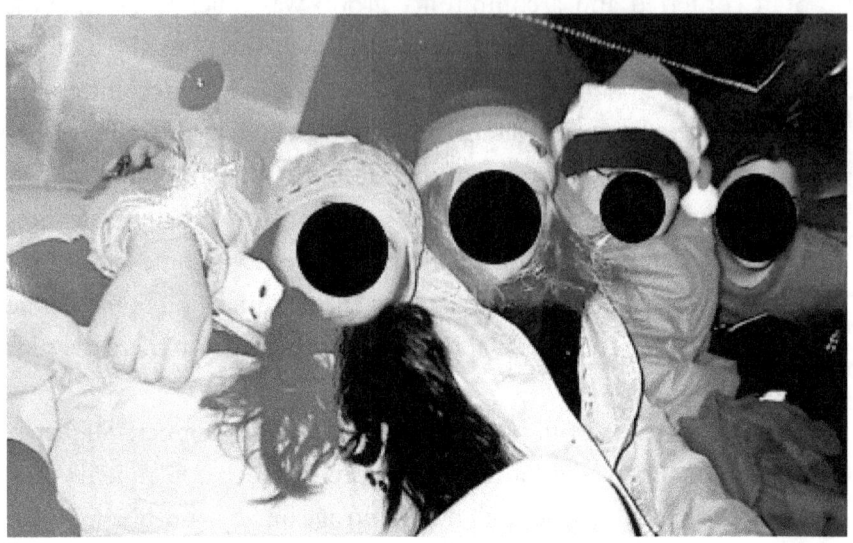

~ residents during a holiday outing

Excited, the staff worked with the Salvation Army to assign her to several more. Because Thea was 17 and progressing in her program, it was decided that she would be allowed to ring bells without supervision, walking to and from the bell ringing location. Thea returned each time in high spirits, seemingly happy to help the cause. Only in later days it was discovered her pleasure was gleaned from the extra change she had stuffed in her pockets from the Salvation Army bucket. Thea is an example of an adolescent with hidden anger at her parents that manifested itself into behaviors she knew would disappoint her parents and hurt them when they found out. Thea was not savvy at hiding her thievery, almost intentionally getting caught or making up such ludicrous lies as to be unbelievable. Subsequent to the bell ringing incident, Thea also stole money from the collection basket at a twelve-step meeting and many items from a locker room at the YMCA. Each time, the incident followed a conflict with her parents or a home visit. Otherwise, mild mannered and non-aggressive, Thea's pattern was to express her repressed rage covertly.

It was the day after Christmas, and we wanted to make it a fun day for the girls. We had free coupons to go ice skating at an indoor skating rink. There was a hustle and bustle amongst most of the girls – wanting to find warm socks, finish their lunch, and most importantly - fix their hair before slipping, sliding, and skating on the ice. However, one of the girls didn't want to go. She was refusing to move out of her chair. Then she started less passive aggressive techniques – such as running around the house and cranking music until you could hear nothing else – to show her displeasure in the upcoming activity plans. When she collapsed on the couch looking exhausted, I sought to connect with her.

I asked her if there's anything I could do. She locked eyes with me and said, "You can't do anything for me, nobody here can do anything. All I want is a family. This is my second Christmas in a row being here!" There was no answer to that and the hurt gleamed in her eyes as all I could do was sit with her and honor that hurt.

HAPPY HOLIDAYS

From Our Staff to Yours

Candlelight Vision Staff

~Candlelight Vision Corp's 2001 Holiday card sent to referral sources and families

23

The Heart of an Angel

Danel

CVC would often attract people who had good hearts and wanted to make a difference in the lives of the girls we served. Of course, we had regular volunteer opportunities like mentoring and tutoring, but sometimes a person would want to help in other ways and offer their own ideas to us. The clients benefited from these often unique and generous ideas. One time, a church offered to landscape the entire campus for CVC, including buying and planting flowers, plants, and decorative stones to help CVC present a warm, welcoming, cheery image to the clients and their families. Another time, a volunteer (who also mentored) offered to start a garden for the girls and teach them how to grow, harvest, and ultimately cook and can the vegetables they produced. This was a wonderful venture that taught the clients caretaking of something living and we found some girls actually bonded with "their" plants, not to mention gained valuable independent living and occupational skills while having fun. No matter the offer, if we felt it could benefit the girls in some way, we would accept.

Early on in my career at CVC, I took a call from a woman, Angel, who had heard about the group home through a newspaper article and was interested in helping somehow. I spoke to her about the usual volunteer opportunities we had available. She listened carefully then let me know she was raising several young children and was expecting to adopt one more at any time so was unable to fit in volunteering in the traditional ways. She then suggested that her and her church group send monthly care packages to the girls at the group home that the staff identified as lacking available family and needing a little extra support. These care packages, we decided, would not be extras or extravagances, but things a normal teenage girl should have, but by virtue of family circumstances, did not.

We discussed this as a staff and pondered if it might raise some jealousies between the girls who received and the ones who didn't. Whether the gifts would encourage the girls to expect the gifts or feel entitled rather than grateful. But in the end, we thought we'd give it a try, hoping that all the girls would understand the concept of receiving and being part of a community that cared about them, as well as the fact that all people did not get the same level of material and non-material items in life. Angel began compiling items for a list of girls we identified. Monthly, Angel and her children would drop off the care packages and spend a few minutes visiting with the staff and clients. Often personal notes of encouragement or comfort were included in the packages.

The girls quickly grew to know her and surrounded her when she came. Her children became used to the group home, and everyone rejoiced when Angel announced she was expecting for the fifth time. We would keep her apprised of the comings and goings of the girls as they were accepted and discharged from the group home. As CVC expanded and opened TLC^2, the Transitional Living Center, Angel and her group took on all of the girls who were admitted into TLC^2 and sent items pertaining to living independently, such as dishtowels, utensils, calendars, and the like.

Angel enjoyed her visits to the group home and would often call me in between to get an update or just to chat. She let me know if there was any other way she could help out, I should let her know as long as it was a once in a while opportunity. I graciously thanked her and promised to keep this in mind.

Her offer came at a time that couldn't have been better. Easter was quickly arriving and as usual several weeks beforehand, the staff meeting consisted of figuring out who had earned home passes and where and how long each girl would be gone so we could figure out staffing patterns. It seemed this year, we had every girl leaving for a period of time except one girl, Rikka, whose dad was out of the picture and her mother in inpatient drug treatment and not able to get a pass to spend time with her daughter that holiday. What to do?

Of course, we could put a staff member on the schedule and they could spend the holiday together doing something special or serving a meal at the homeless shelter as we have done in the past. Thinking out loud, I suggested, I wonder if Angel would let her spend the holiday with her. I knew Angel had connected with this girl during her visits to the group home and Rikka had reciprocated. This was easier said than done, however. Angel had to officially agree, the necessary safety checks had to be done, Rikka's county case worker had to approve the visit, and Rikka had to agree to go.

Though daunting, we believed it could be done and be a wonderful experience for Rikka. Lo and behold, everything fell into place and both parties were thrilled. Thus started a tradition that lasted. When we had a girl or two that had nowhere to go on a holiday and her mentor was unavailable to take her, we would ask Angel and most times she would agree. Angel welcomed them into her home and even shared her time with her extended family. With her new role and her continued presentation of the care packages, she became known as "the caretaker" at CVC. We would make sure any client we presented for her to take in over a day or two for a holiday would interact well with her children, which now numbered six.

Of course, this venture was not without its problems and mishaps. One Easter holiday, a girl, Amara, was not going to have a home to visit as her father lived in another state and her mother was currently in jail awaiting trial on failure to protect a child for knowingly allowing fourteen year old Amara to have sex with her 26 year old boyfriend in her house. Once again, I made the call to Angel, hoping it would work out. And once again, Angel was gracious and did not hesitate in her acceptance. Amara was set to visit Angel's home for one evening and part of the next day. All appeared to go well, and Amara came back to the group home happy, with stories of playing with the children and Easter basket hunts.

Our satisfaction with her visit was short lived, however, when we received a phone call from Angel. She apologetically said,

"I hate to even call you, but I don't know what to do."

"Oh?" I questioned, warily.

"Well, when Amara was here, we visited my sister's house for Easter dinner and now she can't find several pieces of jewelry," Angel stated.

"Hmmm. Do you think Amara took it?"

"I don't know what else to think. We've looked everywhere and we can't find it. I don't want to accuse her if it's not true, but I wanted to call and ask you what you thought."

Angel was talking faster now, and I could tell she was upset.

"It certainly wouldn't be impossible." I said. "I'll ask her about it and get back to you."

Sure enough, after a perfunctory inquisition, Amara spilled everything, not only fessing up to the jewelry, but to taking make-up and other toiletries as well from the sister's bathroom when she was there. The jewelry was recovered, but the make-up had been used and distributed to some of the other girls. A house meeting was called, and consequences were meted out. Amara bore the brunt of making amends and we made plans to visit Angel and her sister the next week after Amara had received her allowance and was able to purchase new make-up items to replace the ones she stole. The whole house received a no make-up or hair accessories ban for one week.

The drive out to Angel's sister's house was quiet, punctuated by a few tears as Amara silently rehearsed what she would say to her victims. I took the time to discuss what damage she had done, not only by violating the trust Angel and her sister had put in her, but to the relationship between the group home and this family. I went on to let her know she had jeopardized the chance for other girls to be able to spend time with Angel and her family for other holidays. After this discussion, Amara arrived at the house feeling meek and humble. She murmured her apology and handed over the items she was returning, all the while looking down at the floor.

Angel and her sister did a wonderful job accepting the apology and letting Amara know how her actions had affected them and their children. This was a very positive experience for Amara, though I'm sure it didn't feel like it at the time. She was able to accept ownership for her actions, positively make amends and face her victims while hearing the impact her actions had. This is crucial for the adolescents we serve to understand that their behaviors always impact more people than just themselves and they often leave a trail of hurt in their wake. For Amara to make this connection in a hands-on way rather than in a group or a lecture, conveyed this powerful message more than any other way could.

I would have loved to tell you this experience changed Amara's outlook completely, but she continued to struggle. One step in the process of change though was she was able to maintain that relationship despite the damage of trust. This demonstrated a powerful message of unconditional love she hadn't received in the past.

24

Lice: A Four-Letter Word

Danel

One of the most dreaded words that staff could hear was the word "LICE." When one of the kids would come home from school reporting a classmate had head lice, staff would get their pencils out and began daily inspections. One thing adolescent girls do not take kindly to is bugs in their hair. The immediate focus became finding the culprit – who is responsible for the bugs in their hair? It was not pretty.

The reason behind the panic involved not only the drama of the girls (staff were known to hide in the closet out of sight of the girls to scratch a simple head itch to avoid causing panic), but it was also a huge expense as the long-drawn-out process of ridding ourselves of the bugs ensued. Buying shampoo in large quantities, often requiring us to go to more than one pharmacy (staff drew straws to see who had to do this chore). To avoid re-infestation, everyone's head and all bedding needed to be treated on the same day. Given we had between eight and thirteen adolescent girls at one time, this was a defeating notion. To accomplish this, we would call in the reserves. Informing our loyal employees why the extra staff was needed was not always met with cheers. In return, of course, we offered a free shampoo.

Staff would be broken up into teams: Delouse the House Team, the Shopping Team, the Nit-Picking Team, and the Laundromat Team.

The Laundromat Team was required to strip all the beds of sheets, comforters, pillows, stuffed animals, and blankets. The shopping list would be drawn out – later just printed off the computer as an already created document; large heavy-duty lawn and garden bags would accommodate the bedding that was headed for the laundromat in town. Their stuffed animals and lovies needed to be bagged up and stored for seven to ten days. Cases of special shampoo, preferably generic, cases of delousing spray for the couches and carpets, twelve packs of Coke and Mountain Dew to keep energy levels up, and chocolate for the girls to quell the whining.

It was not uncommon to begin the delousing procedure after school and still be putting beds back together at eleven or twelve at night. And...we did it all again in two weeks. No one was spared from the tragedy of lice. Even the bookkeeper panicked when he had to shell out money from the already tight budget for supplies.

There wasn't much we could do about the lice that came from school, but with experience, we learned to require the girls that came into the house from jail to shampoo to avoid all out mutiny. Staff would secretly hide in the office and draw straws when we had a client with particularly thick, curly, or exceptionally long hair to pick through, strand by strand by strand. We found it exceptionally humorous that one client had a court order to not contract head lice. Strong on motive, weak on ability to enforce, we thought. We did appreciate the support, however.

It was telling when one of our temporary overnight staff became quite alarmed when lice was discovered, more so than her co-workers. It was revealed that she had been sleeping, in violation of policy, on the couch, where, of course, the girls with lice had been sitting, reinforcing the theory of natural consequences.

Of course, when a breakout was discovered, we were obligated to share the happy news with our soon-to-be not-so-happy parents and social workers. Again, straws were drawn from the administrative team end of things now. Of course, Mary Kay oversaw the Family Program so parent notification fell to her, and I was in charge of calling social workers.

We first did a frantic search of recent passes, hoping we could eliminate some of those unpleasant phone calls. The two most memorable family calls were to the parents who had just sent their other children to camp after having their daughter home from CVC wrestling and snuggling with her younger siblings. The second, a father who had hosted a sleepover birthday party for one of his children and now had more parents to call than we did. As much as parents loved their children, most of the parents requested home passes remain on hiatus until the epidemic was contained.

Staff became hyper-vigilant and kept the community health nurse on speed dial. Any time a client scratched their head more than three times we would call her for a visit. After they were finished delousing at work, all staff had to go home and repeat the same procedures to avoid re-infestation at the group home. One staff person came in one day after this process and soulfully reported that her daughter wanted her to quit her job so she would not bring bugs home.

25

Questioning

Mary Kay

Adolescence is a time of self-discovery, a time that developmentally, a person in between childhood and adulthood may not know exactly who he or she is. Searching for and trying on different identities is sometimes a full-time job for an adolescent. This time gets even more complicated when an adolescent may not have solid, healthy role models for behaviors and values. Abuse, alcohol or other drug use, family secrets, or grief and loss issues may interrupt emotional development, leaving an adolescent stuck as an emotional eight-year-old wearing a teenager's body. Unsure of herself and the expectations and emotionally unable to reason through life's issues, it becomes difficult to make healthy choices for herself.

Many adolescents question their sexual identity as they mature and attempt to figure out where they fit into life and what is ahead for their future. At times, adolescents confuse emotional intimacy with physical intimacy. For example, the adolescents at CVC group homes spent most of their time physically close; They attended school together, activities together, and treatment groups together. The most intimate life issues were discussed. These girls share their lives with each other: tales of being burned by a father's cigarettes, of being forced to stay in the room while their mother turned tricks, of nearly dying of an overdose, of visiting a boyfriend's grave who had committed suicide. Tears were shed every day as the girls worked through these issues, finally dealing with their emotions in a healthy manner instead of destructively, while their peers lent support and often cried with them. There were times that such emotional intimacy was interpreted as a sexual desire, an intimate "love," rather than the emotional support and unconditional love it was.

In other instances, girls have identified their sexual orientation prior to being admitted to the group home, most being confident, sure of themselves, and un-embarrassed. Some identify being "lesbian for now," a reference that often evolved from being in a locked all-female corrections facility where males were simply unavailable. A similar phenomenon is said to happen in prisons.

There were times a resident of CVC struggled with gender or sexual identity issues. Many of the girls we worked with suffered sexual abuse at some point in their lives. Unfortunately, some even suffered ongoing sexual abuse or had multiple perpetrators in their lives. Whether this experience had anything to do with questioning their gender or sexual identity is a mystery. Whether they wanted so badly to reject that person who was abused and create a new persona, perhaps one that would be unattractive to a would-be abuser was surely on the minds of the professionals who work with abuse victims.

Ashland was one of these young women. Stockily built, 15-year-old Ashland carried herself with a masculine gait. She cropped her hair short and even fashioned sideburns out of the dark, thick tresses. Ashland didn't speak much and when she did it was usually cuss words. She worked hard at pushing people away. Sexually abused from age three through age eleven when her mother finally broke up with her abusive boyfriend, Ashland sought refuge in food and misbehavior, and solace in her room with her stereo turned on the highest volume. She dressed in flannel men's shirts two sizes too big and wore workmen's pants or dark jeans with high top tennis shoes. Ashland had no interest in relationships, either with boys or girls; She was a self-identified loner. Quickly noticeable to the staff was her desire to present herself as male in her physical appearance, including her voice which she made an effort at lowering the pitch; her interests, which ran to playing tackle football; and her lack of desire to be involved in anything she considered feminine.

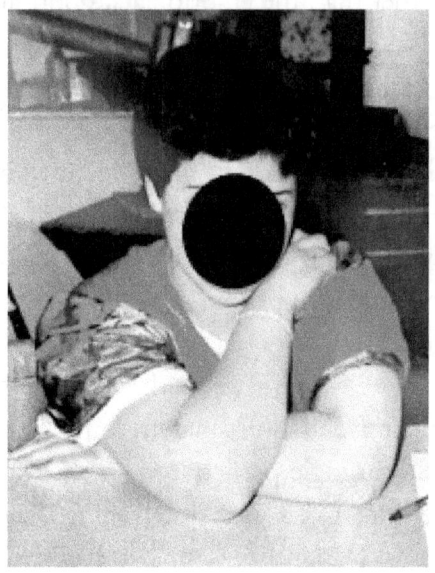

~ A client at ABC group home

Ashland even took this persona as far as refusing to wear tampons or sanitary pads when she menstruated, preferring instead to ignore this obviously feminine process of maturity. This obviously created hygiene problems for Ashland, the staff, and the other girls, especially her room-mates who began noticing bloody underwear being hidden behind beds and dressers.

To acknowledge her period would be to acknowledge her gender, which was extremely threatening to Ashland. She saw being a girl as being vulnerable, being subject to abuse. Identifying with some of the traits of her abuser, she wished to be strong, a trait which she believed was masculine, invulnerable to attack. Ashland was setting the scene for feeling able to protect herself by being stronger and not being as de-fenseless. She was, in effect, blaming herself for the abuse: "If only I had been stronger, I could have stopped it." Her resolve was to be stronger by shunning her femininity. Ashland wore bras deliberately a size or two too small and shirts a size or two too big to reduce the appearance of her breasts. She wore no make-up, nor did she wear jewelry beyond a very thick gold chain, akin to what a teenage boy might wear.

Efforts, even gently couched in identifying feelings of powerlessness, to address this issue with Ashland were rebuffed. Her wall was up, and she was absolutely determined to not let anyone chip away at the veneer. After all, this wall was protecting her and keeping her safe. It made sense to her that adults could not be trusted, and she needed to do what she could to take care of herself. In her mind, her mother would not protect her as she had allowed her abuse by continuing the relationship with her boyfriend during the abuse. Ashland struggled at ABC, lasting just short of two months before her escalating behaviors spurred a quick run through the available consequences and the staff team felt she was presenting too much of a danger and disruption for the other clients at CVC.

26

Finding the "Little Girl" Within

Mary Kay

Girls came to us for a variety of reasons. Initially, what is identified are the obvious behavioral problems – running away, out of control behaviors, drug use, etc. These were the visible symptoms that spurred action and eventual removal from the home. We knew there was much more going on, deeper wounds, invisible damage that drove the outward symptoms. Part of our program philosophy helped to identify for each client the wounded "little girl" inside her. Generally, when trauma or abuse occurred, their emotional development paused, stopping at the age of abuse. We would often ask the girls to describe their "little girl." It was awesome to watch them soften and become more vulnerable.

"Mine has long blonde hair, pigtails with ribbons," one girl would say.

"Mine is in blue jeans and tennis shoes," another girl would report, getting into the idea.

"I am wearing my favorite dress,"

As this discussion continued, we always came to the revealing question: "How old is your little girl?" We asked the girls to picture their little girl and name the age she was at that moment. This was almost assuredly the age at which their trauma had repressed their continued emotional growth. Outwardly, we could see the signs of this immaturity in poor judgment, lack of impulse control, and poor self-esteem. These appeared to be deliberate, willful behaviors when one does not look beyond the behaviors to the root of the problem.

At least 90% of our girls were been abused, physically, sexually, or emotionally. It is not uncommon for sexual abuse victims to manifest behaviors relating to unresolved abuse in several very different ways. Most girls showed ways of coping and dealing with their abuse that were destructive and needed intervention.

Some girls may do anything they can to make themselves unattractive. Common strategies are to overeat until they deem themselves sufficiently overweight to deter any man from wanting to be sexual with them, presenting themselves as more masculine than feminine, and becoming so hostile in relationships that it drives people, especially males, away before they can be hurt.

Another, maybe paradoxical, reaction we see is when a girl who has been sexually abused becomes overly sexual, using her body, sexual attractiveness and flirtation to invite sexual activity. In this way, the girl feels she is in charge of what happens to her body and is no longer helpless. A girl learns that she has power with her body and how to use that for her own wants and needs. Lack of boundaries becomes a huge issue as these girls have never learned where they end and the other person begins. That boundary wasn't respected as they experienced the abuse during those crucial impressionable younger years.

Sexual abuse, being a trauma, often leaves in its wake Post Traumatic Stress Disorder (PTSD), a constellation of symptoms which interfere with functioning. Many families or acquaintances of the victim often feel the length of time between the trauma and the present would be healing. When, in fact, the body stores these trauma memories, and they can be triggered later by very seemingly innocent occurrences. Even a song, a smell, or a body sensation can cause a feeling of reoccurrence of the trauma. Relationships are especially likely to trigger such flashbacks and maladaptive behaviors. Symptoms of PTSD include hyper vigilance, or always knowing what is going on around them, even as far as to sleep with their eyes open; an over-developed startle response, jumping or over-reacting to touch or unexpected noise; and flashbacks. Cutting or self-harm is not an uncommon response to attempt to cope with trauma.

Understanding the extreme responses that the girls exhibited and understanding that they were direct consequences of the abuse and trauma they experienced, we sought to above all else, develop a trusting relationship with the girls. They tended to judge themselves very harshly, taking on their abuse as part of their identity, seeing themselves as labels, such as "the promiscuous one," and "the ho'." Once we established a rapport with the client, we began to educate. It was very important that they understood the relationship between their behaviors and their past abuse. Adolescents are experiential beings. So, along with the education, we sought to use their senses to help them start to resolve the trauma.

In a flashback situation, where the client was physically re-experiencing the trauma, it was important that they learn techniques to keep them in the present rather than totally succumb to the flashback and be re-traumatized. One such method is the metronome. A metronome is used by musicians to keep the beat and set the pace of the music. It is a small battery-run box that would emit a tick tock-like sound at a rhythmic pace.

When working with a child amid a flashback, staff would sit alongside them, talk with them, and tell them where they were, what the date was, and continue to remind them that they were safe. Staff would then introduce the metronome, setting it next to the client and setting it to sound a rhythmic cadence impossible to tune out. The idea behind this method is that it engages both sides of the brain and is clearly a noise that was not present during their abuse, thus interrupting the flashback and grounding the girl in the moment with the continuous, and sometimes irritating, tick-tock tick-tock.

Many girls found this a comfort and would often ask for the metronome if they could predict a flashback was imminent. Other ways to ground the client in the moment were activities like coloring, using stress balls or stuffed animals, or engaging in some physical activity like the treadmill or chores. Self-talk was an intervention that we encouraged, "I am here, not there." "That was then, this is now." "I am safe." "Here are the people around me."

The girls were encouraged to build a safe box to include the tools or techniques that helped ground them the most. Their box might include a favorite stuffed animal, a journal, and a list of self-talk messages. They generally kept this box under their bed for easy access during nighttime incidents of night terrors and bad dreams. We encouraged the girls to journal their night terrors. Physically returning the journal back to the box after their dream would signify containing that moment, making it safe enough to return to sleep.

27

Externalizing the Hurt

Danel

Maureen is an example of a client that responded to her abuse by sexually acting out. We received a referral on this young lady who was residing at another group home in a neighboring community. This was a group home that served adolescent girls that were pregnant or parenting a child under the age of one. It was not the same as the olden day boarding house that the stigma of unwed pregnancy often pushed families to seek, but a state-licensed group home for adolescents on county supervision as either a Child in Need of Protective Services (CHIPS) or a Delinquency petition. The girls had the same behaviors as the girls we served and had often committed crimes. They just happened to be teenage parents as well, complicating the whole treatment picture by adding prenatal and parenting issues to the usual gamut of behavioral, emotional, and family systems issues the girls already had. We knew and were on friendly terms with their staff, and in fact, had two staff members on board that were former employees of this group home.

The county worker called to inquire about an opening for her client. Maureen, she explained, was on a Juvenile in Need of Protection petition (JIPS) and had been placed out of her home for the past six months at the group home.. She had, however, recently decided to turn over custody of her 9-month-old daughter to her mother. This decision made it impossible for her to stay at that group home since its license specifically designated that residents had to be pregnant or parenting. Maureen simply could not handle the demands of parenting an infant, even with the help and support of the group home staff.

Maureen was from a local county, and they were hoping she could still keep a close relationship with her baby while she worked on her own issues. These issues, as we found out later, were numerous and ran deep. We assured the county worker that we would be able to work with Maureen and her family, including arranging for her to have supervised visits with her daughter. Part of Maureen's treatment plan was addressing her unresolved sexual abuse issues which manifested itself in her extreme sexual acting out. She also had a tumultuous and at times, enmeshed relationship with her mother. Maureen's older brother was her perpetrator, which caused a great amount of family tension. Maureen was uncertain whether she wanted to be a mother and would waver between looking at her baby as a status symbol with her peers, and alternatively, an inconvenience to her social life. Maureen struggled with being nurturing, though she was able to show some growth in this area by the time she left CVC.

Maureen was a pretty girl with long blonde hair she wore straight down her back or bunched into a messy ponytail. She was slim, though still carried a bit of postpartum weight when she arrived. One might describe her attitude as bouncy and she mostly always wore a smile, even when it didn't match her mood. Maureen was not one of our clients who were outright defiant or verbally abusive. She complied with whatever directive she was given as long as she was in your sight, and you immediately held her accountable. We noticed problems with compliance when Maureen was trusted to follow a rule without immediate oversight. When Maureen was not under direct adult supervision, such as during the school day where all adolescents have some autonomy to make choices, she usually chose behaviors that were not healthy for her or others.

Most of Maureen's poor choices involved sexual activity. She was able to identify that she still had many feelings about her past abuse by her brother but had difficulty connecting those feelings to her current behavior. Maureen spoke of, thought about, and wrote about sex daily. The fact that this behavior led to her having a pregnancy in adolescence and was currently affecting her mother and her daughter was lost on her. The partners she chose for sexual contact were usually unsavory. Often, they were adults. In fact, the father of her baby was an adult male she had met at the bus station and had had a one-night stand with. A short time later, without knowing that Maureen was pregnant, the father of her baby committed suicide.

Always leaning towards drama and ways she could elevate her status with her peers, Maureen took to telling people she met almost immediately that the father of her baby was dead, that he had killed himself. Maureen enjoyed the shocked looks on people's faces and went on to gather all the "you poor dear" attention usually piled on her afterwards. Her county worker and CVC staff agreed this was a boundary issue and not a healthy way for Maureen to communicate to others. She was told to cease such introductions immediately. She continued to elevate the non-relationship in her mind as a romantic, serious, and devoted bond between them, asking incessantly to visit his grave. To Maureen, to not be loved by a male or have a partner, even a dead one, was unacceptable and she would feel incomplete.

Maureen was kept home from school on several different occasions stemming from her overtly sexual behaviors at school. She was always compliant with whatever consequence she received and was pleasant while she worked on her homework at the group home. We brought her to our treating psychiatrist to determine if her excessive sexual acting out could somehow be related to a manic episode. The manic phase of bipolar disorder (what used to be called manic depression) can sometimes encompass a heightening of sexual activity as a symptom. After examining Maureen, receiving her thoughts on her behavior and the staff's documentation of what we were seeing, announced with a marked no-argument tone, "You aren't going to be able to medicate *this* kind of behavior!" And that was that. We were left with attempting other interventions.

Maureen saw a counselor outside of CVC to augment her work on the sexual abuse. She happily went, though seemed to be making no discernable progress, at least none that was evidenced by her behavior. Only a short time after the fruitless visit to the psychiatrist, did things really come to a head and our skills and therapeutic aptitude were put to the test.

It all started during an evening secrets group. A secrets group would occur at the group home when it was apparent to staff that something was going on "underground." When something negative, or threatening to the treatment environment, is going on, it is usually common knowledge among the residents but not the staff. Whispered conversations, a note left on the kitchen table, or an outright statement from one of the girls might lead a staff member to call a secrets group. Secrets by their very nature are destructive. Family secrets are behind many of the unhealthy behaviors they presented that caused them to be placed out of their homes. Secrets of family alcoholism, of sexual abuse, of parental neglect – all designed to make someone feel helpless and powerless. Secrets were a pattern to be broken if we were to empower these young women to take back their lives and make healthier choices.

Because they didn't happen often, secrets groups held a certain impact and raised anxiety about their behaviors. There were some rumors cropping up that week about unsavory happenings going on at school and the possibility of contraband in the form of cigarettes or drugs in the house. That provided the incentive to do a secrets group.

The girls were instructed to be seated in their pre-assigned "house freeze" seats, which are located apart from each other, but in full view of the staff. They are not allowed to talk while being given a piece of paper and asked to list the secrets they have been keeping. They could be about themselves or someone else. This practice was not to encourage "snitching" or "ratting out their peers," concepts often verbalized by the clients who were feeling persecuted, but to promote holding themselves and their peers accountable. It is not a true friend who keeps the secret that you are using drugs, as that behavior is destructive to you and the people you love. A true friend will risk your anger and perhaps your friendship to do the right thing and let someone know that can help you.

This is a new concept to most of the girls, as most have heard the opposite message their whole lives in the form of "what happens in the family stays in the family," "we take care of our own problems," and "if you tell our secrets, you will break up the family." We supported the girls in creating a new pattern of openness, (not telling secrets to seek revenge on a peer, as sometimes happened), but to tell a secret with the motivation of caring about the other person.

With these instructions, the secrets group that night commenced. For the above reasons, secrets groups are, by nature, very long, taking up most of the evening. As each girl signaled that they were done with their list, a staff member would retrieve it and look it over. Most often the first time the list was turned in, it was given back with the instructions of "what else?" Sometimes this happened four or five times. The lists were compared and if one girl had a secret about a peer on it, that peer's list would not be considered complete until she included it on her list.

As with anything in this profession, sometimes you must be prepared for the unexpected. Mary Kay related that during a secrets group in her home with her adolescent foster children, she started with getting a list that stated, "I taught the bird to say swear words," and ended up with "I had oral sex at school."

This secrets group was no exception. As the night wore on, the lists grew longer and they seemed to be including the things we initially suspected – cigarettes hidden in the rooms, skipping a class at school, etc. I went home, letting the staff know I would look over the lists the next day. When they were satisfied with the length of the lists or when it was time for bed, I'm not sure which, the staff released the girls from the house freeze spots and sent everyone to bed with the anxiety of what consequences lay ahead for their newly exposed secrets.

The next morning, I came in mid-morning, and it was quiet in the house with all of the girls at school. I sat down in the office prepared to review the secrets lists to discuss at our staffing. Beyond the usual confessions, I noticed a few statements by girls buried at the bottom of the pages indicating Maureen was involved in a sexual relationship at school. This got my attention. I looked further and the last list had a proclamation that was not vague in the least, a direct incriminating statement: "Maureen has sex with her teacher Mr. Brood."

Whoa! Wait a minute. We weren't talking about internal group home business anymore. This was serious. I immediately asked the staff to call the school and let them know we would be picking up Maureen from school and bringing her back to the group home for the day. We did not tell them why, nor did we indicate in any way what we suspected. I discussed with the staff about the possible ramifications of this, both on Maureen, the teacher, and the group home. We didn't know any facts yet, only a one sentence statement penciled on a list from another group home resident. If Maureen had truly had sex with her teacher, he had committed a major felony. If Maureen had bragged about having sex with her teacher when she hadn't, she was risking this teacher's reputation and job. No matter what, it was a terrible situation.

Maureen returned to the group home somewhat confused about why she was there. We let her know we were concerned about her safety after some of the secrets were revealed the night before. Not wanting to influence what she said or lead her in any way, we asked her to write down what she thought we may be concerned about. While she was writing, our school liaison staff member, Beth stated she believed Mr. Brood was a student teacher or an intern at the school. She would call the school and inquire as to his role.

Unfortunately, this inquiry set the defenses of the school in motion, and they refused to answer any questions about the man in question. With a teary expression Maureen came to the office with her notebook paper. On it was written, "I had sex with Mr. Brood in the music room at school." Staff stayed with Maureen to process this with her, though I stressed to not question her as to not interfere with what would surely be a police investigation. I immediately called Maureen's county social worker to apprise him of the situation, the local police, and Mary Kay who was out of the country on vacation.

The police arrived in a manner of a few minutes to take a statement. I realized as they were talking to us that a police report would be generated and though Maureen would not be named as she was a juvenile, that public record would show the group home address and possibly the name of the High School. We would possibly have a confidentiality issue on our hands if the media showed up at the group home or managed to figure out who any of the girls were who lived here. Maureen cooperated fully with the police. She was teary and stated she was willing to participate in the "sting" the police proposed to catch the teacher. Maureen identified the teacher as a student from a local college who was at the school on an internship from a domestic peace corp. program that places volunteers in agencies or schools that need additional staff. He had been placed in our district's high school to tutor students who had trouble with reading and math.

The police set up the sting for the next day. Maureen admitted she had Mr. Brood's cell phone number and had in fact pursued a relationship with him. This fact takes nothing away from the fact that he was the adult and was criminal in his behaviors towards Maureen; however, it was a typical pattern in Maureen's self-destructive behaviors, placing herself at risk. After the police left, we put a staff one on one with Maureen and called her sexual abuse counselor to set up an emergency appointment. Maureen's mother had also been called and was beside herself. All in all that day, I didn't spend much time without a telephone attached to my ear.

Our fears and planning were for naught as no news team ever did show up anywhere near the school or group home. Maureen continued to stay out of school, and we were instructed by the police to not tip off the school as to what was happening lest Mr. Brood got ahold of the information that he was busted and took off. Again, our planning was well intentioned but had no effect, as the next day, we found out that Mr. Brood had not shown up for his duties at the school. Maureen spoke again to a police officer and sketched for him a diagram of the school including the room she alleged they had sex in, a closet sized room designed for music students to practice their instruments in. It contained a piano and chair and nothing else. She agreed to call Mr. Brood's cell phone while the police monitored the call in the hopes that she could have him admit what he had done for criminal prosecution. Maureen also saw her counselor this day as she would each day for the foreseeable future.

We cleared the office and put Maureen on our office phone, on which the police had attached a recording device. She was successful in reaching him but unsuccessful in eliciting an incriminating admission from him. In fact, he acted paranoid that someone was on to him and repeatedly turned the questions back onto Maureen. They went around for a few minutes until the police officer signaled that Maureen should end the conversation. After school hours the police visited the school, who by now had been informed of the allegations, to take a sample of the music room carpeting for evidence.

Maureen continued to process what had happened with her outside counselor. Unfortunately, the counselor and CVC disagreed on some important points of treatment, leading to confusion for Maureen and a chance for her to play what she saw as one side against the other. This is an example of what we call "triangling."

A triangle happens when three entities are involved representing the three corners of the triangle. The corners are typically labeled: victim, persecutor, and rescuer. In this case, Maureen was a true victim in one sense as an adult had had sexual contact with her. However, in the aftermath Maureen sought constant attention for having this "relationship," was resistant to looking at how her patterns put her into a high-risk situation, indicating she was willing and available to this man for a sexual interaction. In these ways, Maureen created a false victimization for herself when she complained to her outside counselor about how poorly she was being treated by the group home and how the staff were "blaming" this all on her. This cast the group home and the staff in the corner of the persecutor on the triangle.

Unbeknownst to her, her counselor became the third corner of the triangle, the rescuer, by feeding into this destructive pattern by not checking out Maureen's perceptions with the people that worked most closely with her, the group home staff, in particular her case manager. Instead, the counselor agreed with Maureen and ultimately with a very poor sense of boundaries, gave Maureen her personal phone number to call because she knew she "couldn't talk to the group home staff." This completed the triangle and allowed her to avoid accountability for her resistant behavior.

After several frustrating exchanges, ultimately, a meeting was called between all of the providers and, though we disagreed on the method, all agreed that Maureen's well-being was the top concern. Maureen continued to see her counselor who ended up leaving the agency a short time later. And CVC continued to help Maureen process what had happened to her and support her through the aftermath. Once she realized all her providers were communicating and she did not have the power to manipulate the situation any longer, she stopped most of her resistance. That's the thing with triangling: the players involved have to be willing to communicate or the unhealthy roles continue to be reinforced and the patterns will be repeated in future relationships.

Mr. Brood was finally located and arrested. He was held on a $25,000 bond and ordered to have no contact with children or schools. A subsequent search warrant turned up evidence of other sexual contacts he had had with underage girls, and he was soon charged with similar crimes in two other counties. The criminal case wound its way through the court system and several months later Mr. Brood pled guilty to Sexual Assault of Student by School Staff, a class H felony. For the charge stemming from intercourse with Maureen, he was sentenced to two years in state prison and an additional two years on extended supervision.

Maureen continued to be lovingly challenged on her patterns by CVC staff, though was not able to resolve her deep-seated issues. After a long period of family therapy, her mother, once completely enmeshed, was able to make better decisions for herself, her daughter, and her granddaughter who she continued to raise several years later. Maureen ultimately decided she was not cut out to be a mother and signed over complete custody of her daughter to her mother.

28

Baby, Think it OverTM

—The Development of a Curriculum—

Danel

Even though infant simulators have gained press and awareness over the years, the knowledge that such a thing exists is usually limited to high schoolers who are targeted for their use and professionals in the education field trying to make an impact on teenage pregnancy rates. Most of the older generation remembers carrying around an egg or a sack of flour to represent the awesome responsibilities of parenting. Teachers would find the flour left in a backpack or a morose student standing in front of her with egg yolk on her shirt, the result of too much "roughhousing" with the baby, and use these experiences to lecture about the demands of parenting and the advantages of waiting until adulthood to bring a child into the world.

The newer version of this mantra is similar, almost identical, only using different tools and ever-changing technology to more perfectly replicate the parenting experience. We realized early on that we would have a unique population at the group home to deliver this message to. Not only did we have all females, but we also had a captive (for lack of a better word) audience, high-risk behavior patterns, a twenty-four hour supervised environment, and a host of community resources and ideas at our disposal. Building on the premise that our clients all had the physical capability to have children and a history of poor decision-making, we hatched a plan to educate. We did not want to demonize teen parenting, nor glamorize it. But simply use all the tools at our disposal to give the girls every bit of information they could absorb, the good, the bad, and the ugly, about raising a child so they could make an informed decision.

We also felt it was extremely important to go beyond the typical public school curriculum bottom line of "don't get pregnant," but to educate the girls on *how* not to get pregnant. Ours was not necessarily a prevention program, but an education program with the goal of preventing teen pregnancy and improving knowledge, skill, and attitude about making healthy choices for themselves and their future children. Working with teenage girls offers a chance to see firsthand how girls grow, develop, and emerge into the adult world. A chance to see the struggles and the celebrations of womanhood, the successes and the defeats. Of course, we wanted all our girls to have a chance to make it as strong young women in the world. A greater chance than they may have had without us. It was very important for us to make a difference.

One of the biggest presenting issues that interfere in adolescent girls' development and future success is teen parenthood. We saw it repeatedly on the referral reports: sexually active, high risk sexual behaviors, poor boundaries, male-dependent, prostitution, history of abortion, history of miscarriage, baby in foster care. Unlike some other worrisome behaviors the residents show, sexual activity and the consequences of getting pregnant and or catching a sexually transmitted disease were things that could affect them and many other people for the rest of their lives. These were decisions being made in a typical adolescent way – impulsively and because it felt good, not considering the potential life-long cost to themselves and their family. With teenage birth rates rising, we realized we had an excellent opportunity to put a dent in this crisis. All our girls could benefit from hearing this message whether they had high-risk behaviors or not.

The idea emerged as a tiny tickle of a thought. An idea that we could somehow figure out how to package the message in a unique and attention-getting way, one that would not be easily forgotten after the lesson was over like the material they study for a midterm. A message that they could keep in their heads and feel in their hearts each time they needed to make a choice to be sexually active.

A key part of the idea was to engage the clients before we even started giving the message. It would do no good to lecture, degrade, shame, or embarrass them. We wanted them to be excited to learn this lesson.

It started with some simple drawings – a ripple chart. Was there a picture we could give them about how their choice affected different people and things in their lives? As the idea grew, we realized the girls often talked about *wanting* to get pregnant and parent while they were teens. As much as teenagers think they know, we were certain they did not have the information they needed. Education and information were the keys. We realized the only way this could happen was to have them experience it themselves, or as close to the actual experience as possible. We would give them babies.

Of course, not real babies. My research led me to a company that made electronic babies – infant simulators, they were called. They were out of our price range, but boy, did I want those babies for the girls. I made numerous calls and ended up, by chance, with a lead. The local County Child Support office had purchased a number of the simulators a few years back. Would they be willing to lend us some to use with our girls?

As it turns out, they were willing and excited to. Learning to operate an electronic baby that cried, burped, wanted to be rocked, and needed to be fed and changed was a challenge. There was computer software, printers, and batteries to figure out, not to mention how to read the results. I plugged away, all the while developing what else I wanted to include. Taking care of the babies would be only one part of the program. There was so much more to know.

Finally, I had the babies up and running and a rudimentary curriculum in place. I was ready to try it. A few more details needed to be finalized, however. A few more questions still needed to be answered:

- How long should the girls parent the infants?
- How could I train the staff?
- Would we need permission from the parents for this program?
- How would we handle school?

We decided to debut the Pregnancy Prevention Program during Spring Break. For months, we fine-tuned the curriculum, which by now was about nine days long with the girls parenting for five of those days. We arranged to borrow the babies from the Child Support office and for their lawyer to come and speak to the girls during the program. We trained the staff in the philosophy of the program: nurturing tough love, as well as how to "score" the parenting records the babies would give us, and let the girls know how they were doing. We sent letters to the parents and social workers detailing the plan. We scoured rummage sales to find clothing to dress the babies and other equipment. Finally, we told the girls what would be happening.

There were questions, for sure. The social workers wanted to know what would happen if the girls took to liking parenting the infant and confirmed their belief in teen pregnancy. The parents wanted to know why no home visits were allowed during the program. The girls wanted to know if they could pick the sex and race of their baby, and the staff wanted to know who to call if something went wrong or they did not know what to do. It was going to be a learning experience for us all.

Overall, the first program went very well, and I felt like we were underway with a good idea. The social workers were satisfied when none of the girls continued to want to have babies right away. The staff realized what a powerful tool the program was and what a potent message it sent without any lectures. The girls came to their own conclusion about wanting to have a baby or not – what we did is give them the information they needed to make an informed choice.

More work was needed, of course, and over time different aspects were added and some eliminated as BTIO (Baby Think It Over™) grew to a twelve-day curriculum done once or twice per year. We began to attract the attention of certain counties and eventually were able to write a large grant that was sponsored by one county to obtain our own babies and equipment such as cribs, strollers, clothing, baby books, and car seats.

We scrimped and scraped further and were finally able to buy one of my favorite parts of the program, the Empathy Belly™. A fake pregnancy belly that was worn like a pinafore strapped to the client. The Belly held a bladder that was filled with hot water, 2 lead balls that fit snugly into pockets on either side of the bladder and a small but solid sandbag that secured to Velcro at the bottom of the belly. Amazingly enough, it simulated the pressure on the bladder, the hot flashes, the loss of balance, and the weight of a pregnancy. The girls would wear the belly for several hours while they went about their day – doing chores, homework, or getting ready for bed. Three activities were required while "pregnant" -walking up and down the stairs, looking in the mirror, laying down, and getting back up again.

~ A client with the Empathy BellyTM on

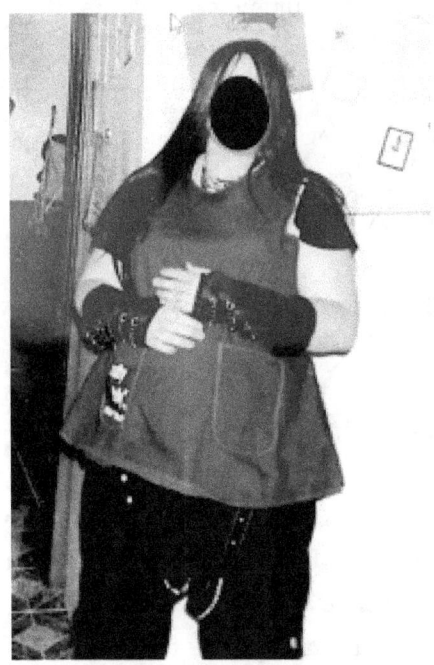

~ More clients showing off their
"pregnant" belly

We added more speakers as it seemed they captured the girls' attention, other field trips and written assignments. The girls relished outside contact. It was a break from their normal routine of groups and interacting primarily with each other and the staff. Outside speakers sometimes lent more credibility with their messages (versus us who were obviously out to make their lives miserable).

Two of the key assignments revolved around their perceptions of teenage parenting. Before they began the program, an essay on their "fantasy" about having a baby was due. On the last day of the program, a similar essay on the "reality" of having a baby was due. We often read both assignments aloud at the end to highlight the always obvious differences in the two assignments.

After the first year, we decided to add one more activity in order to recognize the hard work the girls did by participating in this program, while still keeping true to our message. We introduced the "Celibacy Celebration." This involved a night out for the girls to someplace that they could celebrate the fact that they were still children themselves. A oath to celibacy was not required. Usually, we went out for pizza and to a local arcade or game place where the now non-sleep-deprived non-mothers were very happy to be focusing on their own happiness and wants.

Throughout those first ten years we constantly tweaked, adjusted, and sought ways to make the program better. We ended up catching the eye of the company that created the infant simulators, Reality Works (formerly Baby Think it Over), who contacted us, intrigued by the fact that we were not a school who sent the babies home for the weekend, but in fact, had a sophisticated twelve-day intensive curriculum featuring the babies at the core. The other component that made us unique was that we had a chance to observe and teach over all twenty-four hours of the day. The "mommies" and the "babies" were never without supervision. This created, they said, an ideal situation in which to test new products.

We accepted Reality Work's offer to serve as a test site and in turn, received new, more sophisticated generations of the babies, and new computer software that helped us better track the scores of the "mothers." This developed into such a good relationship that we ended up being featured in the international promotional DVD of their products.

This opportunity did cause a bit of a circus around the group home when during the regular program, there were film crews and people being interviewed. Fortunately, parents of most of the clients gave permission for their girls to be involved and the girls did a fabulous job in their interviews talking about how much this affected them and what they had learned.

The program was truly an evolution and a joy to watch develop from its start to the lengths it grew. To see the light bulb come on in an adolescent's mind that will truly change her life is the greatest reward we could have received. Not only has her life changed, but that of her future children.

—Lessons Learned—

Danel

A Baby Think it Over™ story that pulled at my heartstrings was during the Sunday afternoon when I facilitated a "patterns" group for our young ladies as they looked at parenting styles in preparation for "giving birth" to their "babies". As I created a beaded necklace, the girls noted the pattern that was forming, and some were quick to point out when I deviated from the established pattern.

As the girls were sharing about patterns that they wanted to keep and patterns that they wanted to break, one young lady with tears streaming down her face, sputtered, "How do I know how to parent -- I've been raised by group homes!" Unfortunately, this was not an uncommon phenomenon, abandoned children that would come to us with their entire life's possessions in cardboard boxes, plastic totes, lawn and garden bags, or even garbage bags.

This young lady was so afraid to care for her "baby" and seemed sure that she was doomed to fail – just as her mother had failed in being able to care for her. One night in the beginning of this particular BTIO session, when her baby was crying, she seemed to have so much anxiety and tears that she turned the baby over to the custody of the overnight staff. The staff team encouraged her to keep trying with her baby the following day, and by the end of the program she was averaging 90% on feedback from the baby for "cares." She was so proud of herself!

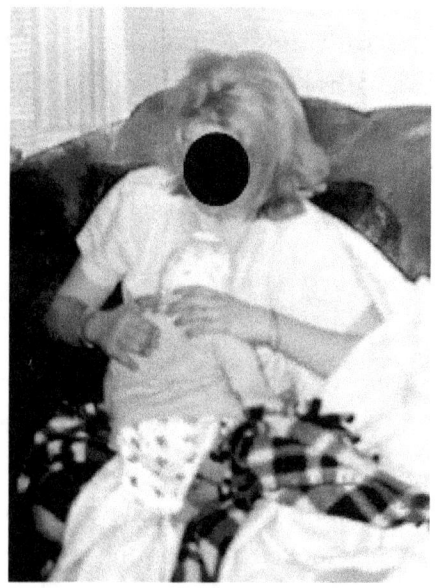

~ A sleepy ABC client holding her "baby"

That was the essence of the philosophy that CVC was founded upon, here was a child that had truly been dealt one of the worst hands of the many girls who had crossed our doorstep. She came to a gut-wrenching realization of what she had missed in life, but with the support and empathy (not pity) of a dedicated staff, she made a decision to do it differently. The effort this child made was as heroic as any war veteran I have encountered.

Each loving, nurturing gesture she made towards that simulated baby reminded her of what she hadn't had. She didn't use her past as an excuse to not make the effort as she well could have. She didn't use this experience to feed a victim mindset, instead she courageously stepped up to the plate and poured out her heart and her effort, motivated by her own mother's inability to provide the loving safe environment she deserved. In a very profound healing, she came to realize that it wasn't because she was unlovable that she had been abandoned by her family, but because of their choices, lifestyles, and priorities, they were unable to give her what she deserved.

It was not a complete deliverance, but in a very significant way the cradle that young woman will rock in the future will provide a gentler more loving mother than she was afforded. In keeping with our theme to make the child raising experience as real as possible, we quickly realized that we would need to come up with an intervention or response to when a client mistreated, neglected, or outright abused her child. This took several forms. In some cases, the offense was simply the result of ignorance and not having learned the appropriate way to parent or treat a baby. This we responded to with education. For example, when a "mother" would leave her baby unbuckled in the car seat and balance it precariously on the edge of the dining room table.

Another case was lack of effort. The "mother" was in too much of a rush or too tired to properly parent the infant. An example of this is waking up late for school and piling books and folders on top of the baby in the car seat in order to carry everything down the stairs for school to avoid having to make two trips. We would respond to this by redirecting the "parent" to a more appropriate way of handling her responsibilities in a manner that would not harm the baby.

The girls would have many learning experiences as parents. The electronic baby responded instantly and loudly if the head was not completely supported, as a newborn's head needs to be. The response the baby gave was to scream uncontrollably for about two minutes to let the mother know that they were hurt. Another often-experienced parenting error was when a girl was holding the baby in a nice cradle hold in one arm and did not realize that the baby's head extended from their arm a few inches. Thus, when they walked through a doorway the baby's head would smack, often quite audibly, against the door-frame, causing the impact sensor to register an abuse incident and the baby would cry loudly, again for about two minutes. Staff's reaction and response to these situations was minimal. Usually, the parent got instant feedback about their mistake from the baby that came through loud and clear and rarely was that mistake repeated.

Unfortunately, another type of lapse that happened was out-and-out neglectful or abusive behavior. In one case, a girl ran away, leaving her baby hidden in the bushes of the back yard in subfreezing weather. Of course, if it was a real baby, it might have died. Other cases occurred in which the baby was deliberately shaken in frustration registering on the impact sensor as a "shaken baby syndrome" incident. This, again, could kill or seriously injure an infant. A serious and lengthy education group was held on this topic prior to the girls receiving their babies.

These offenses of abuse or neglect were much harder to overlook and to do so would be detrimental to the program and any future child the client might have. These were perfect opportunities for a "real-life" learning experience – or as close to real life as we could make it. We worked together to devise a Child Protection Court, held at the group home. Other clients were cast in the roles of jury and a staff member played the judge. The neglectful parent was brought before the "court" to be confronted on her behaviors and how they affected others, specifically her child. At no time during the program or this exercise was the baby referred to as "it" or a doll. The "parent" was given a chance to respond to the and a ruling was made.

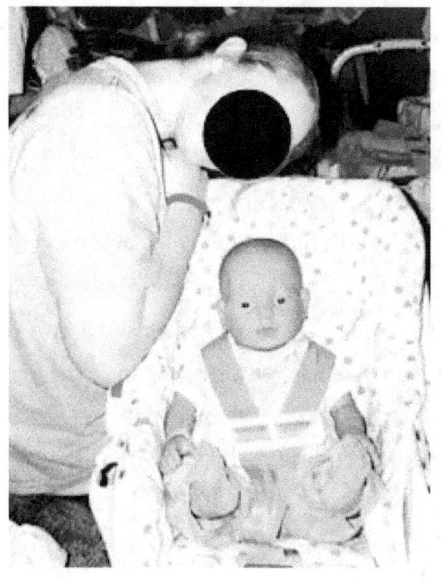

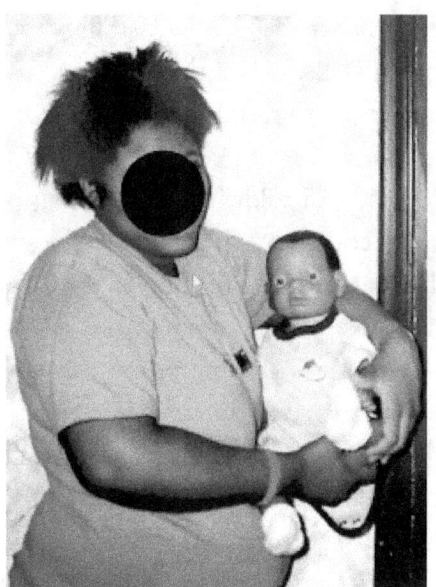

~ ABC clients with their "babies"

Of course, we approached this exercise as we did the entire program, with a nurturing kind of tough love. We *knew* caring for an infant was difficult. We *knew* the clients were not emotionally or psychologically mature enough to handle the twenty-four hour per day pressure of putting another, completely dependent, person's need above their own. We did not expect perfection or even competence at parenting a newborn. What we felt important to get across during the program is that each of the clients was *physically* mature enough to have sex, become pregnant and end up in the very situation we were asking them to simulate. In fact, most of the girls would freely admit, if not for some stroke of luck, they could have become pregnant by now. What we were successful in communicating to the girls with the groups, the speakers, the field trips, the babies, the budgeting, the homework, and the Child Protection Court, is that with continued high-risk behavior this situation could indeed become real for them.

In fact, we stressed repeatedly to the girls that this was not about making them never want to be parents. In fact, some of them had very good instincts and would make fine parents when they became adults. BTIO was not designed to be a scared straight type of program in which we only emphasized the bad things about parenting newborns. Of course there were good things. We presented both equally and realistically. One of the best clues there was to knowing if someone was going to be a good parent, I told them, was if that person understood that the best gift they could give their future child was to wait to have that child, until they could fully and completely care for him or her.

Slowly over the course of the days that they parented and attended groups a predictable change occurred in the attitude of the girls. Prior to receiving the babies, there was an air of excitement and anticipation. "Can I have a girl?" "I want twins." Requests came fast and furiously. Baby naming books were placed strategically about the house and girls made plans to babysit each other's babies.

"I watched my cousin after school for three years. This will be no problem." Confidence exuded from the house and in some of their minds, this program was a chance for them to show us that we were wrong – that they were perfectly capable of parenting – a classic win-lose situation.

At this point, we just smiled, nodded, and shared their excitement. The babies were "born" several days into the program and each girl was handed her randomly chosen infant (no requests were honored – you can't pick the gender in real-life). Squeals of delight erupted as the girls named their babies and filled out the birth certificates we provided. They compared infants and immediately began cooing over them and dressing them in the clothes they had purchased at our "Mall" with the dollars they were allotted from the budget exercise. Early on, wails were heard when a head wasn't supported, or a baby decided he was hungry in the middle of a complicated outfit the parent was putting on. There were a few tears from the more anxious girls in these early hours when things weren't going quite as expected or another girl made a nasty comment about another's parenting abilities. Excitement, adrenaline, and tensions ran high. We excused the girls from treatment work for the evening as they settled into their rooms with their babies to set up the nurseries (bassinets, blankets, and car seats).

Interestingly enough, several days into the parenting experience, a slightly different opinion would begin to emerge. As a day or two passed without showering, interrupted meals, and strange looks from people out in the community became a reality for the new "parents," the excitement and optimism waned.

"This isn't what it's *really* like!" "You set this baby on 'hard' on purpose." A cry went up about the unfairness of it all. We continued to reinforce the message that, yes, we knew parenting wasn't easy, but the babies were programmed randomly and followed a real infant's schedule. In fact, the recording of the cry was a real infant's cry. That it was okay if you were having trouble. It doesn't mean we win. We are here to help you learn as much as possible. This was a hard pill to swallow for some of them, as their baby's computers were read and they received their scores each night, a sullen attitude or tears could follow.

The computers embedded in the babies scored the girls in several different categories. The mothers were allowed two minutes to respond to a cry by figuring out what the baby needed. There were four choices:

bottle, diaper, rocking, or burping. A motion sensor determined if the mother was rocking to the satisfaction of the infant. If so, the baby responded by making cooing noises, burping, or breathing sounds to give the mother feedback. If the mother did not figure out what the baby needed within those two minutes, an episode of "neglect" would be recorded on the baby's computer. Though two minutes seems like a lot of time, neglects were frequent, especially for nighttime crying. Like real infants, these babies often had their days and nights mixed up the first few days.

In addition, the babies recorded the total number of minutes of crying time. Now this varied greatly from baby to baby depending on the temperament of the infant. However, if the baby was registering an inordinate amount of crying time in comparison to its "brother and sister" babies, we knew the baby might have been left to cry somewhere unattended. This proved a more useful tool during the outpatient sessions than during the sessions we held at the group home where we could supervise the interactions and baby care twenty-four hours a day.

Most telling were the "head support," "shaken baby," and "abuse" scores. Each time the head was not supported, the baby registered an "improper head support" incident. Each time the head went unsupported three times in two seconds, the baby registered a "shaken baby syndrome" incident. Each time a baby sustained a blow to its head or torso, the baby registered an instance of "abuse."

The scores were added up and privately reviewed with each mother each night with the goal of giving them feedback on how to improve in the care of their infant. Some girls took this feedback to heart and were determined to improve their scores. Some used it as an excuse to give up and repeat their mantra that somehow, we were trying to "trick" them into failing.

Towards the end of the seven or eight days we assigned the girls to care for the babies, a new tune was being sung by the majority of the girls: "I am never having sex again!" "This is totally not worth it." While gratifying to hear this, we knew the experience might fade if we did not reinforce what they learned and the feelings they were having at this moment. The last few days of the program consisted of the girls attending groups specifically designed to figure out *how*, exactly, they were not going to end up in this position. Peer pressure groups led to role-plays of turning down activities that were risky or dangerous. They taught how the girls could say no and still save face or "be cool." These role plays were discussed using scenarios the girls volunteered from their own lives. Values were discussed and reworked. Birth control and other resources were reviewed.

For these reasons, and the fact that we recognized the best people to speak about certain subjects were the experts themselves, as part of the Pregnancy Prevention Program curriculum, there were scheduled field trips led by experts and speakers we brought in. In the beginning, we started with just a few, but as they were so well received, we expanded the pool of speakers and soon had speakers on topics such as: car seats, shaken baby syndrome, child support, adoption, STDs, birth control, teen pregnancy, fetal alcohol syndrome, labor and delivery, and others.

~ ABC clients on a walk with their "babies."

—Listening to the Realities—

Danel

The speakers who came to the group home to talk to the girls were people in the local community who volunteered their time to help our clients get an understanding of how much is involved in parenting an infant, especially as a teenager. The labor and delivery speaker showed a video of an up close and personal real birth and had plastic props to show the baby emerging from the womb. The child support speaker conducted a mock child support interview and talked about how, unfortunately, only a fraction of the money owed is ever collected and given to the custodial parent. However, the speakers the girls liked the best were those that bravely told their own story.

The shaken baby syndrome speaker was a woman who had had a baby shaken by her day care provider. It was a testament to being aware of the damage shaking can cause as well as the wisdom of choosing a babysitter you can trust. After the slide show the girls were in tears. The two adoption speakers, who we usually tried to schedule on the same day, came at the topic from different directions, but always with the same message: adoption is a loving choice and gift you can give your child if you are not ready to parent. For some reason I have yet to figure out, the teenagers we had at the group home invariably were dead set against adoption and viewed it as a betrayal of sorts. Perhaps it was because the adolescents in placement with us usually had their own abandonment issues. Or perhaps, at their maturity level, they still saw the baby as a possession they wanted to own, rather than a person who needed a certain level of care to survive. Whatever the reason, the adoption speakers were able to at least plant a seed and make a dent in the idea of adoption as an act of disloyalty.

Lisa spoke from an adoptive mother's point of view, as she adopted two children, one an open adoption and one closed. Kelly and Sue spoke from the adopted child's point of view. Both had a unique point of view, so we tried to include both if possible. Kelly came from a family that adopted after they had three biological children, then went on to adopt a sibling set from Korea. Kelly found her biological mother while in her twenties and was very positive about her birth mother's decision. Sue was an identical twin who was adopted while her twin remained with the birth parent. Sue spoke about being grateful for the decision and finding out her sister did not fare so well, struggling in many areas of her life. She knows, but is not close to, her birth family.

We had a young mother of three girls that came in and spoke to the girls about the son that she had placed for adoption when she was sixteen. She and her now husband had conceived a child when they were teenagers and made the difficult but loving decision to choose the adoptive parents through open adoption. She shared her picture album of the photographs she received every year on his birthday. She shared the letter she wrote to him the day he left with his parents to go home. Their son was being raised with full knowledge of the circumstances of his birth, and that he had two sets of loving parents. The plan was for him to meet his birth parents when his adoptive family believed it to be the appropriate time. She was a very credible and genuine speaker. She graciously shared her story many times. We were grateful for her courage.

One of the most powerful speakers we brought on board was Christine, a former client who actually went through the Pregnancy Prevention Program herself. She completed the program but was unsuccessful at avoiding an untimely pregnancy as she had a baby at sixteen. Christine was one with aspirations and dreams and hopes of a happily-ever-after relationship with the baby's father. The father, an undocumented immigrant, was deported.

—Baby Think it Over™ in the Field—

Danel

The three field trips that were essential to the program were the labor and delivery field trip, where a nurse would lead the girls (who had not received their babies yet) through the labor and delivery ward of a local hospital. If we were lucky, there would be an actual delivery going on. While the girls were not allowed to be present for the delivery, there was a time or two when they returned wide-eyed to report the screams and other sounds of distress they had heard. The nurse, a very dynamic woman who was an exceptionally good educator, would enthusiastically choose a "volunteer" from our crowd to demonstrate different labor positions and breathing techniques, including hopping onto a bed, legs spread and "pushing," while other girls would be labor coaches. Despite the giggling, the girls sensed the excitement and drama and got into their roles.

They went onto the nursery and viewed the newborns there, oohed and aahed at their tiny feet, wisps of hair, scrunched up faces, and stumpy belly buttons. By this time, they were getting pretty excited about their whole pending experience and would begin asking *WHEN* exactly would they get their babies.

"We don't know," we would tell them. "Your due date is only a guess by the doctor. When you go into labor is up to your body and the baby." Trusting the process was clearly outside of their comfort zone. For a group of adolescents who are used to doing what they want and controlling what happens in their environment, the powerlessness could be unbearable.

Another outing we scheduled soon after they received their babies was a trip to the WIC office. The Women, Infant and Children program was a county run nutrition and food subsidy program designed to offer women who were pregnant or had children under the age of five grocery supplements of healthy, nutrition-packed food items to ensure proper growth and development despite low income. The girls heard "free food!" Now this was something to get excited about. The chattering settled down a bit after we handed out the ten-page application form to fill out.

They dutifully bundled up all of the babies into the properly installed car seats and headed over to the WIC office (during a time there were no clients scheduled) to register the babies and hear about how to enroll in the program. Sometimes the presenters would covertly ask me if I wanted them to talk about the program in such a way that it seemed negative or undesirable. They were concerned about the excitement of the girls and worried we were encouraging them to want to have children at an early age if they saw all of the perks they may be able to get. I reassured them that it was okay to present the program exactly as they would to a new client.

The girls had a knack for telling if we were glossing over something or spinning the truth for our own purposes. Much better to present everything – the good, the bad, and the ugly (which was sure to come in a few days) - and let them make their own decisions with all of the accurate information. After all, they were going to make their own decisions anyway. We could only hope to influence them with the truth.

After both being weighed and measured (babies AND the girls), the girls watched a video about nutrition and were told about the expected meetings, weigh-ins, and paperwork expected for participation in the program. They also found out, to their dismay, that not all food items were WIC –approved. Only certain nutritionally sound items qualified to be bought with their WIC coupons. The logistics of the purchasing were a hard swallow for the girls as well. All WIC items needed to be separated from the rest and purchased separately with the WIC coupons before the rest of their groceries were purchased. For anyone, but especially a teenager, this spelled embarrassment. Hmmmm....this was looking less appealing as the field trip wore on. The girls left with handfuls of pamphlets about nutrition and breastfeeding and thoughtful expressions.

One field trip that was planned with purpose and good intentions, but never got off the ground, eventually being eliminated, was a trip to Child Support court to watch the (mostly) fathers show up (or not) to face charges of failing to pay child support. So many of the girls had fantasies about both the state of their relationship with the baby's father and their finances that even showing them the statistics did not deter them from thinking they were going to be the exception to the rule.

"We will be together always and love each other and give our baby anything she needs because she deserves the best," wrote one 14-year-old participant who already picked out the father of her baby. While we did not contest that her baby would certainly deserve the best, we felt obligated to let her know in any way possible that the odds were against this particular fantasy coming true if she had a baby while she was still a teenager.

Therefore, off we went to Child Support court. Unfortunately, the men scheduled to appear proved our point by consistently not showing up. While it was a good lesson, it lacked the excitement and action to keep the girls engaged and we gave it up in favor of having the girls create a budget using statistics to determine whether the baby's father was going to contribute any money towards the child rearing costs.

Our final field trip prior to the birth of their child was scheduled as part of the budget assignment; the girls were required to figure out how much they could afford to spend on baby items and costs of raising an infant. They were given the option of working full-time and not going to school or working part-time and finishing high school. They had to pick a job that they could realistically get considering their age and experience and use the wage that was being paid for that kind of position. They also chose whether they were going to breastfeed or bottle-feed, how often they would do laundry, and how important certain "extras" were to them, such as cable TV or cigarettes. Everyone picked a card that indicated whether the father of the baby was involved and whether he contributed any money toward the budget. Despite their fantasies, that was what they used for their budget.

With notebooks and worksheets in hand, we caravanned to the local discount retail store to itemize our necessary items – car seat, formula, diapers, wipes...was a baby bathtub really necessary?? "No, but it is very helpful." "Yes, you do need winter outwear for your baby. We live in Wisconsin." Staff was on hand to answer questions and help them price the items. Once the worksheets were filled out, we headed home to finish the assignment.

Calculators came out and compromises were made as the girls tried to get their budget to fit the dollars they had available. Promises to quit smoking and breastfeed were common as they shaved off dollars to remain in the black at the end of the month. When the dust settled, we hit them with one more shocker. Pick another budget surprise card. "Unexpected $100 car repair bill," "Prescription for an ear infection – $20," or "Receive $50 as a baby shower gift" were handed out to the girls and back to the drawing board they went.

After the budget was completed and approved by the staff (no 16-year-old was going to be earning $15 dollars an hour in the year 2000), the staff highlighted the amount of money they had budgeted to spend on clothing and led them into the "Mall" we had created in another building on campus. The "Mall" was carefully set up with donated clothing separated into three wings. One wing we labeled "Baby Gap", another "ShopKo," and the third, "Goodwill." Clothing was sorted and priced accordingly. Initially all of the girls swarmed the "Baby Gap" table with all of the cute, in-style clothes. Reality hit when they saw the prices. They were given a list of the minimum items they needed to purchase and were left alone to shop. The only requirement was that the minimum amount of clothing they needed fit into their own personal budget they had created. It was a fantastic hands-on experiential exercise. The girls loved it. Though some were disappointed they could not buy everything they wanted, most were very careful shoppers and made their dollars go far.

Once stocked, the girls were ready to receive their babies. We started to call for the girls one at a time to another room, the "delivery" room, where I had donned scrubs and was passing out their newborn babies.

—On the Front Line of Baby Think it Over™—

Danel

Some scenarios we could not script if we tried, though we've had enough years in to know that anything can happen, and you cannot predict how other people may react to something you find completely normal. Electronic babies for instance. One way to make two weeks of multiple screaming babies and multiple surly, unwashed teenage girls bearable is to recount the humorous stories that inevitably accumulate over the years.

One of our favorite stories came out of the outpatient program for girls held on campus. Each day girls would come to a day treatment setting for groups, speakers, and activities revolving around the realities of teen parenting. Each afternoon they would leave with their "baby" to parent in their homes as staff held their collective breath that they (both babies and girls) would return the next day unharmed and in one piece. This particular time we had eight girls participating, referred through their delinquency Case Workers, their parents, and their schools. All were identified as high risk for becoming pregnant while in their teens. In fact, some had indicated themselves that they were trying to get pregnant because they thought having a baby sounded like fun and felt they were definitely ready for the challenge, citing babysitting a younger sibling as their experience and expertise in this area.

Most began the program with an excitement that gradually wore off as the demands grew greater and more grueling. The girls had different ways to cope with these feelings of being overwhelmed and exhausted. Some cried; most cried. Since we did not have the luxury of 24-hour supervision in this case, we watched them carefully for signs of self-harm or drug and alcohol use, some of their typical coping patterns. In one instance, one of the outpatient girls ran away. Running away is a "fight or flight" reaction typical when a person feels cornered with no way out, a not uncommon feeling for a new parent, especially a teen. This afternoon, we began group short one client. Querying the others, we discovered no new information as to where she could be, and no one answered at her home. Unfortunately, this was a Friday afternoon, our last session for the week, and we would not reconvene till Monday.

Getting no answer at the Case Worker's office, we resigned ourselves to the fact that we would probably not know what happened until Monday at the earliest, when we were next scheduled to meet.

Monday came, but before the afternoon session of the program began, a phone call came into the group home. I watched the staff member who answered the phone, as she appeared confused. I was able to make out that the phone call somehow had to do with babies, so I stuck around, sure I would end up taking the call. The staff member's confusion heightened, then blossomed into amusement as she handed the phone over to me saying only, "You gotta hear this."

"Hello. This is Stephen from the Outagamie County shelter care."

"Yes, how can I help you?"

"We think we have one of your babies here," Stephen told me. "It won't shut off and we don't know what to do. Can you come get it?"

As it turns out the saga of this particular faux infant led him on quite a journey. Our no-show from the Friday before had apparently ran away, leaving the baby behind. She didn't think to leave the "key" with the baby, (the sensor the teens wore around their wrists to let the baby know the right mother is taking care of it). So, she ran, with the key fastened to her wrist by a hospital band. Now, without the key, the baby cannot be silenced, as it will not recognize anyone besides Mom trying to care for it. This is very helpful when you have a teenager trying to avoid parenting duties, but unhelpful in this situation. So, without any recourse, the shelter care staff simply had to let the baby cry.

The teen and parents had co-signed an agreement that they would need to pay for any damage incurred to the baby. Since the battery compartment was tamper proof it was not possible to shut down the baby without damage. By the time the police arrived at the home to take the runaway report, they found a flustered set of parents with a crying electronic baby who were anxious to resign as grandparents. The police assumed that Candlelight Vision Corp. was an outpatient clinic and would be closed until Monday, so the police took the baby into custody and placed it in shelter care. The shelter care staff had apparently tried to care for the baby all weekend to no avail (the batteries were still strong on Monday morning), and the baby continued to scream all weekend. They finally called us, thinking we were now open for business. Bringing the remote to turn off the simulator, we retrieved the baby from the desperate shelter care staff and returned it to our collection. The girl never returned to our pregnancy prevention program, Although, when the police caught up to her some time later, she was brought to the same shelter care her baby resided at.

Another real-life learning experience that is realized quite often is keeping track of your things with a baby is essential to reduce stress. We had closed up for the night after an Outpatient program had finished their groups and as Mary Kay was locking the doors, a car pulled into the driveway next to the building. A harried looking woman stepped out of the car almost before it had stopped moving, while a curly haired girl with her head down remained in the passenger seat. The familiar sound of a wailing baby filled the air when the car door opened.

"Get out here!" yelled the woman, apparently the girl's mother.

The girl stepped reluctantly out of the car.

"Tell her," the woman demanded.

Mary Kay listened while the girl explained that she was in the Pregnancy Prevention outpatient program and had lost a diaper for her baby. The babies come with diapers with sensors sewn into the lining, so the baby knows if the "clean" diaper is on, or if the mother is simply replacing the "dirty" diaper. Though no bodily fluids actually emerge from the baby, it will cry until it has the correct diaper on. Each girl is issued two diapers. She had lost one and the baby was letting her know it was wet. The girl's mother interrupted several times to make the point that a new diaper was needed ASAP. The girl was close to tears and the baby continued to wail.

"Well," said Mary Kay. "You could come upstairs and we can see what we have."

Everyone trooped up the stairs after Mary Kay sent the girl back to the car for the baby so it would not be left alone. Mary Kay sat the trio down and went into the storage closet, rummaging around for a bit before coming up with a diaper with the correct sensor in it.

"Oh, thank God," stated the mother. The girl looked brighter as well.

"That will be six dollars," said Mary Kay.

They both froze.

"What?" said the girl, sneaking a peek at her mother who seemed to be escalating in frustration again.

"Well," said Mary Kay," If you run out of diapers when you have a baby what do you do?"

"Buy some more," said the girl after a long pause.

"Welcome to CVC – Mart."

Mary Kay then spoke to the mother to suggest she pay for the diaper and have her daughter make a payment plan for how she would pay her back since the baby was her responsibility. The mother, daughter, and baby left the campus with the baby now quieted. Soon afterwards the diaper appeared and was returned. We surreptitiously paid the mother back her six dollars and called it a lesson learned.

Sometimes the clients were more clever than we gave them credit for as one found out how to bypass the bottle sensor by placing a diaper flat across the baby's mouth with the diaper sensor connecting to the feeding sensor. This was a loophole in the baby's computerized system and allowed the parenting teen to simply lay a diaper on the baby's mouth during the night if the baby requested feeding rather than getting up and feeding the baby. This bit of feedback was given to the Reality Works company which refined the sensors in the next generation of simulators it produced.

29

Overcoming County Concerns

Mary Kay

Overall, the policies CVC created in order to work with girls through their unhealthy patterns served the clients well and gave CVC the reputation for being a placement that was meant to last throughout the good times and bad until resolution could be found, and healthier patterns could be developed.

However, a county department that placed a significant percentage of our clients was led by a woman named Trisha. Trisha developed a concern that eventually led to several clients being pulled from the group home prematurely and placed elsewhere in an untimely manner and definitely not in the best interest of the clients' treatment goals. Trisha approached CVC to question parts of CVC's program, specifically a perceived conflict of interest with Mary Kay being the founder as well as the person conducting family restructuring sessions (family therapy). Without any concrete evidence to point to, she mused that surely a person would be tempted as a counselor to recommend the client stay in placement for a longer time than needed for financial gain. CVC countered citing one of the very things that kept us unique and able to treat hard-to-place adolescents was the fact that we hung in there with them throughout the tough times. This was one time when our policy of "stubbornness" was misinterpreted and hurt us, temporarily at least.

From the onset, CVC decided to meet increased scrutiny and rigid State licensing criteria to avoid having any one county having too much power to compromise our program. By working with all counties, we attempted to insulate ourselves from political frays and power struggles that threatened the autonomy of our philosophical base.

Trisha, however, had enough political power within the county to execute the decision to remove the clients from CVC's care despite several attempts by CVC to negotiate, and re-assure county personnel that we had both internal and outside accountability. Nothing short of re-structuring our program to Trisha's specifications was going to be acceptable. We decided to respectfully refuse to alter the basic tenets of our program.

Unfortunately, four girls were removed and sent home prematurely or to another placement outside of the community. The decision to not compromise the integrity of the program by bowing to one county's unreasonable demands, although one of the most stressful and costly in CVC's history, was the right decision. Unfortunately, we lived with the remorse of the treatment impact for the four girls caught in the cross-fire. Several more meetings were conducted and eventually Trisha stood alone on this issue within the county. She subsequently left on medical leave for serious health issues and was out for quite a while.

During this time, the county began placing clients at CVC again with successful results. Trisha did eventually return to her role within the county, however, having survived a strenuous treatment for cancer seemed to have either mellowed her on her position of wanting to determine our programming, or she found other more lucrative polit-ical fish to fry. After moving into another position at the county, she eventually left.

The four county placements were sadly not the only casualties of that power struggle. Approximately three years later we received a referral to our transitional living program, TLC^2 from a neighboring county. After chatting and conducting the usual conversation:

"Yes, we have beds, can you tell me a little about the client."

"She's 17 living with her mom and stepdad."

"What kind of issues is she having?"

"There have been some physical fights between her and her parents, running away; the police have been called several times when things have been broken."

"Anything else I need to know?

"Well, you might know the mother."

"Oh?"

"Trisha _____ says we can't place her daughter there because it would be a conflict of interest since she licensed you to begin with. Is that true?"

Well, of course it was not true. Trisha had merely been a referral source and then not a referral source at all. Her daughter was, however, welcome at TLC^2 as she met all the placement criteria. The placement never materialized. Perhaps the county changed its mind; perhaps, Trisha was unable to resolve her personal history of conflict with CVC Administration. Whatever the reason, we considered this yet another casualty of a senseless power struggle, another missed opportunity for a hurting child and family to heal and have a healthier future. What a reminder of how interconnected our circles of life in this world can be, and how decisions, no matter how right or wrong, remain a part of our past and can sometimes carry significant consequences into our futures.

30

The Hats

Danel

While most of our time at the group home was spent dealing with up to 14 adolescent girls and the various problems, conflicts, moods, and behaviors each day, we also had an assembly of staff members to manage. Staff management at a twenty-four-hour organization brings its own issues including scheduling, time off requests, staff conflicts, and disagreements over how to best handle a client, work performance, and keeping everyone on board with state licensing requirements, to name just a few.

For the most part, we expected staff to handle themselves in the same way we expected the girls to handle themselves. In other words, part of their job was to be a good role model and practice the skills they taught, even if the girls were not present. The majority of the staff had no problems with this expectation, and we strived to handle conflicts directly and respectfully.

However, there were times that this simply did not happen, or times where staff were stuck at an impasse with resolution being nowhere in sight. Because of the caring and emotive nature of most of the staff, conflicts tended to come up over decisions about clients. Hashing it out at staffing seemed somewhat effective but was often reduced to repeating the same information over and over with no compromise being sought. Problem-solving was lengthy.

~ Two staff members of ABC and TLC2

While surfing the internet, we hit upon a solution with the discovery of "The Six Thinking Hats" created by Edward de Bono. The

Hats were a tool meant to assist groups in making reasonable and efficient decisions that everyone could live with. The concept was to leave no stone unturned while simultaneously disallowing repetitive or unhelpful statements. The Hats could hopefully keep us on track and at least make a completely informed decision, even if everyone did not agree with it.

We decided to try it. Now, change is a mysterious thing. It is always happening, yet most people are very uncomfortable and resist it. When we introduced the Hats, there was some resistance and doubts expressed. It seemed like more work, and it certainly was outside most of our comfort zones. Nevertheless, we plowed forward, determined to improve our decision-making process.

We set out six popsicle sticks on the table with pictures of differently colored hats stuck to the top of each stick. Each "hat" represented a certain type of statement a person could make. No other types of statements were allowed when holding that hat. For example, the White Hat represented data, facts, and measurable things. "Sarah ran away four times last month." That is measurable. Not, "I can't believe Sarah ran away so many times last month, she obviously is trying to send her mother a message." That is an assumption.

The White Hat always comes first and it's helpful if someone takes notes. Collecting all the facts takes the whole team, and it was our policy to ask everyone to participate in every color hat, regardless of what their views were. This was harder for the hats that came later.

After the White Hat came the Yellow Hat, the optimistic, positive, pros hat. What is good about an idea? How will it help us? Statements like "Sarah should be discharged because it will benefit her to be in a more secure placement to keep her safe." Or "Sarah's discharge may have a positive effect on the other girls as staff will have more time to give them." Staff members opposing Sarah's discharge may be hard pressed to find a pro about something they disagree with, but we strongly encouraged staff to offer something for each position.

~Staff members at a CVC talent show

The Black Hat followed the Yellow Hat and symbolized pessimism, the downside or the con to the issue. This was sometimes called the devil's advocate. "Sarah should not be discharged because our philosophy is that we do not give up on kids." Or "Allowing Sarah to stay could help us have more time to connect and work with her family which will ultimately benefit her."

Red Hat time was everyone's favorite. Only here were we allowed to state our emotions, our gut instinct, or our first reaction. No reason was necessary, no facts were needed. "I just hate it that she is getting away with running away so much." Or "I just know this kid has a chance. I can feel it." Red Hat generally took a while but was well worth it as we could acknowledge the feelings involved in the decision, but not be overwhelmed or controlled by them.

The Green Hat was next and was the meat and potatoes of what we were doing. After all the pros and cons were voiced and emotions vented, it was time to problem-solve. During the Green Hat time, only suggestions, solutions, or compromises could be made. Again, it was helpful if someone took notes, and we could hash out a reasonable compromise that seemed best for the client based on everyone's input.

The final Hat did not fall into a certain order but was a moderator's hat. Anyone could pick up the Blue Hat at any time to keep us on track. "I think that what you are saying is more Yellow Hat, than Green Hat. Could we stick to solutions, please?"

Now this process took time, sometimes lots of time. It did not always go as planned and there was some resistance every time the staff saw me reach into the closet and take out the popsicle sticks. However, it was unmistakable that we were making clearer and more professional decisions about the girls. It was clear that there was less infighting and jockeying for position when we discussed emotionally charged issues. Undeniably, the process worked, and for that, it was worth it.

31

Unexpected Events

Danel

We are well aware the group home life can lead to and create its own adventures, chaos, and general craziness. However, we cannot take credit for all chaos and adventures that ultimately find us. Some simply appear without regard to who we are or what we do but seem to intertwine together in mysterious manners that sometimes stumped even us.

At one point in time we were anxiously seeking the return of a longer-term runaway. This client was gone much longer than a usual runaway, and concern was beginning to arise about her safety. One afternoon the second shift staff returned giggling from the transitional group home's (TLC^2) basement, which was accessible only via the exterior garage. She reported that one of the mattresses we had stored in the basement was down and there were blankets strewn about. She also noted several food wrappers, leaving the impression that someone was using the basement for a safe house or sanctuary and was not interested in paying rent. We assumed our runaway didn't want to be far away from home and it was her resting her weary bones in the basement. We even left her a note of a pending court date she was required to appear at, lest a warrant be issued. We will never know for sure if it was really her, as she was later apprehended several weeks after being discharged from CVC.

During approximately the same period, we saw a crisp fall day whipping the leaves to the ground piling up against fences and doorsteps. Late afternoon was giving way to dusk as the fall season afforded us less and less daylight. All the girls were behaving well that day and packing up their notebooks to ready themselves for a process group starting in a few minutes. Process group is a type of group therapy where staff or client-selected issues are processed, and feelings expressed in order to gain insight into how they interact with others and the effect this has on them and the other person. It is an excellent process for relationship building. I was in the office chatting with Mary Kay about group topics and the direction we would like to take the girls that day, when a staff member came running up to the office door and stated, "We need you, Mary Kay," (an oft heard phrase over the years). She was winded and gasping for air having come from the opposite end of campus, behind TLC^2, where she had been unloading and rearranging several bigger furniture items in the TLC^2 basement and garage, which were being used for storage at that time.

"What's up?" asked Mary Kay, used to last minute needs and interruptions.

"Someone ran into the garage. WITH A CAR!" replied the staff member.

"I've got group," I stated, letting her go, picturing an interloper on campus, perhaps a runaway or someone that the girls had planned to meet up with. I knew Mary Kay would make short work of the situation and probably join me before we were halfway through the group.

Mary Kay

You did not have to get too far downwind to come to the instant conclusion about why it took the garage to stop her. As a woman climbed out of her car, it was obvious she was intoxicated. However, we were quickly distracted by the contents of her car. There was the immediate question of where she sat in this vehicle.

The rusty white four-door sedan with a large crack in the windshield was packed with numerous household items, appliances, bedding, tools, and clothing. The trunk was tied shut with a lawnmower hanging off the trailer hitch, a microwave tied to the top of the lawnmower supposedly, to stabilize the lawnmower that balanced precariously on the hitch. Garden rakes were propped up on one side with a shovel on the other. There were gas cans and kitchen chairs, an electric chainsaw, and a weed eater in the backseat, along with numerous items we recognized from the basement at TLC^2.

The woman had driven up the driveway and had not stopped for whatever reason at the end of the driveway, but had taken a sharp right turn, narrowly missing our industrial-sized fenced in dumpster, and plowed into the side of the garage, denting the siding and ultimately stopping her car.

You would anticipate that when a person plows into your garage, they might approach you with some kind of remorse, or at least some minor embarrassment. While we were evaluating the wide array of contents of the car, this woman was obviously offended that we were interested in the location and contents of her car. She expressed her sentiments in a very hostile way using many X-rated phrases.

A staff person immediately left to call the police. We recognized a few of the objects in the car, including a blanket. We had some concerns, although we couldn't substantiate them, that the toolbox might belong to the contractor that had recently been pouring concrete and had left his tools in the garage. There was also a flowerpot we strongly believed belonged to CVC. While evaluating the contents of her car, we began to wonder if this wasn't the person sleeping in the basement of TLC^2 rather than the runaway client we originally suspected.

With her alcohol-induced rage still going strong, she greeted the Neenah Police officer much the same way as she greeted us. By this time neighbors, too, were observing the commotion from their backyards. Our staff was trying to occupy the clients that were now out of group, and we suggested to the staff that they take the girls off campus. If the neighbors were concerned about the noise level, the whole block prob-ably became concerned when we suggested to the officer that some of the things in her car might belong to us and we suspected this woman had been sleeping in our basement without invitation. She became fur-ther enraged using profane language, tearing out things from her car, pointing out cigarette burns on the blanket we identified, and throwing things from her car all over the lawn. The officer, and frankly, us as well, were more interested in quelling the storm rather than pushing the issue of ownership. There was nothing in that car worth this kind of continued escalation.

The officer spoke with the intoxicated, raging woman and allowed her to leave the premises to retrieve a truck to load her things appropri-ately and legally. She and the police officer both left the property with no tickets issued, no DUI, no criminal damage to property, no posses-sion of stolen property, nothing! The officer did share that the woman's partner was affiliated with a notorious and violent biker gang that could prove to be a threat to her and to our facilities. It appeared to me he was suggesting not making a lot of waves and letting this girlfriend clean up and disappear so as not to bring attention of our agency to this gang and its members. He supposed aloud that she could very likely have been sleeping in the basement, entering through the outside access door to hide from her partner. This relationship was obviously well-known to the police, and we awaited the next chapter.

She returned, still intoxicated if not more so, about three hours later and driving a truck. She had a very difficult time getting the objects from the car into the truck. Given the information shared with us, we were more than anxious to assist her in hastening her exit. After her truck was filled, she precariously backed out, missing the corner of the house by a quarter inch, swerved down the driveway, and continued to swerve into the horizon. The car remained for another three days at which time she returned with her insurance information and drove the damaged car out of the corner of the damaged garage and down the driveway, a good distance from the house this time. We can only hope this woman found the help she needed to cease running from her danger and creating it for others. We, by the way, put a lock on the basement door and avoided further visits by strange interlopers in need of refuge.

32

A Surprise from the Photo-Mat

Mary Kay

A bit of history, pre-dating the beginning days of the opening of our very first house is necessary to thoroughly comprehend the panic and wave of emotions that ensued following this gruesome discovery.

Prior to our opening, there had been a very newsworthy and shocking discovery in the surrounding community. A state-licensed facility for juvenile troubled boys, well recognized by the county it served, was exposed for abuses by the owner towards his employees and the clients. It was revealed that the well-respected owner had been grooming and videotaping lewd and lascivious behaviors with the young clients placed in his care by several counties. The investigation had also revealed that there were cameras in all the bathrooms, including those used by staff members. Needless to say, this was big news for a long time.

As the 94 counts of abuse he was charged with wound its way through the system and wreaked havoc with the county that had licensed him, scrutiny rained down upon us as we journeyed through the licensing process for the opening of A Better Choice Group Home for juvenile delinquent girls. The similarities in our populations were not lost on our licensors, our prospective referral sources, or us. We needed to meet and exceed the highest standards and expectations, lest we be painted with the same brush.

Shortly after we did achieve licensing I took a walk with one of our young residents to the local drugstore. I was anxiously anticipating picking up a roll of film at the photo counter that I expected to be from a baby shower that the girls had thrown for a staff person. They had done this as part of an independent living exercise. The girls were given an allotment of money and had to plan the shower, invite the guests, and buy the gifts. Providing the girls with the opportunity to develop the ability to work together, develop empathy, time-management and budgeting skills while developing rapport and hopefully some social graces. The event was a great success. The girls felt great about it, and the pictures would be proof positive of what a good job they had done.

I had found the film while cleaning the office the week before. It had been sitting on the desk for some time and the discovery prompted me to get the film developed immediately. It had become necessary to clean the office because we had recently had a rash of runaways that had returned to the group home. It was standard policy to pack up the belongings of the client who had run away to deter theft and to see if there was anything that may give us a clue to their whereabouts. In addition, when they returned, all of their belongings were confiscated, and they were given pajamas to wear as a deterrent from continued runaway behavior. All of this was done with the client's safety as the goal. Now, mind you, everything except the changing into pajamas was done in the front office, a generous sized room, but not big enough to be a storage facility. When we had more than one runaway, things piled up.

Oftentimes, when a client needed individual attention, we would invite them on a walk to get them away from the hustle and bustle of an adolescent-filled house. That was the case this afternoon. With film in hand, I approached a teary young lady who was asking for individual attention and said, "Sure, let's go for a walk. I want to pick up some pictures." Out the front door we went, and I listened all the way there.

Picking up the pictures and checking out was uneventful. In hindsight, surprisingly uneventful. I continued to listen to the young lady after we left the store and absentmindedly opened the envelope to glance at the pictures – I'm not very good at delayed gratification. *"Oh my God. Oh my God. Oh. My. God!"* I was no longer listening to the client who continued to talk beside me. I don't think I was breathing. In retrospect, I don't know how my legs continued to carry me around the block with that young lady continuing to carry on beside me. With each picture I looked at, my heart beat faster and faster. My mind was going a thousand miles an hour. *"Where were these pictures taken?"* I was looking for familiar things in the background. I sure did not want to look at the shockingly disturbing images in the foreground. I occasionally responded with open questions or responses to the young lady beside me to avoid letting her see my escalating panic.

We had finally rounded the corner and the group home was in sight. I was grateful to see the van full of girls just getting ready to pull out of the driveway. I flagged down the staff person driving and quickly hustled the client into the van with everyone else. Now, with time to breathe and collect my thoughts, I once again viewed the pictures in my hand and realized this was not a nightmare. I really was in possession of some terrifically graphic child pornography pictures. Each one was worse than the next. It suddenly hit me that I recognized at least one of the subjects in the photos, a past client. The panic hit again with this realization.

I picked up the portable telephone and thought, *"Where the Hell do I start? Who do I call first?"*

The recent scandal in the community flashed through my mind all over again. *"How could I defend myself? Why weren't the police at the drug store? How could they even develop them? Were the police on their way over? Were they going to set up a sting?"* My mind was going wild. The thoughts were spilling over each other and racing.

When I was able to settle my thoughts down, I realized the film I originally thought I had must have been mixed up with some of the confiscated belongings that had been kept in the office. As I regained my composure, I realized that we had to do what we would expect anyone else to do – be honest and make a police report. I cannot tell you what order I made the calls in, but I called the county abuse and neglect hotline, and the police liaison in charge of sexual abuse investigations. Luckily, we had a positive reputation and a good relationship with both of these people as well as a good work history with both departments.

The police liaison to social services came immediately over to the house. Bless his soul – first, he comforted me and assured me he knew this was not the same situation that had previously taken place in the other community. Then he very anxiously and carefully examined the pictures.

He knew almost immediately where the pictures had been taken – at a home not unfamiliar to the sexual abuse investigators in an adjoining community. He took into evidence the offensive pictures with hopes that they might help him solidify the growing case against this pedophile. Obviously, someone in our care had been the victim of this disgusting degenerate. Unfortunately, she was no longer placed with us so that was the last we heard about the case and to this day I am unsure of whether that man was ever prosecuted for this or any other crime.

I was just glad to be rid of the pictures. To top it all off, I never did find the pictures of the baby shower. Just my luck. I certainly could have used something else to replace those pictures in my mind.

33 |

Unusual Antics

Mary Kay

The nature of the group home business with a constantly changing cast of characters lends itself to stories that are off-the-wall, heart wrenching, unbelievable, or funny, but never mundane.

—Rae—

Rae was a young lady from a nearby county, but one that did not place adolescents in group homes very often, instead preferring to use foster homes even for children with out-of-control behaviors, and then advocating for placement in corrections should these placements fall through. It was not a philosophy we agreed with as it often set up the child with higher needs for failure in the foster care system and then to be exposed to and possibly learn worse behaviors in the corrections system. Not to mention being unfair to the county foster homes. A possible reason for this strategy was that foster care reimbursement was significantly less than group home reimbursement as there was no paid staff, treatment plans, or other services the kids received in group home care. While a bed at Southern Oaks Girls' School certainly was not cheap, the state of Wisconsin would reimburse the county for a portion of the costs incurred when a child was placed there. This strategy may have been good for the pocketbook but did not always prove successful for the children they were serving.

The group home setting offered a nice compromise as a less restrictive setting, yet a higher level of care than foster care. So, when we received Rae's referral from this county, we knew this would be an unusual child, one that even the higher-ups at the county did not feel would make it in foster care. Yet they probably didn't have enough criminal history to place her straight into corrections. With this grain of salt, we interviewed Rae and, though we found her a bit off, we liked her and felt she could do well with us.

Rae was very pretty with flowing dark brown wavy hair. Tall and mature looking, the other girls initially clamored to be her friend. Rae soon proved to lack a few of the basic social skills that would be required to keep these friendships afloat. She displayed hyperactive behaviors, missed social cues, and laughed uproariously at things the other girls did not find funny. Because of her tenuous hold on friendships and difficulty with social interaction, Rae ended up appearing needy and could suffocate those around her for attention. The other girls began keeping their distance and Rae, feeling left out, escalated her attempts to capture their attention.

Unfortunately, the pattern of seeking attention in a negative way was so ingrained in Rae that it had become her default way of behaving rather than attempting to use the skills the staff were teaching her at ABC. In one case, during a staff meeting, we were treated to a display of Rae's attention seeking behaviors.

During staff meetings in the summer when the girls are home from school, we would have them go upstairs into the common area to read, work on treatment work, or, occasionally, watch a movie.

The staff would turn on a noise machine to drown out our conversations and assign one staff member to regularly check on the girls during the meeting. Usually, these times were incident free, and the girls enjoyed a bit of semi-unsupervised time while the staff was able to concentrate on house business. It was Leah's turn to make the trek up the stairs every 20 minutes or so.

Leah had been a Case Manager at ABC for over a year and knew her way around the clients and several effective tricks to ensure her visits were somewhat random, including avoiding the squeaky stair on the front staircase or using the back staircase occasionally. Leah had also seen a lot of unusual client behavior and was pretty good at maintaining her game face, as it were. It is a good skill in the field to not allow the clients to see that they have shocked you as this, in itself, is a reward and highly reinforcing even if they don't ultimately get what they are after.

Leah was gone a good deal longer than she usually was on this check and staff were beginning to speculate what was going on. Another staff member was just about to take leave of the meeting to check if she needed assistance when Leah reappeared looking a bit perturbed.

"I have never...I mean...I need to go to my happy place!" Leah stammered each word out.

Finally, she started laughing and spilled the story.

"So, I'm heading up the stairs and I hear some giggling and ruckus, so I know, you know, something's up," she began. "Well, I see most of the girls huddled on the couch when I got up there, and Rae standing up with her back towards me."

Leah paused here, the giggles starting to rise up. After she caught her breath, she continued,

"She was dancing. There was no music mind you, but it was some dirty dancing, bumping and grinding, all by herself. Since her back was towards me, the other girls saw me, but Rae didn't so she kept on. Once she noticed the girls had stopped laughing, she turned around and saw me, and I saw IT!"

"What did you see?" we wanted to know. What was going on?

Leah turned red but finished the story.

"She had stuffed two or three socks down her pants and was pretend-ing to dirty dance with herself as a GUY! She was stroking herself and generally getting off, or at least pretending to. The other girls seemed embarrassed, but Rae just smiled and laughed when she saw me."

Leah had, appropriately, asked Rae to remove the socks and moved her to the learning center desk out of view of the other girls. She had made sure everyone had work to do and let them know we would be talking about this later. Rae had succeeded in holding onto her peers' attention for a few minutes with her outrageous behavior and might have gotten even more favor from them had Leah reacted in an overt way.

Another incident involving Rae's untoward behavior in her attempt to seek attention and get what she wanted occurred again during a staff meeting. This time, she had no audience of peers, but was home alone on a school day having been kept home for behaviors at school that were inappropriate. By this time, Rae was savvy to our attempts to make the random checks during the meeting. During the first few checks she appeared to be working on what she was supposed to be doing and was well behaved and cooperative. During the second check, Rae asked if she would be allowed to watch a movie. She was told "no" due to her sanction status and the fact that she was supposed to be at school. Rae seemed to take this answer in stride and did not make one peep of a complaint.

On the third check, the staff member headed up the stairs and immediately we heard a shout for help. Three of us went up to assist, wondering what could be going on with only one girl home. We soon would find out how creative Rae could be.

Rae was on the floor shaking and jerking and gnashing her teeth. It looked like an all-out seizure. She was unresponsive to her name or any attempt to connect with her. We moved all the furniture away and decided we needed to call the ambulance. The paramedics responded within minutes and two medics plus a stretcher came up the stairs. All this while Rae continued to shake, spittle flying out of her mouth. We cleared the room as best we could but a couple of us stayed to watch the medics work and give them the scoop on what we had seen so they could best treat her.

"RAE! RAE!," they shouted at her.

No response.

One of the medics commenced a sternum rub. This was something I had only seen on TV but was pretty sure it had something to do with whether she was faking it or not. They must have gotten some kind of clue that it may not be a genuine seizure. It looked painful, and Rae winced a bit then went back to shaking. I watched as the medic glanced at his partner and a message seemed to be telegraphed between them. They loaded her on the stretcher and bundled her into the ambulance, still shaking.

We sent a staff member to follow the ambulance with her medical information and Medicaid card. Rae was seen in the ER and discharged quickly back to the group home with a diagnosis of a pseudo-seizure. In other words, she had an event that mimicked a seizure, but was not neurologically a seizure. It could have been brought on by psychological symptoms or she could have been faking it. I certainly would not have thought she was faking, but a seizure, especially after she didn't get what she wanted, seemed too much of a coincidence.

Soon after we talked to the county about the appropriateness of the placement for Rae, feeling she may benefit more from being in a Child Care Institution (CCI), a level higher care than us. CCIs have their own nurses and psychiatrists on staff and can respond better to Rae's needs regardless of whether she was faking, or an event was brought on by mental health issues. The county declined to follow our recommendations and instead convinced the judge that Rae was appropriate for corrections since she was not successful at the group home level.

Several months later, we received a call again to ask if we would consider taking Rae back to the group home. We had not received any more referrals from this county in the past months and were hoping they weren't unhappy with the services or the outcome of how Rae had fared with us. In consideration of all these unanswered questions, we decided, with some trepidation, to interview Rae again for placement. Hopefully she matured a bit and would be a better fit for our environment.

The interview took place at the jail. Rae was sullen as we walked in but brightened some during the interview. Our attempts to try and elicit some ownership for her behaviors fell flat and Rae had a manipulative quality about her even though she was being pleasant and seemingly cooperative. Our gut and professional experience told us nothing had changed, and we would continue to have a crisis on our hands if Rae returned to the group home. Reluctantly, but firmly, we conveyed this to her county Case Manager. He thanked us for interviewing her and hung up. We didn't receive another referral from that county for two more years. Was there a connection? We aren't sure.

—Tiana—

Tiana was another case of a socially inept teenager. Behaviors like standing too close to her peers, using "weird" language, and talking in strange voices drove her peers away very effectively and Tiana spent her time alone and defeated in her attempts to fit in. She, unlike Rae, did not look "cool," hampering her efforts even further.

Tiana was being raised by her aunt and had not had any contact with her mother for years. She was an ungainly adolescent, not fitting into her skin and walking with her head down most of the time. She was overweight and did not keep up good hygiene, needing to be reminded to shower on a regular basis. Tiana had short blonde hair and glasses she had the habit of pulling off and sucking on, unmindful of how that behavior was perceived by others.

Since Tiana was getting no positive feedback from her peers and discounted any positive feedback from the staff, some of her behaviors were simple measures at self-soothing and providing self-comfort. She had a blanket she carried around no matter what. Staff tried to discourage this behavior as it set her up for more ridicule. Given the age range we worked with, self-soothing revolving around sexual gratification was not uncommon. Our policy was that any individual sexual activity needed to be done in private behind closed doors. What was brought to our attention when Tiana was a resident made us realize our policy was not nearly specific enough.

To our horror we discovered that Tiana had been creatively utilizing the group home silverware for her own pleasure as well as the office pens that were adorned with plastic flowers to discourage theft. Thankfully, the *used* silverware had never been returned to the general population of silverware, but was hidden in her room, discovered during a room search along with the pens. Tiana tearfully disclosed the purpose of the items when questioned. Staff, wearing rubber gloves, quickly tossed the stash into the garbage bin and we splurged on a new set of silverware and fresh office pens.

Through this experience we learned we had to set very specific and clear boundaries at Tiana's intellectual level, which altered how we communicated with her. We resumed efforts to try to modify our approach while continuing to be non-shaming and supportive. It saddened us to see the result of this and other socially unacceptable behaviors that set her up to be set apart from the community, which only fed her low self-esteem.

34

Search Party

Danel

While we didn't conduct personal or room searches on a regular basis, there were occasions where it was simply unavoidable. We may have believed there was contraband hidden in a room, something that would threaten the recovery of the clients such as drugs, weapons, or information about running away. Or we may have believed there was theft going on; items from the group home or other clients were missing, food and clothing being the two most common items to be taken.

State regulations gave staff leeway to search a client's person, never body cavities, if we had documented reason to believe that that client was hiding something dangerous to themselves or others. On the other hand, we were able to search lockers and the group home rooms, including bedrooms, randomly to prevent and deter any contraband being available to the clients. It was the rule that if we were searching a client's room that one client assigned to that room would witness the search so there was no accusation of staff members stealing or planting items. We did, however, keep this practice to a minimum as it was very time intensive, dirty, and laborious. We also often found things that we did not expect.

On one occasion we had been discussing in staffing that an inordinate amount of girls had access to cigarettes, somehow, and that certain areas of the house smelled like smoke. The belief was that cigarettes, lighters, and matches were being hidden in the house somewhere. This was not good for several reasons, the first being that it was against the law for anyone under eighteen to smoke and while we were not the nicotine police, we did not want to have it on the property. Second, and of most concern to us, was the risk of fire. Clients had been known to light their cigarettes with the toaster or stove burners, smoke in bed or other dangerous places that affect the safety of all staff and clients in that home. We believed a search was in order. All available staff stayed past their shifts to help.

We donned the required plastic gloves and worked in pairs, each assigned to a room or area. The common areas were searched first before the clients returned from school. A moderate number of notes, food wrappers, candy, and other articles of minor offense were found, as well as a personal razor a staff had forgotten to check back in, and several long overdue library books. As the girls began returning from school, they were informed that the search was in progress, and it would be in their best interest to tell us now what we might find. Most of the girls were complacent and a couple fessed up to the candy. We asked everyone to go to their house freeze spots. Each team of staff members asked one of the girls from each room to accompany them to her room for it to be searched. Noalee, a Case Manager, and I were assigned Amber's room. Amber was the only one in her room at the time, so she was the one who needed to be present while we conducted the search.

"Anything you want to tell us before we do this?"

Amber refused to answer, sullen. Her long black bangs hung in her eyes as she plopped down outside her door.

"We're going to start now," Noalee told her.

"Whatever," mumbled Amber.

Amber was a young lady who had a low tolerance for frustration and was often quick to escalate, not able to handle her emotions. We wanted to watch her carefully. She had a notebook and was apparently doing schoolwork while we searched. Methodically, we worked our way through the room. Noalee, a police officer before coming to Candle-light Vision, took the lead, having conducted many searches before. As we worked our way through the room, we found several interesting things. First, a good number of cigarettes, rolled up and stuffed into the battery compartment of her alarm clock Second, a book of matches and two lighters apparently stolen from staff members. These were tucked into a hole in the box spring of her bed.

Noalee and I started to notice a pattern in Amber's behavior in relation to when we would find something of interest. In fact, only moments before we discovered something Amber's behaviors would escalate and she would begin to misbehave to direct our attention towards her and away from the room search, perhaps hoping we would lose our place or maybe even give up the search altogether to focus on her behaviors. A rollercoaster of sounds emanated from our area of the house drawing curious staff to see if they could assist. We waved them away and assured them Amber was simply announcing that we were close to finding something she didn't want us to. She was simply performing verbal antics, nothing physical and we did not feel threatened by her presentation, so we let her be.

Noalee and I caught each other's eye as my move over to the bookshelf resulted in a wail from Amber. Sure enough, behind the neatly stacked books was a glass jar full of a pale yellow liquid. We weren't sure what it was, but we were certain it didn't belong in Amber's room. Amber's early warning system had identified it for us as contraband. I brought it to Noalee and we examined it. Amber was mum as to the contents and as we slowly opened the jar, it became immediately apparent that it was urine.

"What the...?" I exclaimed, bouncing my eyes back and forth between Amber and Noalee.

Amber's eyes were down and Noalee shrugged. This was the last item we discovered that evening. A full paper grocery bag full of contraband not including the jar of urine was found, as well as burn marks on her comforter and a dryer sheet through which she had been smoking to try and disguise the smell. Staff gathered in the office to try and determine the reason and/or the origin of our most unusual find. Suggestions were made that she may have been storing clean urine in case she had to take a drug test. Other thoughts laid out the possibility of it being related to sexual abuse. Amber stayed mute on the subject, and we never did find out the purpose behind the liquid stockpile. We disposed of it and dished out consequences for her other contraband and for smoking in the house.

35

Cultural Barriers – Finding Out
What We Don't Know

Mary Kay

While Candlelight Vision Corp was located in a fairly homogenous area of the Midwest, we had our share of different cultures that made their way through the door. Several Native American Reservations are within an hour's drive, African-American clients were occasionally placed from the more urban counties, and several Asian refugee cultures were present in the community.

Jessy was a Hmong client. It is unusual in Asian culture for families to be involved in the social services system, as a principle of their culture is to take care of one's problems within the family or the extended Asian community. To bring in "outsiders" meant shame upon the family. Jessy, though, had been causing enough trouble in the community to warrant outside involvement by the Juvenile Justice Unit and subsequent placement at the group home. Jessy was a second-generation refugee, very Americanized at 13 years old. Slim with straight black hair, she bounced around like an excited puppy. She thoroughly ensconced the material world of American teenagers. No wonder she had given her parents so many problems. Her parents, by contrast, presented as very quiet and timid. It was established early on that there would need to be an interpreter present to communicate regarding their daughter. Though not ideal, an older sister stepped forward.

The sister, bi-lingual, also straddled both worlds, though had taken a more conventional route, was working and had not fallen into the temptations that Jessy had with drugs, sex, and rule-breaking. Jessy's sister accompanied the parents to every staffing and meeting that was held, patiently keeping both sides up to date. Of course, she couldn't be with us all the time. Teenagers are fairly good at manipulating in a normal circumstance, and when Jessy saw her chance, she took it.

One Sunday afternoon after what seemed to be a successful home visit, the staff person checking her in smelled alcohol on Jessy. She immediately began questioning her about her activities. Jessy, thinking quickly, moved from denial to a strategy she thought would be much more effective.

"Jessy, what's going on? I can smell alcohol...what happened?"

"What? I don't know."

"Come on now..."

"What?? Are you accusing me of drinking?!?!?"

"I'd like to know what happened so we can decide what to do."

"Okay, I KNEW you'd get all pissed off, so I didn't want to tell you"

"Are you going to tell me now?"

"You know we had a ceremony this weekend and part of it is for beer to get passed around to everyone, even the kids...it's not illegal...it's just what we do...the Shaman gives it to us."

"Oh...well put your things away now and we'll talk later."

Being Sunday, the staff person documented what was said, and it was not addressed until Monday. Because of the many players in this story, it actually took days and a family meeting before we figured out this was a completely made-up story by a fast-thinking teenager trying to avoid trouble and take advantage of our naivety. We worked very hard at being culturally sensitive and allowed as many cultural practices as possible to remain in place when the child is in placement. This experience helped us realize we didn't know what we didn't know and there were going to be times we would have gaps in our knowledge.

Ultimately Jessy showed enough improvement to be returned to her home. During the last meeting, as we were wrapping up, Jessy's father, surprising all of us, addressed us in English, stating "Thank you for all you have done." As it turns out, Jessy was not the only one in the family who felt safer relying on cultural barriers to keep distance between them and the providers. We had a good chuckle about that one.

36

Family Work

Mary Kay

Family Restructuring work was essential at CVC, where the adolescent is the identified client, but for all intents and purposes, only a portion of the problem. No child exists in a vacuum, and while most parents tried their best, often, unhealthy patterns got the best of them, sometimes even unknowingly. The following profiles are cases in which CVC undertook the family as a whole in hopes of creating and practicing healthy patterns. In each case, there was a family member that was threatened by this, as patterns, even unhealthy ones, are comfortable and difficult to change.

Tia's referral came in through the county the normal way. The unusual aspect about it was that it was her first referral to a formal program. Most girls that came to us had a series of other placements prior to coming to us. It always made us hopeful to receive referrals for younger clients that had been less involved in the system and hadn't become jaded at the thought of participating in treatment. On the other hand, it made us sad to see such a young girl placed out of her home.

Tia's parents had moved her to her aunt's home after her father, Seth and stepmother, Linda had exhausted years of interventions in attempts to provide a stable, nurturing environment. On the surface, it appeared that Tia was the typical child caught in the middle of her parent's divorce, unable to accept the reality that she couldn't make her wish for her original family come true. Her mother, Brenda, and father met very young and had an unstable relationship from the beginning. Paul, Tia's older brother, and Tia were very close in age. He was the most consistent and stable thing in Tia's young life. Though Brenda and Seth tried hard to keep the marriage and family together, their struggles with addiction wreaked havoc on the marriage and the children. An encounter with the law was the turning point, at least for Seth. After a period of incarcerations and intense treatment, he made the hard decision that he would be unable to maintain his sobriety in his marriage to his wife, an active alcoholic.

Brenda was angry and resentful, indoctrinating the children, now toddlers, with the message that their dad had abandoned them and did not love them anymore. Early in Seth's recovery he met and dated a woman, Linda from the church he attended while in treatment. This relationship developed and became a stabilizing force in his's life, enabling him to seek the lifestyle he dreamed of. He, himself, grew up with two chemically dependent and violent parents. Neither his needs nor the needs of his siblings were met. Life was hard and unpredictable, opening the door for his own addiction. He was determined to avoid this same road for his children.

Brenda was very angry about the new relationship, blaming it for his unwillingness to return to her. This resulted in her denying him contact with the children for extended periods. During these times, Brenda would reinforce the fact that Seth had left them for another woman and "ruined their family."

Brenda's progressive addiction to alcohol created deterioration in her ability to provide a stable and safe life for her children. There were numerous incidents of homelessness, neglect, and increasing safety risks as the children were exposed to drug and alcohol use and unsavory, even dangerous, men. This culminated to a crucial point when Brenda left both children, now preschoolers, with Seth's mother, also chronically addicted, and did not return for a week. The grandmother, with the understanding she would only have the kids for an afternoon, quickly tired of them and called her son, to "Come pick up your goddamn kids." That was the catalyst for Seth and now step-mom, Linda to pursue custody of both children.

Both Seth and Linda held hope and optimism for their ability to create a happy home for them and the children. They threw themselves into the day-to-day parenting responsibilities and went out of their way to make sure the kids knew they were welcome. They and both kids were soon in counseling trying to make sense of the past year's events and process their feelings about them. In the meantime, Seth and Linda did the best they could do to maintain contact between the kids and their mother, despite serious misgivings and their mother's inconsistent presence. Brenda was increasingly spiraling downward into the depths of her addiction, into a darker and darker world of self-destruction.

After their intermittent visits with Brenda, the kids' behavior would escalate beyond what you would expect in a standard divorce situation. They would lash out at Linda, their stepmom (not at Seth), stealing things from her that they knew were important to her, like her grandmother's jewelry. They would kick, stomp, and be physically abusive towards her and make false accusations of abuse and neglect. It was later discovered that on their rare visits with Brenda, she was scheming and deliberately plotting with the children to try to destroy their marriage so Seth would return to her and their family could be "whole" again. Over and over this message was given. The children were fast learners and wanted desperately to please their mother and have an intact family again. The behaviors escalated as they grew and became more sophisticated.

Linda continued to be patient and committed even in the face of such hurtful behavior. She continued to try and get them help. Even the counselors didn't understand the depths of the children's anger towards Linda and were floundering to find interventions. Tia's brother, Paul, was thoroughly indoctrinated with Mom's messages of hate towards Linda and encouraged this in Tia, in fact, chastising her when she allowed Linda any affection. Tia was so attached to and dependent on her big brother, the one person that was always there for her, that she acquiesced to his demands and continued to punish Linda.

By the time Tia was on the cusp of adolescence, her brother was incarcerated at a youth facility, and she was acting out even more. Seth and Linda were running out of patience and felt like prisoners in their own home. Still, they looked for help and held out hope that at least with Tia they would be able to create their dream family. Out of desperation and exhaustion, they sent Tia to live at her aunt and uncle's house, hoping for a miracle and salvaging at least one of the children.

Tia's innocent façade and good behavior lasted for only so long in this new environment. She quickly reverted to acting out. The final straw was when she stole money from their small child's piggy bank and ran away. The county agreed to place her out of the home. Perhaps the county's decision to look at group home placement immediately rather than try a less restrictive environment like a foster home was based on Paul's intense criminal thinking and behavior. This was, hopefully, an effort to prevent Tia from walking that same path. Thus, the referral was made.

The thing that sticks out the most about Tia's arrival was how childlike she was. Her appearance was sweet and angelic with big brown eyes, long eyelashes, a petite frame, brown hair pulled back into a perky ponytail. She presented as vulnerable and innocent, and we were immediately worried the other kids at the group home would corrupt her. How naïve we were.

Our severe underestimation of Tia ultimately led to serious crises and consequences for the group home. Though she appeared young and vulnerable, we soon learned many of Tia's sophisticated patterns. We started with family sessions right away, including both sets of parents separately. It was amazing how she could engage her mother into defending her against Seth and particularly Linda. On the other hand, our amazement continued in sessions with Seth and Linda that she could elicit the same emotions from them in protecting her from her mother.

Tia was playing both sides to the middle and doing so unashamedly and, unfortunately, very successfully. These early signs of manipulation required us to invoke a rule in family sessions: "No talking about the parent that wasn't there." Even this was difficult to enforce for a long time. Nevertheless, the families kept coming.

At the group home, Tia was what we called a "pot-stirrer." Like a master puppeteer, she would pull the strings and watch how peer conflicts would play out, all the while maintaining her innocent façade. Tiffany would go to one peer and report that another peer had said she was a "ho" and wanted her boyfriend. She would then go to the other peer and encourage her to pursue the boyfriend because he really liked her. If you want to get adolescent girls stirred up, talk about each other's boyfriends. Tia, apparently, was an expert at this and quickly had the house in an uproar. She covered her bases well when she would surreptitiously go to staff and report being worried and scared that the two peers were fighting and making it unsafe for her. Not only would she report this to staff, but she would also report her feelings of fear and how unsafe she felt to her mother because all her peers were fighting and teaching her bad things.

Brenda, who was eager to rescue Tia, would then call staff and social workers vehemently objecting to her placement at the group home and demanding she be returned to her. This cute, innocent, naive, young lady that we perceived walking in the door at intake, kept things quite lively on several different fronts.

Seth and Linda, seasoned by years of Tia's deceit and acting out, were able to hold her accountable for her behaviors and her part in conflicts. This fueled Tia's fire and antagonism against Linda. It soon became obvious that Seth and Linda were safe people to be angry with in that Tia was assured that no matter what, they would continue to love her and remain a constant in her life. Her mother, on the other hand, had disappeared several times in Tia's young life for extended periods of time. It was of the utmost importance for Tia to not be perceived as disloyal to her mother lest she leave again.

In the sessions with Brenda and Tia, on the surface it appeared that Brenda was genuine and open to feedback about the presenting patterns of behavior, at least Tia's patterns. She would vigorously confront Tia on her manipulative behavior and encourage her not to let "those other girls" deter her from getting home. It was well known by this point that Seth and Linda were willing to surrender physical custody to Brenda, not because they didn't want or love Tia, but because they were willing to sacrifice what they wanted for what they thought Tia truly wanted, to be with her mom. Then maybe, just maybe, she would stop acting out.

Tia did have a very stable and promising period while at the group home. She was a bright and insightful girl who could easily pick up on skills that we taught. Continued family sessions raised her awareness of the pain her behavior had caused Seth and Linda, as well as reinforced the stability of their continued presence in her life. She also gained insight into her mother's incongruencies and lack of follow-through on her promises. Tia began to realize the influence Paul had on her life and her decisions and how her mother had indoctrinated their thinking, preventing her and her brother from bonding with her father and attaching to that family unit.

No matter what she realized on an intellectual level, there was still a little girl inside who was fearful that Mommy would disappear again. The logical conclusion for a little girl to reach was to obviously avoid upsetting her mother so she didn't leave again. Children's processing ability is skewed and affords them magical thinking that gives them some sense of control over the overwhelming chaotic and uncontrollable circumstances in their environment. The inability of Tia and her brother Paul to reconcile reality with the haunting fears of their early childhood clearly left them unable to attach to the family unit created by Seth and Linda. The childlike magical thinking that prevailed (and was fed by their mother) was that if they could somehow eliminate Linda from the family portrait, their mother would resume her rightful place and the original family unit would be restored. Thus, their mom would be happy and not feel the need to leave them, and they would not ever have to face the possibility of abandonment again. Often the case with children and even adults who are driven by compulsive self-destructive behaviors is the inability to resolve what they know intellectually with the sometimes unrecognized childlike emotions that drive the self-sacrificing and primal survival behaviors. This pattern becomes a self-perpetuating cycle of toxic shame. The unconscious driving the conscious behavior.

In the group home, Tia was holding her peers accountable, achieving high levels, being congruent in the home, in the school, and in the community. Discussions had begun regarding the wisdom of placing her back with her mother who had not done any significant work on her own issues. Throughout Tia's placement, her mother's instability was demonstrated by her continued inability to follow through on promises to Tia, and her continued dangerous choices in boyfriends. There was even a drive-by shooting at her home. After this incident she moved to the same city the group home was located in.

Tia's healthy thinking was proven at one point when, upon the arrival of Brenda for a family session, she reported to staff that she thought her mother was drunk and may even hurt Mary Kay. This was a serious situation. Rules of the group home stated no one under the influence was allowed on campus and certainly no one who was a threat to the safety of clients or staff. Mary Kay grabbed a portable breathalyzer we kept on campus and invited mom to demonstrate her sobriety. She not so politely refused and began screaming and cussing while she stomped down the driveway, threatening in language that would embarrass even a trucker driver. More than one neighbor's face appeared in the window. Thankfully, she did leave the campus quickly enough to avoid a call to the police.

With Brenda's cover blown, there was no longer hope for further engaging her on a therapeutic level. After her departure, Tia was found inside the house sobbing hysterically and fearful her mother would never talk to her again. Nevertheless, Brenda and Tia continued to have family visits according to the county's wishes. One such pass took place when she and Tia were signed out to attend her brother's graduation ceremony at the youth detention facility he was held at.

Everyone was encouraged by Paul's progress and was hoping some of his new positive behaviors might rub off on Tia as she still looked up to her big brother for guidance. Tia arrived back at the group home happy, full of encouragement and optimism about her brother's progress. Brenda also talked about what a good experience it was to see her son doing well.

Questions arose about the legitimacy of this pass a couple of weeks later when we found out Seth and Linda were unaware that this graduation occurred. These questions spurred an investigation on the group home's part. A call was placed to the county who checked and reported to us that no such graduation had taken place. The obvious place to address this deceit was in an upcoming treatment team review which occurred monthly. This was a regular meeting for each client and included social workers, parents, the county worker, the group home Case Manager, and the Treatment Director. Treatment plans were reviewed, and goals were set for the next month.

When the topic of Paul's graduation was addressed in the meeting, Brenda became defensive and insisted repeatedly that they had indeed gone to Paul's graduation. She was quite offended that we would accuse her of lying. When asked why Seth and Linda were unaware of the graduation, she took the opportunity to, one more time, talk about Seth's failure as a parent, alluding that Paul did not want him there. Brenda's statement would have, in the past, triggered an escalation as Seth and Linda responded to accusations, defended themselves or perhaps attacked back. However, the progress Seth and Linda had made in family sessions was evident during this meeting and we were proud to see them not allow Brenda's attempts at changing the focus of the conversation. This was a new pattern for the family and a healthier one.

We were encouraged by Tia's strength during the meeting when she admitted that there was no graduation and they had gone to visit her mother's relatives. Brenda was silent and seething with anger at Tia's admission. Tia maintained herself throughout the rest of the meeting. Home passes with her mother were put on hiatus. Visits were allowed only on campus and closely monitored by staff.

It was shortly after that meeting that Tia's behavior once more deteriorated. She began to fall back into old patterns. She began acting out on home passes with Seth and Linda, triggering painful memories for them. Brenda and Tia colluded together against staff and the county workers to get what they wanted. Tia began running away, stealing from local stores, and being verbally abusive to staff. We received reports of acting out and truancy at school. We strongly suspected Tia would run to Brenda's house, which was in close vicinity to the group home. Upon one return from a runaway, it was discovered Tia had been found at Paul's girlfriend's house who had maintained close contact with Brenda during Paul's incarceration. The obvious conclusion was that Brenda was harboring and encouraging Tia's runaways to circumvent her supervised visits.

Tia's behavior grew more and more unmanageable and covert. Many interventions were attempted to no avail, including short jail stays invoked by the county. These interventions seemed to fuel her fire and made Tia more determined to win or get her way. It was obvious to all that Tia's honesty in the Treatment Team Review and her mother's reaction had triggered her fear of her mother's abandonment. Nothing we could say or do brought Tia back to her higher level of stability. She was becoming a safety threat to the group home and the other kids, forcing us to request her removal from the group home.

The county invoked their contractual 30-day notice rule, which meant that Tia needed to remain at the group home for up to 30 days until they had found another placement for her. We argued for immediate removal as she was taking other girls with her when she ran away, placing them in danger. We did not feel as though we had a safe place to maintain her apart from the other clients. No matter how valid the criteria was for Tia's immediate removal, the county maintained their adherence to our contractual agreement of 30 days.

Upon Tia's last return from jail, it was determined that it was not safe to room her with any of the other clients. There was an empty room that had been used as an office in the past. During a staff meeting, it was decided to separate Tia from the clients by creating a bedroom out of the empty office so she would not be sharing a room with another, more vulnerable client. It was a solid plan – one designed to protect both Tia and the other clients. We felt it was the best we could do in such a dire situation. To prevent Tia from locking staff out of her new bedroom, the doorknobs were reversed, placing the locking apparatus on the outside.

A specific plan was developed to meet Tia's needs, including treatment work designed to help her see the destructiveness of her patterns. Ultimately, she was removed and placed in a different facility and things settled back in at the group home and the chapter on Tia ended, at least so we thought.

A few months later Danel and I were on one of our famous road trips when we received a call from the group home reporting that our State Licensor was there to investigate a complaint that someone had been locked in a bedroom. It's never comfortable when the Licensor comes, but this was such a preposterous accusation we were not the least bit alarmed. After all, such a thing was totally outside of the principles we stood for as an agency. I told the staff we would call back after our interview.

"Make sure you provide whatever she needs," I directed them and hung up. Danel and I briefly pondered which client would have made such a report. We concluded that it could have been any number of clients or parents that were unhappy and wanted to create crises. After all, it was a very litigious population we worked with, and no matter how hard we tried there was generally always someone who was unhappy. With that, we pulled up at the institution we were headed for and went in to interview a prospective client.

We began our return trip as we usually did, discussing the area of needs of the prospective client. It was always a great balancing act; can we be effective with this young lady? How would she impact the general milieu?

Often there were girls we really wanted to and could make a difference for; however their placement would tip the scales negatively within the therapeutic community. Some examples of this could include behaviors of running away; having too many runners that were not stabilized could pose a threat. Having a more sophisticated runner from say Milwaukee or Racine could mean one of our more vulnerable, younger kids could end up on the streets of the inner city and be eaten alive. We also had to be wary of not creating a subculture. Too many gang members, too many big city tough gals, too many with issues of violence, too many of a specific diagnosis, etc. This balance was vital to providing a therapeutic experience and environment for all. Declining a placement because they wouldn't fit with the current milieu was always difficult, but it was our responsibility to provide as safe and as therapeutic an environment as possible. Thus, much of our return drive was always weighing the pros and cons and deciding whether to proceed with the placement process.

I do not remember which client we interviewed that day, but it is a date etched in my mind forever. I can tell you where we were on the interstate, the billboard I was looking at, the song playing on the radio, the look on Danel's face, and the nauseating breathless feeling that overcame me when I made the return call to CVC to check on the Licensor's visit. I could hear in the staff's voice the hesitancy as I asked "How are things going?

"It's true" was her response. In utter shock and dismay, I responded: "*WHAT! THAT CAN'T BE POSSIBLE...WHO, WHAT, WHEN, HOW?*" This all might sound a little melodramatic to some of you, but for me in hindsight it was probably one of the defining moments of my life both personally and professionally. The staff at the other end of the phone was not only a colleague but a good friend and I could sense her desire to take care of me as she covered the who, what, when, and how of the day's events.

The overarching principle that we hung in there with even the toughest girls, we realized was, sometimes to a fault. The complaint had been lodged by Tia, and the investigation of her report revealed that the incident had occurred on her last return from jail. We had made the request of the county to remove her as her behavior was a threat to the other girls. The county had invoked the 30-day notification rule and the decision was made to isolate her from the rest of the girls, putting a more concentrated effort at supervising her. As we discussed earlier, we created an area for her out of an empty office that we thought would provide just such an environment. The locks we had reversed in order to prevent her from locking us out were the downfall. The new staff person working the weekend interpreted the reversed handles as an indicator that the door should be locked. Thus, for the shifts that this person worked, she personally supervised Tia and locked the door.

Through the grapevine we had heard that Tia had run from another group home shortly after she had gotten there. Approximately six months later we had confirmation from her stepmother, Linda, that Tia was still missing. It was obvious that she was beside herself with worry. According to her, Dad was just waiting fearfully for the call that every parent of a runaway is terrified to receive: "Would you please come and identify the body?" More times than not the "little darlings" were tucked away at a friend's house, getting more sleep than their fear ridden parents. However, there are those pictures you see at Wal-Mart and Sam's Club of those innocent faces of children missing for years, and those horrifying stories of children sold into human trafficking or found tortured and killed. Or worse yet, you hear nothing for days, months, years and are left with the tragic nightmare that never ends.

It is impossible to work with a child for that long without feeling a continued connection to her and her future, especially knowing the potential Tia had. There was great relief for all who had worked with Tia at the group home when we heard she was alive and incarcerated at

Southern Oaks Girls' School. The news came by way of a social worker who was equally invested and concerned about Tia. The rumor was that Mom had had continuing contact with Tia throughout her disappearance, revealing her whereabouts to the authorities only after finding out Tia had been being held in the adult unit of the Cook County jail in Illinois, certainly no place for a 15-year-old. It appears Tia had given a false name and age when arrested for soliciting in Chicago. Once her identity had been straightened out and all parents had been notified, Tia was placed at the more appropriate juvenile facility.

As if once around was not enough for us, the possibility of saving Tia from herself and her history was simply too tempting. We had so much invested in her both treatment-wise and emotionally. When the call came from her social worker that Tia was being discharged from Southern Oaks, we accepted her for placement once again after a long and grueling pre-screening interview with Tia, and a long discussion at the weekly staff meeting. The meeting with Tia revealed a very remorseful and motivated young lady. At the first sight of Mary Kay at the interview, Tia burst into tears, and hugged her. She apologized for all the chaos of her last stay. She withstood the intense questioning about why we should take her back and truly appeared motivated to have a different life for herself.

After these considerations, there appeared to be more pros than cons and we tentatively accepted placement with strict conditions. In our defense, the exact same mistake was not made twice as one of the conditions of accepting Tia was that we would not work with her biological mother as that had proved to be a toxic relationship to Tia's recovery the last time around. Her identified long-term placement would be with Seth and Linda and that's what the family sessions would focus on. We did expect Tia to follow through with what she stated at her pre-screening interview and show consistency in her commitment to recovery.

Sadly, after some intense effort towards change on Tia's part, she succumbed once again to her fear of losing her mother and she began her pattern of running away once again. Despite this seemingly unhappy ending, we know Tia did some good work during her time with us and left with a very different understanding and insights about herself and her family system. We hope Tia will resurface someday safely and seek the help she needs to continue to face her fears.

37

Entitlement

Mary Kay

Most people assume that the behaviors of the girls in our care were the result of bad parenting, sexual abuse, physical abuse, or neglect that led them to seek out such a destructive lifestyle. A lot of the stories we have shared with you so far could be attributed to any of the reasons above, but by far the most difficult teens to treat were the ones that came from solid healthy family systems. These kids have a severe case of entitlement. They have the mindset that their parents are around solely to provide for their every desire. Many of them come from family systems that the rest of the girls would die for. There is no such thing as a perfect family, and all families have things to work on, however in these cases the biggest sin of the parents was that of loving too much.

One such young lady came in at age 15, she was the oldest of two children with an eye-opening list of charges. Her mother was a professional woman who had worked with impaired children all her adult life. Lyla was in direct competition with her mother for Daddy's attention. She had managed to drive quite a wedge in the marital relationship. Dad was a blue-collar worker whose only goal was to provide for his family a better life than he had. Lyla's younger sister came along 8 years later and seemed to have really put a wrinkle in Lyla's reign over her kingdom.

With mother able to give us some childhood background, the warning signs of big problems to come were apparent as Lyla's tantrums and defiance increased throughout her early years. Mom set up behavioral programs, initiated counseling for Lyla and the family, and was consistent in follow through. Dad followed suit, but was never really sold completely, wondering if mom wasn't being just a bit too unreasonable. After all, Lyla was just a kid, and when she turned on those tears, Dad's heart melted. The older she got the more sophisticated she became at pulling those heartstrings.

Mom put up a valiant effort, and Dad tried to toe the party line, but would inevitably succumb to guilt and subtly rescue Lyla. This, of course, created conflict between Mom and Dad which eventually, like water running over a rock, created a widening channel in their relationship. The younger sister learned early on to either stay out of Lyla's way, or keep her mouth shut. Mom, after years of trying to do it right, was weary and lonely while Dad grew sullen and angry at his powerlessness to make it better for his family. Little sister spent more and more time away from home as Lyla was running the show. At the end, her behavior and drug use escalated into law violations, but it was violent behavior towards her younger sister that finally prompted the social worker to make a referral to the group home.

For the first three months Lyla was not brought into family sessions. It was necessary for the rest of the family to reunite and look at the patterns that were feeding Lyla's unhealthy control over them. Both parents were shocked and angry when Lyla's little sister, now seven years old, began to disclose how afraid she was to be home, how she had been threatened and intimidated by Lyla and her unhealthy friends. She laid out in detail how and when Lyla would sneak in and out of the house, where Lyla hid her drugs (in Mom and Dad's bedroom), and which outfit Lyla stole from which store.

Dad and Mom needed to reunite outside of the parent role, and work through the blame and finger pointing those years of chaos had woven through the foundation of their marriage. Until this could be resolved, there could be no unity, and without unity in the parental units, there could be no success for Lyla. Through all of this Lyla did her best to regain control, at least of her father. She would call him at work from school and cry, telling him the horror (some fabricated, some not) of the issues, crimes, and family status of the other clients. She would plead with him that she "wasn't like those other girls" and she "didn't belong here." She would call and scream at her mother and barrage her with accusations of neglect and abuse, accusing mom of never loving her and only wanting the younger sister "that's why you put me here... you just want your perfect little baby." Mom and Dad fought courageously to stand up to these escalating attempts at bringing chaos back into their fragile relationship.

Eventually Lyla was brought into the family sessions. It didn't take long before she was presenting herself as the victim, (this place isn't fair, there's no time to do homework, my roommate is stealing from me, and they don't like me) pretty much what all the girls reported to parents and social workers in the beginning, hoping to find a "rescuer." The earlier work with mom and dad paid off. As a result of opening the communication between the two of them, her father immediately saw the manipulation. The exchange that ensued went something like this:

Mary Kay: "What do you see happening here, Dad?"

Dad (with tears in his eyes): "Lyla wants me to feel guilty that I put her here."

Mary Kay: "Are you responsible for Lyla's placement here?"

Mom: "No, she put herself here!"

Here was Lyla's chance to shift the blame and focus.

Lyla: "WHY DO YOU ALWAYS DO THAT, WHY DO YOU AL-WAYS HAVE TO TALK FOR HIM? I just want to do these sessions with my dad. Mom just wrecks things for us."

Mary Kay: "We can talk about those feelings that you're having, but first let's talk about whether you think Dad should feel guilty about your being placed outside the home?"

Mom had responded to my signal asking her to wait. She was already on board and aware of the tactics used by their daughter. Dad, on the other hand, was just beginning to see things as they really existed, making it vital to keep this exchange focused.

Lyla (sobbing): "Daddy, I can't believe YOU signed those papers, you knew they would take me away; I thought *you* loved me at least!"

In a dramatically different tone of voice, quiet and dejected, she said in a deliberately audible whimper, "Now I have no one to take care of me..."

Mom reached over and quietly held his hand, hoping that this time they would stand together in the battle for their child. It was obvious by Dad's body language that he was appreciative of her support.

Dad: "Lyla, I do love you, but I don't want to live like this anymore. Until you were placed here, I didn't realize just how crazy and chaotic it was at home. It was like a war zone, Lyla. Your mom and I fought all the time. Your little sister is home now. I didn't even notice how much she was gone until now."

By now Dad was sobbing and Mom was very teary hanging on to Dad's hand for all she was worth. Lyla was scowling with her knees held tight to her chest continuously looking up at the ceiling, feigning rolling her eyes, but in reality, fighting the tears that were welling in her eyes.

Dad: "Do you know your little sister is afraid of you? I can't believe things have gone so far that home isn't safe for my children, WHY Lyla, did I never see that side of you?"

Mary Kay: "That's a really good question Dad. (Turning to Mom) Mom, did you ever see that side of Lyla?"

Mom: "That is the only side I have seen for over a year. I just quit fighting and let him deal with her. It was just easier... less conflict. I guess I've just been staying busy and being gone too."

Mom seemed surprised by this discovery. Looking at Lyla, she said, "Just like your sister."

With this, Dad openly cried. Putting his arm around his wife, he pulled her close and said, "I'm so sorry, Honey."

Before dad could go any farther Lyla jumped to her feet screaming. "This is fucking bullshit!" She threw the chair she was sitting in and stomped toward the door.

Dad raised his voice calling her name and asked her to pick up the chair and sit down.

Mary Kay: "You know Dad, I think Lyla has handled all she is capable of at this time."

I sent Lyla to wait in the group room and called a staff member to pick her up. The truth of the matter was I thought we all had reached our capacity for this session.

38

The Final Word

Danel

Writing these stories has allowed me look back over the years that I was with Candlelight Vision Corp with a sense of gratitude for the lives I encountered, the learning I did, and the professional and personal growth I went through during my ten years at CVC. I was lucky enough to be mentored by Mary Kay in my role as Lead Social Worker which allowed me to gain confidence in my role as a group facilitator, a grant writer, a first contact with the clients, and completing assessments. Additionally, I was able to be witness to insightful and effective family work, composure when events took an unexpected turn, and above all grow in confidence in myself. As I observed the evolution of an idea to an agency that continued to grow to meet crucial needs for at risk teenagers, it challenged me to see more big picture ideas.

It was a hard decision to leave Candlelight Vision, moving on to other positions in which I carried my lessons to clinical work with adults, doing discharge planning for a inpatient psychiatric ward, facilitating domestic violence offender treatment groups, functioning as lead therapist in the OCD program at a nationally known clinic, and landing where I am now, providing therapy as an outpatient therapist.

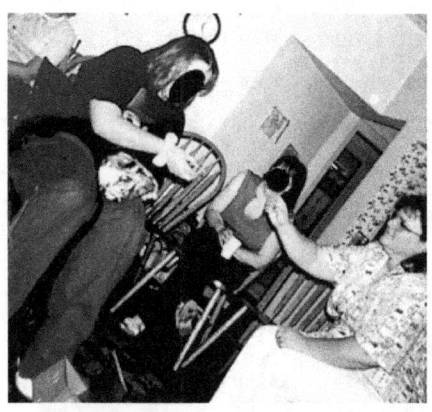

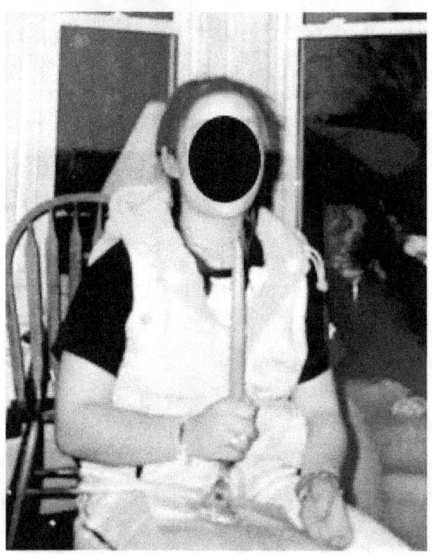

~ A Graduation ceremony at Candlelight
Vision Corp.

Personally, I found it difficult to have uncertainty about where the clients of Candlelight ended up, or where their journey took them as they moved into adulthood. There would be the occasions in which I would run into a former client or a parent in the community and hear a bit of an update. Likewise, I keep in contact with several of the staff members I worked with at Candlelight over the years who have also heard tidbits here and there about our girls...we thought of them as "our girls." Even with the little I found out over the years, I had a good sense that there were success stories, incredibly, seemingly unrealistic, success stories given what we knew of them and their environment, that we could celebrate. And the worst-case stories. I'm sad to have heard of the deaths of several of "our girls" as they were unable to escape the reaches of their upbringing and toxic patterns. With many unknowns I choose to lean into hope that there are more success stories out there and realize there may be more sad outcomes.

As I continued with my career, I took my knowledge from Candlelight with me. As I look back there are things I wish I had in my professional toolbox when I worked with the clients of CVC. Candlelight had a way of sucking you in...the drama, the one more thing, the staff updates, and the general time spent debriefing this hectic ever-changing job. I've gotten better at setting boundaries in subsequent jobs, making sure I could separate from the pull of the job in this field where there is always one more thing to do. I also think, for better or worse, I carried the knowledge of what "could" happen into my own family, being over-attuned to the dangers in the world as I parented my own children. I wish I could have been able to find a realistic middle ground to land in my worry.

Of course, as technology has exploded and teens are finding new and creative ways to get in trouble via the internet, I reflect back with gratitude that we were not attempting to keep ahead of social media or needing to add cell phones to our list of contraband. Even though it was a full-time job keeping the girls in our care safe, it could have been much more difficult. No one knew what sexting was. Arranging a ride to run away was difficult and required physical note passing. Low self-worth and bullying were bad enough without social media and curated images to contend with. I empathize with the group homes of today who battle with the downside to technology as they try to maintain safety and order. And I'm grateful they continue to do it.

I thank Mary Kay, all the staff, the mentors and volunteers, and especially the clients of Candlelight Vision Corp. for being part of my life and my family for understanding that I was a part of theirs.

Mary Kay

Even when writing and revising this book, Danel and I would giggle at some of the memories and antics of the girls of Candlelight. Sadly, many of them brought tears to our eyes. These are real life stories. Real people lost and confused, damaged individuals. In some cases, life was not good to them, and in some cases, they were the ones doing harm to others. All of them, however, deserve to be held with unconditional regard. Without fail, every one of our clients was damaged and traumatized. My own philosophy and the underpinnings of the philosophy of the group home's programming hinged on two things: honesty and accountability as the key to recovery.

One of my most gratifying moments was reading "Oh, the Places You Will Go," by Dr. Seuss at the graduations of the young women that persevered through stressful and painful times of facing their realities, earning the recognition of persevering, and role modeling for their peers. There were girls that did not graduate for a variety of reasons that were, nonetheless successful. They all took solid life lessons from the program, and whether they applied them to their lives or chose a different path, we may never know. All of them brought joy, some by coming and some by leaving.

I will always be eternally grateful for the Founding Mothers who served to hold me up when I could no longer. Each of them was the heart of the program. Without them, the lives of the girls we served would not have been impacted as greatly.

Thank you to Michele Hutchison, Marn Gibson, and Danel Burchby. Thank you to Danel as well for her patience and perseverance to bring this book to completion. She is a saint.

In this world of no absolutes, children scramble to find structure and consistency when little is provided. The same life principles of Candlelight Vision Corp. still apply yesterday, today and tomorrow.

Love thy neighbor as yourself and let your "yeas" be "yea" and your 'nays" be nay"

God Bless you all and thanks for sharing our journey.

~ An ABC client graduates successfully from the program

www.ingramcontent.com/pod-product-compliance
Lightning Source LLC
Chambersburg PA
CBHW071143130626
46553CB00004B/1501

* 9 7 9 8 9 8 8 8 5 4 3 6 4 *